afro am

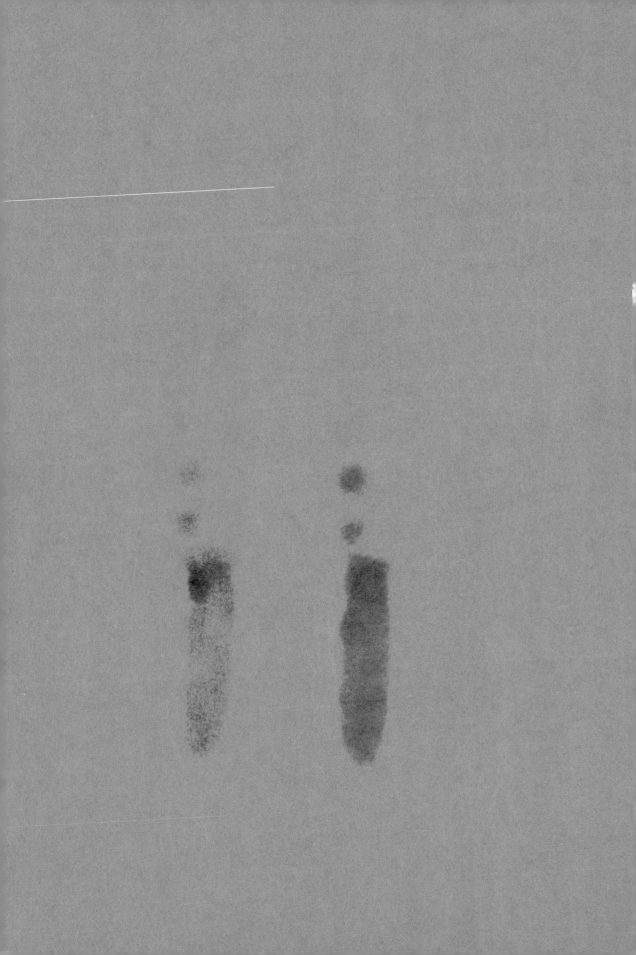

The Kansas City Monarchs

JANET BRUCE

The Kansas City

# MONARCHS

Champions of

Black Baseball

 University Press of Kansas

© 1985 by the University Press of Kansas
All rights reserved
Printed in the United States of America

Published by the University Press of Kansas (Law-
rence, Kansas 66045), which was organized by the
Kansas Board of Regents and is operated and funded by
Emporia State University, Fort Hays State University,
Kansas State University, Pittsburg State University, the
University of Kansas, and Wichita State University

Library of Congress Cataloging in Publication Data

Bruce, Janet, 1955–
    The Kansas City Monarchs.
    Bibliography: p.
    Includes index.
    1. Kansas City Monarchs (Baseball team)—History.
2. Afro-American baseball players—Kansas—Kansas
City.
3. Baseball—United States—History. I. Title.
GV875.K29B78    1985    796.357′64′0973    85-8535
ISBN 0-7006-0273-9

To Mom and Dad, with love

# Contents

# Acknowledgments

**m**y fascination with the Monarchs began quite accidentally. I needed an exhibit idea for a museum-science class I was taking. It was spring semester, and having grown up in a small town where baseball was *the* summer activity, I turned to Kansas City's baseball past. Although volumes have been written on the national pastime, Robert Peterson's pioneering *Only the Ball Was White* was about the extent of the literature I could find on the Negro leagues. My friend Cathy Rocha and I arranged an interview with the famed Monarchs pitcher Hilton Smith—so that we could get enough information for the exhibit labels. I came away with more than an exhibit. That afternoon I treasured details about games forty years gone by. But beyond the statistics, I was profoundly touched by the dignity and courage of this gentle man. My idle curiosity soon became a passion.

Undoubtedly, my greatest debt in writing this book is to the players: Newt Allen, Hank Baylis, Allen Bryant, Connie Johnson, Roy Johnson, Buck O'Neil, Othello Renfroe, Hilton Smith, Al Surratt, Jesse Williams, and Maurice Young. Newspaper accounts by black sportswriters A. D. Williams, Fay Young, and Wendell Smith provided the skeletal structure of life in the Negro leagues, but the players filled it with its humanity. Newt Allen was in a wheelchair, crippled by a stroke, when I interviewed him in 1980. But that afternoon we were in 1925—as he vividly recalled making a triple play by himself. These men told me of the joy of being traveling ballplayers, but they also openly shared the pain of discrimination, which left me silent.

In addition, wives, children, civic leaders, bartenders, and beauty queens told me about the throbbing community life in black Kansas City and what the Monarchs meant to them. Like the players, Gladys Wilkinson Catron, Guy Davis, Jesse ("Kingfish") Fisher, Milton Morris, Mary Jo ("Josette") Weaver Owens, Alberta Gilmore Penn, Ted Rasberry, Bob Sweeney, Harriett Baird Wickstrom, Lee Wilkinson, Richard Wilkinson, and, especially, Georgia Dwight generously and graciously opened their homes and shared stories and scrapbooks with me. The friendships of all these wonderful people have enriched my life and make me feel very lucky.

The Friends of the Library, University of Missouri, Kansas City, provided funds for the oral histories. I also received grants from the Women's Council Graduate Assistance Fund and the Office of Research Administration, School of Graduate Studies, for completion of the research. I appreciate their help and vote of confidence.

Many have helped me in locating the photographs that illustrate the text. I thank all of them: George Brace, Bob Peterson, Bill Curtis, Gladys Catron, John Holway, Alberta Penn, Ocania Chalk, Art Carter, Lee Wilkinson, Josette Owens, Ted Rasberry, Phil Dixon, Craig Davidson, Mamie Hughes of the Black Economic Union, Linda McKinzie of the Urban League, Emmett Morris of the 18th and Vine Heritage, Inc., Horace Peterson of the Black Archives of Mid-America, Ira Herman of the Negro Baseball Hall of History, Paul Eisloeffel of the Kansas City Museum, Marge Kinney of the Kansas City Public Library, Nancy Sherbert of the Kansas State Historical Society, Tom Heitz of the National Baseball Library, and Joe Anzivino of the Harlem Globetrotters. Phil Dixon was a great help to me in identifying the photos.

Thanks are due also to the interlibrary loan staff at the University of Missouri, Kansas City, for their diligent work in processing my many requests; to Gordon Hendrickson of the Western Historical Manuscript Collection for his research advice; to Cliff Kachline, who was librarian at the Hall of Fame during my week in Cooperstown; and to Dick McKinzie as my thesis adviser. Special thanks go to Donn Rogosin for allowing me to use his many taped interviews with the players, but most importantly for his encouragement and support as I struggled with the story.

Thanks also to Bob Richmond of the Kansas State Historical Society, who first put me in touch with the University Press of Kansas, whose staff understood how much this book meant to me and urged me to persevere.

Finally, friends and family—can you believe it's actually in print? For sharing the frustrations as well as the joys, my thanks and love to all of you.

The Kansas City Monarchs

# ONE

## Before 1920

"The Monarchs was Kansas City's item. They made Kansas City the talk of the town all over the world."—Jesse Fisher

**W**hen the Kansas City Monarchs opened their season in 1923, a leading black newspaper reported that people in the black community came "out like a lot of bees hidden away all winter, . . . getting active when the sun shines."[1] Kansas City blacks loved their Monarchs baseball team. One of their strongest fans, Jesse ("Kingfish") Fisher, the bartender at the Blue Room in the Street's Hotel, put it simply: "They were the life of Kansas City in the Negro vicinity."[2] The Monarchs occasioned and provided a show, almost a carnival; there was a kind of magic about the heartland's most popular black baseball team.

To the players who created the magic, being a Monarch also meant a life of riding and sleeping in buses, because white-owned hotels in small towns often refused to give them overnight accommodations. It meant a precarious existence, full of stiff competition for the few positions on the league rosters. Every player knew that black children across the nation dreamed of being a "dusky Babe Ruth" and of breaking away from the stone quarry, the celery farm, the meat-packing plant, and the steel mill. Players who suffered injuries or long slumps knew they could be easily replaced by young men who were so determined that they learned to pitch by throwing rocks when they could not afford baseballs. The Monarchs and about fifteen other teams were the "majors" for black Americans from 1920 until Branch Rickey, president of the white Brooklyn Dodgers, signed the

3

The Kansas City Monarchs, World's Colored Champions in 1924. From the left: George Sweatt, Bill Drake, Carroll Mothel, Bill McCall, Frank Duncan, Lemuel Hawkins, Cliff Bell, Dobie Moore, William Bell, José Mendez, Bullet Joe Rogan, Newt Allen, Harold Morris, Heavy Johnson, Newt Joseph. Courtesy of National Baseball Library, Cooperstown, N.Y.

Monarchs' rookie Jackie Robinson in 1945. After nearly a century, the struggle for integration had been won.

Black participation in baseball before the Civil War was very limited. After the war, black teams provided weekend entertainment for urban populations in both the North and the South.[3] Key players on many teams were former soldiers who had learned the game in military camps during the war. In these early years, baseball was a gentleman's recreation. One journalist asserted that like the white New York Knickerbockers, the early black teams were "composed of very respectable colored people, well-to-do in the world."[4] Accordingly, these early contests were accompanied by appropriate entertainments. Women "lent value by numbers and general attractiveness," recalled black historian William Carl Bolivar. "There were picnics, dances and lunches showered upon the players."[5] Sometimes the team itself hosted the event. Records from the Philadelphia Pythians include receipts for ham, chicken, cheese, ice cream, cake, coffee, and cigars—staples for a pregame picnic. Although the black community generally supported these early teams and entertainments, a few black leaders attacked the sport as a dissipation of energies that should have been directed to political causes. William Still, a Philadelphia abolitionist and author of *Underground Railroad*, stated their case: "Our kin in the South famish for knowledge, have claims so great and pressing that I feel bound to give of my means in this direction to the extent of my abilities in preference to giving for *frivolous amusements.*[6]

The popularity of the game increased nonetheless, and in October 1867, the Excelsiors of Philadelphia and the Uniques of Brooklyn engaged in a contest that was described by the press as the "championship of colored clubs." Even by that time the image of black teams as associations of elites was beginning to slip. A large crowd, about half white, at Satellite Grounds in Brooklyn watched the Excelsiors strut around the field, headed by a fife and drum corps. The teams had brought a "pretty rough" crowd with them, according to decorous observers, and the contest was "in no respect credible [*sic*] to the organizations." In fact, the rowdy spectacle brought to mind "the old style of nines which used to prevail among the white clubs." In any case, this championship game among amateurs ended after seven innings because of darkness: Philadelphia Excelsiors, 37; Brooklyn Uniques, 24.[7]

In December 1867 the black Pythian Club of Philadelphia sent a representative to the organizational meeting of the National Association of Base Ball Players (NABBP). The nominating committee, however, voted "unanimously . . . against the admission of any club which may be composed of one or more colored persons."[8] Although the delegates allegedly "all expressed sympathy" to the Pythians, the secretary justified the decision by noting that "if colored clubs were admitted there would be in all probability some division of feeling, whereas, by excluding them no injury could result to anybody, and the possibility of any rupture being created on political grounds could be avoided."[9] The NABBP drew the color line, and although the organization

lasted only a few seasons, it established a precedent that lasted nearly a hundred years.

Although black baseball players never achieved full equality, they did experience a limited integration. Bud Fowler, who played in 1872 with a minor-league club in New Castle, Pennsylvania, was the first black known to have played baseball in the white leagues.[10] Moses Fleetwood Walker, a black catcher, was the first in the major leagues. Upon graduation from Oberlin College in 1883, Walker joined the Toledo Mudhens, a minor-league team in the Northwest League. He became the first black in major-league ball in 1884, when Toledo joined the American Association, a major league from 1882 to 1891.[11] Before 1900 more than sixty blacks played in the white leagues, but they found their situation increasingly precarious as the threats of violence from white fans became more intense. Indeed, some owners began to commission investigations of a few players who were suspected of having a black family heritage. Skin color—not genealogy—was the primary determinant in the unwritten law barring blacks. Men with light complexions "passed," while players with "swarthy" skin often had abbreviated careers.[12]

The individual who is usually blamed for bringing segregation into organized baseball is Adrian ("Cap") Anson. Anson was a versatile, talented athlete who played and managed the Chicago White Stockings during this period of increasing intolerance, and he certainly expressed his dislike of blacks. Although he claimed some responsibility for the exclusion of blacks, Anson was not the only voice.[13] A writer for *Sporting Life* in 1891 admitted that white baseball fans and players were "willing to permit darkies to carry water to them or guard the bat bag, but it made them sore to have the name of one on the batting list." The article continued with the claim that the feet-first slide was developed in order to cripple black opponents.[14] *Sporting News,* the self-proclaimed "Bible of American baseball," conspired against blacks by the use of silence. From 1886 to 1942, only twice did the magazine mention a black player. And in the early 1900s a sketch of black children watching a white team in training carried the caption "Coons."[15]

That blacks were squeezed out of organized baseball at this time is not surprising. Acquiescence to southern demands that racial issues be resolved locally set back the cause of equality. The postwar weakness of the old abolitionists and the efforts to reconcile the North and the South meant that long-present fears and animosities would again dominate relations between the two races. The nineteenth century witnessed the growth of racial stereotypes and the emergence of a new "scientific" racism. Dominant social theories reinforced the belief that there was something inevitable and rigidly inflexible about a segregated social structure. White Americans relied on these scientific findings to justify the growing "institutional racism" which segregated blacks in restaurants, theaters, and other places of public accommodations. The Supreme Court mirrored the mood of the times, culminating in *Plessy* v. *Ferguson* (1896), in which the majority of the justices acknowledged that law was powerless in eradicating "racial instincts." This decision established the idea of "separate but equal" as a justification for discrimination. The *Richmond* (Va.) *Times* spoke for most white Americans in 1900 when it demanded rigid segregation "in every relation of . . . life," on the grounds that "God Almighty drew the color line and it cannot be obliterated."[16]

Though blacks were excluded from white teams, some black clubs continued to play in the white leagues. In particular, the Cuban Giants, who had long been recognized as a drawing card, enjoyed a full schedule against white teams for several years. They defeated all of their white opponents, and by 1888 the *Indianapolis Freeman* hailed them as "virtually champions of the world."[17] This team of former waiters from the Argyle Hotel in Babylon, New York, was sensitive to the growing racism of the era, and as "Cubans," clowning in a gibberish Spanish on the field, they were safer from white fans when they defeated white teams.[18]

Faced with increasing discrimination from white players, fans, and booking agents, black baseball players—like the majority of black Americans in the late nineteenth century—adopted the accommodationist philosophy of Booker T. Washington. Segregated institutions were viewed as a temporary expedient, not as a substitute for the ultimate goal of integration into the mainstream of American life. Black leaders continued the struggle for full integration, appealing on the basis of democratic principles:

> If anywhere in the world the social barriers are broken down it is on the ball field. There many men of low birth and poor breeding are the idols of the rich and cultured; the best man is he who plays best. Even men of churlish disposition and coarse hues are tolerated on the field. In view of these facts the objection to colored men is ridiculous. If social distinctions are to be made, half the players in the country will be shut out. Better make character and personal habits the test. Weed out the toughs and intemperate men first, and then it may be in order to draw the color line.[19]

But as black players were forced out of regular competition in organized baseball, they formed separate teams in segregated leagues.

The first attempt to organize a black baseball league appears to have been made in the South in the spring of 1886. In March of that year, brief newspaper ads asked "captains of all colored baseball clubs of Georgia, Florida, South Carolina, Alabama and Tennessee" to join the Southern League of Colored Base Ballists. Owners, claiming assets of nearly $100,000, did schedule a few games. The ten-team league broke up almost before it had started, but the regulations that governed membership provided a model and a standard of comparison for black leagues in the future. The entrance fee was $5, a sum required to cover the league's costs for printing, advertising, telegraphing, and postage. The rules required the host team to guarantee board, lodging, and travel expenses for visiting clubs. Teams could be expelled for "repeated disorderly conduct, cursing, fighting, drunkenness, etc." Owners were required to subscribe to the *Jacksonville* (Fla.) *Southern Leader,* the league's official organ.[20]

In 1887, teams from six cities tried again, with the formation of the League of Colored Ball Clubs. The press, at least, had great expectations for the new league. *Sporting Life* indicated that one pitcher had signed for $75 a month. More importantly, this league held the promise of feeding blacks into the white organized structure: it was recognized as a legitimate minor league. But the league was short-lived; active by mid April, it was a "failure" by the first of June.[21]

At least three other attempts to establish a black baseball league ended in failure before 1920. The Inter-State League, composed of teams in New York, New Jersey, and Pennsylvania, was organized in 1890 but collapsed during the same season.[22] In 1906, four black and two white teams called themselves the International League of Independent Professional Base Ball Clubs. The organization survived but one season, the victim of changing franchises and financial instability.[23] In 1910, teams in Chicago, Louisville, New Orleans, Mobile, St. Louis, Kansas City (Mo.), Kansas City (Kans.), and Columbus (Ohio) sent representatives to Chicago for the organization of the Negro National Baseball League. Under the guidance of Beauregard Moseley (a black lawyer, businessman, and politician in Chicago), this league adopted a statement of purpose that was a clear exposition of Booker T. Washington's doctrine of self-help. Negroes, he said, were "already forced out of the game from a national standpoint" and were finding it difficult to book games against white semipro teams locally. Moseley feared that the situation presaged "the day when there will be [no opportunities for Negro baseball players], except the Negro comes to his rescue by organizing and patronizing the game successfully, which would of itself force recognition from minor white leagues to play us and share in the receipts." He appealed to the other midwestern representatives: "Let those who would serve the Race and assist it in holding its back up . . . organize an effort to secure . . . the best clubs of ball players possible."[24] Although the owners were enthusiastic, few had the financial resources to support a league. The organization died without having sanctioned a game.[25]

Despite the failure of the leagues, black baseball grew in popularity. From 1900 to 1925, the number of blacks living in cities doubled, to four million. At the same time, the number of black baseball teams began to

Rube Foster (in suit) posed with his 1918 Chicago American Giants, one of the top black teams in the nation. Courtesy of Negro Baseball Hall of History, Ashland, Ky.

increase dramatically, especially in the northern industrial centers, which fostered enough stability and prosperity among the large black populations to sustain professional teams.

On the east coast, New York was the capital of black baseball. The East supported a number of semipro teams, but Harlem's was one of the best in the country. "Cyclone" Joe Williams and "Cannonball" Dick Redding pitched the Lincoln Giants to victory and regional fame.[26] Chicago was the hub city in the Midwest. The black population in this most segregated city in the nation grew by more than 65,000 between 1910 and 1920. In addition, Chicago's black leaders actively tried to counter the discrimi-

nation of organized baseball by establishing black teams and other recreational enterprises. Frank Leland's Chicago Union Giants, and later Andrew ("Rube") Foster's Chicago American Giants, dominated the strong, integrated Chicago city league and served as models for other midwestern teams. During the August-September harvest season, when rural Americans had little time for baseball, many midwestern barnstorming teams converged on Chicago for a month of keen baseball competition.[27]

Black baseball teams almost always started as weekend diversion for the steel workers, meat packers, and railroad workers. With proper management and good booking, several of these weekend teams soon became professional: the players devoted all of their time to playing baseball.[28] Even though these teams sometimes played as many as two hundred games a year, writers for the black *Chicago Defender* insisted that they were merely semipro because player contracts were not in writing and because team rosters varied from game to game.[29] Some black clubs, such as the Cuban Giants and the Page Fence Giants (from Adrian, Mich.), paid good salaries and traveled comfortably by private railroad cars. But Dave Wyatt, a black sportswriter and former member of the Union Giants, contended that the majority of black players were easy victims for white exploitation: "The colored people practically know nothing of baseball and the theories upon which it is based. He knows less of the business side."[30] Players were paid according to their position; fielders received from $12 to $15 a week, and a pitcher who was also a fielder could hope for $18 a week plus expenses—starvation wages according to Wyatt.[31]

In addition to the economic exploitation, black players suffered increasing social problems. Sol White, who played for the Cuban Giants in the 1880s and 1890s, said it was "a common occurrence" for the team "to arrive in a city late at night and to walk around for several hours before finding a lodging." White complained that this was far different from the relatively integrated 1870s.[32] During games, some white teams found ways to humiliate their black opponents. Some would contrive to hold the score at 11 to 7, a "craps score," or would break a watermelon in front of the black team's bench.[33]

Despite the high wall of segregation, black ballplayers were never completely isolated from their white counterparts. The black players continued to compete against the white players on semipro teams and in all-star barnstorming and winter-league games. As the two races continued to compete, more and more white sportswrit-

ers, owners, and managers recognized the talents of black players. Writing to its white constituents in 1912, the *St. Louis Post-Dispatch* wondered "if baseball, after all, is the great American game. We play it, to be sure, but the colored people play it so much better that the time is apparently coming when it shall be known as the great African game."[34] John McGraw, manager of the white New York Giants, admired the ability of John Donaldson, a black pitcher for the All Nations team and later for the Kansas City Monarchs. "If Donaldson were a white man," said McGraw, "or if the unwritten law of baseball didn't bar negroes from the major leagues, I would give $50,000 for him—and think I was getting a bargain."[35] Because of the peculiar nature of white racism, American Negroes were barred from organized baseball, but Cubans were accepted. Some baseball officials saw this as a potential loophole that would allow them to make use of black talent. A club in the New York State League made an unsuccessful offer to Donaldson of $10,000 to go to Cuba, change his name, and then return to their club as a Cuban.[36] The black *New York Age* even encouraged blacks to "keep their mouths shut and pass for Cubans" until the public became accustomed to seeing dark-skinned players in the majors.[37] When the Cincinnati Reds signed two Cubans in 1911, the black press optimistically predicted a fading color line: "Now that the first shock is over, it would not be surprising to see a Cuban a few shades darker . . . breaking into the professional ranks, with a coal black Cuban on the order of the black pitcher, Mendez, making his debut later on."[38]

Despite recognition of their athletic prowess, black baseball players found themselves increasingly segregated in organized baseball as well as in most aspects of their

Left-handed pitcher John Donaldson (seated in the center) posed with the All Nations team, sponsored by Hopkins Brothers, about 1916. Courtesy of George Brace.

lives. World War I and the subsequent rush of blacks to the factories in the northern cities destroyed the notion that the race issue would remain a southern problem. During the recession after World War I, racial animosities exploded into riots, most notably in Chicago. The relatively fluid patterns of race relations in the 1870s hardened during the war years, and white Americans established rigid patterns of discrimination. Baseball officials continued to hold the game up as a reflection of America's democratic principles: "That is the American way, and baseball, as America's National Pastime, offers an easy entry into the field of opportunity."[39] But by 1920 it was clear that this myth of equality did not include black Americans.

# TWO

## Baseball's Shadow

"The much heralded Negro Base Ball League was launched into actual being when a three-day deliberation by the high satelites of the diamond pasttime ended one of the most peaceful and harmonious gatherings ever witnessed among our people."—*Indianapolis Freeman*

Earlier efforts at league organization failed because of financial instability and the lack of strong leadership. The first great economic improvement for blacks came with World War I. Deprived of immigrant labor during the war, factories began to hire black workers. The Great Migration of blacks from the South to northern cities during the war years swelled the black population by as much as 611 percent, in the case of Detroit. As the black population grew in urban centers and as blacks were separated physically from the white city, they began to structure their own communities. And with the resulting prosperity of World War I, they found that they could *afford* to support these separate institutions. Most blacks looked with pride at their accomplishments in constructing a social network: "Why should these dollars be spent with white men or wasted in riotous living? If white men are so determined that Negroes must live separate and apart, why not beat them at their own game?"[1]

For years, black ballplayers had suffered the oppression of white booking agents and owners. Dave Wyatt, writing in the *Indianapolis Freeman*, railed against "the white man who now and has in the past secured grounds and induced some one in the role of the 'good old Nigger' to gather a lot of athletes and then used circus methods to drag a bunch of our best citizens out, only to undergo humiliation, with all kinds of indignities flaunted in their faces, while he sits back and grows rich off a percentage of

11

Andrew (''Rube'') Foster, like other baseball pioneers Spalding, McGraw, and Comiskey, rose through the ranks from star pitcher to manager to owner to administrator. Foster dominated Negro baseball from 1910 until 1926. Courtesy of Robert Peterson.

The Paseo YMCA, where the NNL was organized in 1920. Courtesy of William J. Curtis.

the proceeds."[2] Black sportswriters called for "the Moses to lead the baseball children out of the wilderness."[3] Moses came in the figure of Andrew ("Rube") Foster. A giant, charismatic man, Foster earned his nickname by winning a pitching duel against George ("Rube") Waddell, ace for the American League champion Philadelphia Athletics.[4] When Foster took over the booking of the Chicago Leland Giants and later formed the Chicago American Giants, he commanded respect from his white semipro opponents and 50 percent of the gate receipts. Regarded as the "John McGraw of black baseball," Foster was keenly aware of the drawbacks of playing independent baseball and of depending on white booking agents. In calling for the league meeting, Foster urged owners to unite "in not allowing white men to own, manage and do as they feel like doing in the semi-pro ranks with underhand methods."[5]

Following preliminary meetings in Chicago and Detroit, Foster invited several owners of midwestern black teams and sportswriters from prominent black newspapers to meet at the YMCA and the Street's Hotel in Kansas City, Missouri. The men who attended the meeting on 13 February 1920 were Rube Foster, representing the Chicago American Giants; J. T. ("Tenny") Blount of the Detroit Stars; John Matthews of the Dayton Marcos; Joe Green of the Chicago Giants; C. I. Taylor of the Indianapolis ABCs; Lorenzo Cobb of the St. Louis Giants; J. L. ("Wilkie") Wilkinson of the Kansas City Monarchs; Elwood C. Knox of the *Indianapolis Freeman;* Dave Wyatt of the *Indianapolis Ledger;* Cary B. Lewis of the *Chicago Defender;* and A. D. Williams of the *Indianapolis Ledger.* Elisha Scott, a black attorney from Topeka, Kansas, also attended. Scott's sons would later argue for school desegregation in the landmark *Brown* v. *Board of Education* case.[6]

Foster dreamed of creating a league structure "on the same identical plan as both big leagues and all minor leagues."[7] At the apex of the nationwide professional structure that dominated white baseball after 1900 were two major leagues, the National and the American. Numerous minor leagues, ranked according to quality, completed the vertical structure of organized baseball. The players signed contracts and received regular salaries from the franchise owners. The teams and leagues were governed by an intricate set of rules and agreements. Semipro teams operated outside this structure and employed men who made the bulk of their money at other jobs and played baseball for entertainment. These teams of local amateurs usually divided the gate receipts; the owner (who provided the equipment) took a certain share, and the players split the remainder. Foster hoped that an identical structure in black baseball would "pave the way for [the black] champion team eventually to play the winner among the whites."[8]

After hearing the owners' debates and arbitrating their disputes, the sportswriters and Scott labored through an entire Friday night writing a constitution to present on the next day. The owners adopted the constitution of the National Association of Colored Professional Base Ball Clubs. They envisioned it as the parent organization for all black baseball leagues; they also expressed this hope in their slogan—"We are the Ship, All else the Sea." The constitution outlined rules for the western division, the Negro National League (NNL), which became the first enduring black league.[9]

The constitution provided that (1) managers and owners would be fined for ungentlemanly conduct; (2) managers could

National Association Professional Base Ball Clubs

TELEPHONE DOUGLAS 6059
BASE BALL COMMISSION
A. R. FOSTER, CHAIRMAN
JOHN T. BLOUNT
C. I. TAYLOR
J. L. WILKINSON

CABLE ADDRESS "RUBEFOS"
BOARD OF DIRECTORS
A. R. FOSTER, CHAIRMAN
T. W. CHAMPION
JOE GREEN
C. I. TAYLOR

WE ARE THE SHIP        ALL ELSE THE SEA

DETROIT STARS            AMERICAN GIANTS
TAYLOR'S A. B. C'S.      CHICAGO GIANTS
KANSAS CITY MONARCHS     ST. LOUIS GIANTS
CINCINNATI (CUBAN STARS) COLUMBUS (BUCKEYES)

BASEBALL WESTERN BOOKING AGENCY BUREAU

OPERATING THE NEGRO        NATIONAL LEAGUE, INC.

BACHARACH GIANTS, NEW YORK AND HILDALE, DARBY, PA., ASSOCIATED MEMBERS

The letterhead for the NNL, which expressed the owners' hope for controlling Negro baseball: "We are the ship, all else the sea." Courtesy of Robert Peterson.

not take a team off the field in the middle of a game—a game had to be completed, even if under protest; (3) ballplayers were to conduct themselves properly on and off the field; (4) jumping from one team to another was forbidden; (5) players who jumped their contracts were to be suspended from organized baseball; (6) teams had the right to refuse to play clubs that were not affiliated with the National Association or were in violation of its constitution; (7) owners had the right to trade or sell the services of their players; (8) borrowing players for league games was forbidden; (9) violation of the rules was to carry a heavy fine; and (10) each owner would pay $500 to bind him to the terms of the constitution and as a guarantee of salaries and fines.[10] Foster of Chicago, Taylor of Indianapolis, Blount of Detroit, Green of Chicago, Cobb of St. Louis, and Wilkinson of Kansas City signed the constitution. Ill and unable to attend, John Matthews of Dayton sent a special-delivery letter saying that he was in agreement with the majority decision. Abel Linares's Havana Cuban Stars, represented

by Foster, became the eighth team in the NNL.[11]

Of the owners, only Wilkinson was white. Because of the previous economic exploitation by white owners and booking agents, and in response to the increasing discrimination from white Americans, many black owners and sportswriters hoped that the NNL would be an all-black operation. In a very real sense they saw the NNL as a self-help organization. Foster hoped to confine "a lot of money to the pockets of men of the Race that is now going daily into the pockets of other fellows."[12] In addition, Wilkinson was the only member who did not have a professional black team that was already playing across the nation. Foster wanted Kansas City to be the natural rival for St. Louis and Chicago. Wilkinson had established himself as a baseball force in Kansas City with his popular All Nations team. Somewhat reluctantly, Foster invited Wilkinson to join the NNL.

J. Leslie Wilkinson—"Wilkie" to his friends—was born in Perry, Iowa, in 1874, the son of the president of Algona Normal College. While attending Highland Park College in Des Moines, Wilkinson pitched on the side for a variety of professional and semipro teams in Iowa under the assumed name of Joe Green. He later signed on with

a team sponsored by the Hopkins Brothers Sporting Goods Store in Des Moines. After the team's manager had vanished with the money, Wilkinson's teammates voted him in as manager, deciding that he would be a better manager than player. And Wilkinson was to continue in the management side of the game for the rest of his life. In 1912 Wilkinson and one J. E. Gall organized the All Nations team, which was exactly that—a team with blacks, whites, Cubans, Indians, Mexicans, and Asians. Wilkinson also hired a woman, whom he advertised as "Carrie Nation," to play second.[13]

The All Nations club crisscrossed the Midwest, playing in Missouri, Kansas, Iowa, Nebraska, Minnesota, and Wisconsin. The team traveled in a specially built Pullman coach (said to have cost $25,000) in which the players both ate and slept. Like other nomadic baseball clubs, the All Nations traveled with other entertainers—in this case a wrestling team and an orchestra.

Pitcher J. Leslie Wilkinson (front row, left) with the Hopkins Brothers team. Courtesy of Gladys Wilkinson Catron.

The outfit pulled into town and staged a ball game, a dance, and a wrestling match. Wilkinson even brought his own bleachers and canvas fences. The ballplayers had to be more than good athletes; they were also members of the band. Pitcher José Mendez played cornet. Completing the entourage were Wilkinson's wife, his young son and daughter, and sometimes his younger brother Lee. Pitcher John Donaldson, who became a lifelong friend of Wilkinson, recalled, "We all ate, slept and played together. There was never any trouble. We were a happy family."[14]

The traveling show attracted big crowds, but the international team soon earned a reputation that went beyond novelty. And with good reason. The roster included John Donaldson, José Mendez, and Bill Drake,

Wilkinson managed the interracial All Nations team,
which Hopkins Brothers', Schmelzer's, or Goldsmith's
sporting-goods stores sponsored in various seasons.
Courtesy of Gladys Wilkinson Catron.

who later starred with the Monarchs;
Cristobel Torrienti, who went on to the
Chicago American Giants and the Monarchs; Virgil Barnes, Art Dunbar, and Art
Smith, who then played, respectively, for
the New York Giants, the Chicago White
Sox, and the Kansas City Blues. *Sporting
Life* reported that the All Nations was "an
outfit that baseball sharps claim is strong
enough to give any major league club a nip-
and-tuck battle."[15] In 1915 and 1917 the
"much heralded All Nations" beat Rube
Foster's Chicago American Giants. In 1916
they won two games straight from the
Indianapolis ABCs, who claimed the black
world championship that year.[16]

Like many independent ball clubs, the
All Nations fell apart with the World War I
draft. Wilkinson once related with a chuckle
how the team was playing in Casper,
Wyoming, in 1917 when the draft took five

The All Nations team provided its own bleachers,
canvas awnings, and fences. Courtesy of Gladys
Wilkinson Catron.

The All Nations team traveled first class in its own Pullman coach. Courtesy of Gladys Wilkinson Catron

of the fourteen players. Left with only nine men, the All Nations finished their thirty-five-game schedule, losing only one game—and that by a score of 1 to 0. The All Nations disbanded in 1918, and the remaining players scattered to the American Giants or to other semipro teams. Wilkinson reorganized the team for a short season in the fall of 1919.[17]

The All Nations had originally been based in Des Moines, but by 1915 Wilkinson had moved the team to Kansas City, Missouri. With its meat-packing plants and good railroad connections, Kansas City had both the black population and the access to other large cities that Des Moines lacked.[18] Kansas City also had a lively tradition of black baseball. The "first uniformed colored ball team" in Kansas City was Wall's Laundry Grays, which took the field in 1897. Sponsored by Chinese laundryman Quong Fong, the Grays were reportedly known for their "superior ability at fisticuffs and not at the bat."[19]

At about the same time, J. W. Jenkins, the owner of Jenkins Music Company in Kansas City, Missouri, organized another black club. A strict Methodist, Jenkins withdrew his support when the team started playing Sunday baseball; the squad then took the name Kansas City Monarchs. After Wilkinson organized his team in 1920, fans designated the previous group the Original Monarchs. A. W. Hardy, who often played against the semipro Original Monarchs, remembered them as professional men who had been college athletes. A. E. ("Chick") Pullam worked for the post office; Tom McCampbell, who had previously played with the Laundry Grays, was a pharmacist and owned a drugstore with manager Bill Hueston. The team played into the early 1910s and may have represented Kansas City at the league meeting called by Beauregard Moseley in 1910. But by the time Foster organized the NNL, fans said "the name Monarchs was just a memory around there."[20]

At this same league meeting called by

The Original Kansas City Monarchs in 1908. Courtesy of National Baseball Library, Cooperstown, N.Y.

Moseley, Kansas City had also been represented by the Kansas City, Kansas, Giants.
Politician, gambler, and owner of the
Subway and the Sunset nightclubs, Felix
Payne was also coowner of the Giants
baseball team. He attended the 1910 league
meeting and may have been included in the
preliminary discussions for the NNL. The
*Indianapolis Freeman* listed the Kansas City
Giants as one of the prominent black clubs
in 1917, but the team apparently disbanded
during World War I.[21]

As Foster began to organize the NNL, he
at first tried to work without Wilkinson. He
authorized Dr. Howard Smith, superintendent of Kansas City's black hospital, to form
a team. Smith had no baseball experience
and reportedly lacked the financial basis for
supporting a league team. More importantly,
he lacked a lease for the only suitable
stadium in town, the American Association
Park. Foster was then forced to compromise
and work with Wilkinson, who did hold the
lease for the American Association Park.[22]

Wilkinson received a nod of approval from
the *Indianapolis Freeman* for being an
owner who believed in playing clean ball.[23]
He also evidently won the confidence of the
other owners, who elected him secretary and
Foster president of the NNL.[24]

During his long tenure in the black
leagues, Wilkinson won the respect of those
who worked with him. Wilkinson loved
baseball as a sport, but the game also
offered him a livelihood. Many of his
players believed that as a white owner,
Wilkinson was able to strike better deals
with other white businessmen for leasing
stadiums and booking exhibition games.
When racial tensions occasionally boiled up
during games, a white owner helped to
defuse the situation. Quincy Trouppe recalled an argument with a white player over
an umpire's decision: "I think having a
white owner was the only thing that kept a
real free-for-all from busting loose involving
everybody."[25] Sportswriters praised Wilkinson for his promotion and understanding of
the game. A. D. Williams of the *Kansas
City Call* referred to the stocky, pleasant-
voiced owner as a "baseball genius."[26] Fay

Wilkinson, the only white man in the Negro National League, earned the players' respect by operating like a major-league owner. Courtesy of Gladys Wilkinson Catron.

Young of the *Chicago Defender,* who often echoed the opinions of his close friend Rube Foster, declared: "Wilkie gets credit for being the outstanding baseball promoter in the country and a believer in winning teams."[27]

Shrewd businessman, hustling promoter, Wilkinson earned the esteem of his players by maintaining a first-class operation. When the NNL established a payroll limit, Wilkinson was the only owner who maintained the same salary scale by reducing the number of men on the roster rather than cutting wages. Wilkinson reportedly mortgaged his house during the Great Depression in order to make a payday.[28] According to Newt Allen, "He was the swellest guy in the world. You

could go to him in the winter and borrow against your summer salary."[29] And loaning players money was no guarantee of their services the next season. Many players broke this vicious cycle of living on next year's wages by jumping to another team. Most importantly, the players liked Wilkinson for the way he treated them. Newt Allen, who spent most of his career playing for Wilkinson, explained: "He was a considerate man; he understood; he knew people. Your face could be as black as tar; he treated everyone alike. He traveled right along with us."[30] Allen ("Lefty") Bryant concurred: "Wilkie was a heck of a man. You couldn't ask for a better person to work for. He was due respect, he got it, and he respected you. He was just a fine fellow, that's all."[31] Roy Johnson dismissed the idea that there was any resentment against Wilkinson because he was white: "We all called him Wilkie. He treated us fine. He was accepted by the players. This controversy stuff was up in the office, higher up, with Rube Foster."[32] The Monarchs paid public tribute to Wilkinson in the *Kansas City Call:*

> The best club owner in the world to work
>     for—
> who is familiar with the game as it is
>     today
> who knows how to plan for the future
> who believes in us at all times
> who stands for a fair and square deal to
>     all
> who gives the best and expects the best in
>     return
> who loves and is loved by his players
> who believes that charity begins at home
> who knows and appreciates real ability
> who instills the fighting spirit in his club
> who practices what he preaches
> who never turned on a friend.[33]

The 25th Infantry team provided the core for the first Monarchs team. Bottom row, from the left: Dobie Moore, Bullet Joe Rogan, Lemuel Hawkins, an unidentified player, Heavy Johnson. Andy Cooper and Hurley McNair are in dark sweaters in the upper row at the right. Courtesy of John Holway.

Among black Kansas Citians, Wilkinson also had a good reputation for being diplomatic, unassuming, and easygoing. Robert Sweeney, a recognized leader in the black community, said: "Wilkie stood pretty well with the Negroes. He gave employment to several Negro families. He had a good image in the Negro community—all over the country."[34]

Wilkinson, like the players, had found a way to make money at something he loved. As an entertainment promoter, Wilkinson's role was similar to that of Milton Morris, a white night-club owner in Kansas City. Morris offered no apologies for having made money in jazz: "I'll have somebody accuse me every once in a while, 'You just used the black musicians to make money.' I say, 'Sure I did. What was good for them was good for me.'"[35] Wilkinson's being the only white owner in the NNL never again became an issue after this initial meeting.

After the owners adopted the constitution, they traded some players in order to make the member teams more equal. Foster's overarching desire for a league forced him to trade the future Hall of Famer Oscar Charleston—called "the Franchise" by his teammates—from the American Giants to Indianapolis. When fans complained about losing good players, Foster argued that "only in uniform strength is permanent success."[36]

Many players opposed the league organization because it eliminated their opportunity to make more money by jumping. "Jumping" was the practice of agreeing to play with a team, even accepting a cash advance, and then going elsewhere for more money. Long a problem in professional baseball, jumping kept many midwestern owners from traveling east, because there the relatively more prosperous teams frequently stole players. "It has gotten so bad," the president of the NNL explained, "managers do not trust players, nor do the players trust the managers. It's folly to teach a player to jump and not pay the manager he leaves and expect that same player to be honest with [the new manager]."[37] To the players' complaints, Foster answered that organization and stability would bring money into baseball so that parks could be built, salaries could be higher, and players

The 1920 Monarchs in Kansas City's American Association Park. Top row, from the left: John Donaldson, Sam Crawford, Rube Currie, J. Rodrigues, Zack Foreman, an unidentified player, George Carr, Bullet Joe Rogan. Bottom row, from the left: José Mendez, an unidentified player, Bartolo Portuando, Dobie Moore, Jaybird Ray, Hurley McNair. Courtesy of National Baseball Library, Cooperstown, N.Y.

could have an incentive to develop their talents, believing there was a future in the sport.[38]

In forming his team for the segregated league, Wilkinson chose the core of his All Nations club: José Mendez, John Donaldson, Bill Drake, and Frank Blukoi. He recruited other players on tips from John McGraw, owner of the New York Giants, and from Charles ("Casey") Stengel, manager of the New York Yankees. These two men told Wilkinson about a former army team stationed at Fort Huachuca, Arizona. From that 25th Infantry Unit, Wilkinson picked up Wilbur ("Bullet Joe") Rogan, Dobie Moore, Oscar ("Heavy") Johnson, Lemuel Hawkins, and Bob Fagin.[39] Walter Muir, J. Rodrigues, Jackson, Bartolo Portuando, Sam Crawford, W. Harris, and Bernardo Baro completed the first roster.[40] Because Wilkinson acquired so many of the original group from the 25th Infantry Wreckers—the club that "refused to let any other team hold the championship in Hawaii for years"—the early Monarchs were sometimes known as the "army team."[41] In

describing Kansas City's "rattling good club," one sportswriter explained: "The fielders are sure army men. One went back into the crowd Sunday and got a drive that was tagged for three bases. A sensible player wouldn't have attempted the feat, but the army men know no fear."[42]

When Wilkinson organized this team for the NNL, many players suggested it be called the Kansas City Browns. Pitcher John Donaldson, perhaps harkening back, suggested Kansas City Monarchs. It was an appropriate name; the *Call* sportswriter would later declare the club "MONARCHS OF ALL THEY SURVEY."[43]

Wilkinson had several important links with the black community. In many respects he used Dr. Howard Smith and Quincy J.

Gilmore as his "public face" for the
Monarchs. A well-known small businessman
in the black neighborhood, Gilmore may
have played a role in negotiating the initial
differences between Wilkinson, Foster, and
Smith.[44] Gilmore and Smith often attended
NNL meetings, and during the opening
game ceremonies they, instead of Wilkinson,
rode together in the head car. Smith went on
to be part owner of the Columbus, Ohio,
team and served as one of the four
commissioners for the first Negro World
Series in 1924.[45] In addition, Wilkinson had
early gained support from Judge William C.
Hueston. Hueston, who was active with the
National Association for the Advancement
of Colored People (NAACP), was later
elected president of the NNL.[46]

Q. J. Gilmore served as the traveling
secretary in the Monarchs organization.
Wilkinson had an attack of appendicitis
while he was in Chicago in 1921 and wired
for Gilmore to assume his on-the-road
responsibilities. Throughout the 1920s
Gilmore reserved hotel rooms, made arrangements with restaurants, collected tickets and the Monarchs' share of the gate
receipts, doled out the players' meal money,
kept score, and reported it to the press.[47]
Although his official title with the team was
secretary, the etiquette of segregation made
Gilmore *the* public figure. Gilmore's wife
remembered: "Mr. Wilkinson always kinda
used Gilmore to make his public appear-
ances and addresses and things for him.
Whenever they had to appear in public, Mr.
Gilmore would go and kinda front."[48]
Gilmore—not Wilkinson—rode in the car
with the owners of the opposing team in the
opening-day parades. Gilmore spoke to the
City Twilight League as the Monarchs'
representative and wrote articles about the
team for the black *Kansas City Call*. In the
Monarchs' headquarters—across from

Quincy J. Gilmore, who served as the Monarchs'
traveling secretary and organized the Booster Club.
Courtesty of Alberta Gilmore Penn.

Street's Hotel, above a pinochle and roulette
room at 1517 E. 18th—Gilmore ran the
news room, where players and fans could
receive more information about the team.
Gilmore and the Monarchs' pitcher "Bullet
Joe" Rogan also operated what they termed
the "official headquarters of the team"—the
Monarchs Billiard Room.[49]

The manager, who had responsibility for
the team on the field, was the pivotal
member of the squad. Sometimes a player-
manager, he coached and kept the men
working as a team. Most importantly he
passed along his years of baseball knowledge to the younger men. NNL President
Rube Foster freely taught a whole generation of managers. Newt Allen and Newt
Joseph acquired much of their baseball
wisdom from long talks with the master.

The manager was also the one who disciplined through his power to fine. Fines were levied for a variety of reasons, although "indifferent playing" and fighting probably were the most common ones. As owner, Wilkinson retained the final decision about hiring and firing, but he almost always consulted the manager. Younger players, on the road for the first time, looked to the manager for advice on everything from homesickness to hitting slumps. He might control their spending or advise them when it was time to go home to a steady job and raise a family. Jesse Williams, who came up under managers William ("Dizzy") Dismukes and Andy Cooper, spoke fondly of the manager: "He was the pitching coach, batting instructor, manager, your father away from home. We were his kids out there."[50] One team member was considered the captain. Usually a veteran player, he helped the manager and coached.

Frank ("Jewbaby") Floyd—known simply as "Jewbaby" to players and fans—served as the Monarchs' trainer for more than thirty years. An old baseball scout and Kansas City's only licensed black chiropractor, Jewbaby traveled with the team to give rubdowns and ease the pain of charley horses, lame shoulders, bad ankles, and cuts. The sportswriter of the *Call* joked about Jewbaby's "valiant attempts to poison the squad with various concoctions of his own manufacture, carried over from the days when he doctored the nags on his farm. Jewbaby can't seem to be able to differentiate between ball players and mules."[51] Team trainers sometimes filled another role—that of cupid, carrying messages between female fans and players. A friend once said of Jewbaby that "his advice extended to the moral and psychological as well as the physical well-being of his players."[52] When the Monarchs played in Kansas City, Jewbaby distributed placards advertising the games, supervised the locker room at the stadium, and maintained the headquarters office when Secretary Gilmore was away. In the off-season, Jewbaby operated a massage parlor for the public at the Belleview Hotel and served as trainer for the Kansas City Greyhounds hockey team.[53]

Finally, the Monarchs had a mascot, a youngster aspiring to be a player, who posted each inning's tally on the outfield scoreboard and carried the players' luggage and equipment. Though the players boasted that their mascot was "the best in the league," his name often went unrecorded. Wilkinson, Bullet Joe Rogan, Frank Duncan, and Hilton Smith all had sons who assisted as bat boys at home games.[54]

The number of players on the team's roster varied from year to year. Black teams could not afford to carry many reserves. The largest roster was reported in 1922, when the Monarchs left for a series in St. Louis with twenty-one men; most teams traveled with sixteen.[55] In a joint meeting in 1924, the Negro National League and the rival Eastern Colored League (ECL) agreed on an upper limit of twenty. By 1928, however, sportswriters had convinced the owners to reduce their rosters to fourteen, a limit that they maintained as long as the leagues lasted. A. D. Williams, sportswriter for the *Call*, always advocated twelve or thirteen players plus a manager—in his view, those who could not sustain the pace were not worthy of being members of the team. While financially beneficial, a small roster had disadvantages. The worst was that injured players were almost obligated to continue playing.[56] While the permissible number of players varied from year to year, the Monarchs' roster also fluctuated during the course of the season (see Appendix A

Kansas City's sandlot teams served as training ground for several future Monarchs. Courtesy of Urban League of Greater Kansas City.

for yearly rosters). Some of the new recruits did not last; some players quit in midseason or jumped to another team. Like their counterparts in jazz, ballplayers with talent and ambition moved at will from one team to another. The pitching staff, in particular, appears to have been extremely fluid. The Monarchs generally signed five pitchers; in 1925, however, Wilkinson started the season with eight.

Many young men clamored for a tryout with the team. Pitcher Hilton Smith claimed that "everybody, *everybody*—anybody that played baseball wanted to play with the Monarchs."[57] The *Call* announced that any local boy who wanted a tryout could call the Monarchs' headquarters to make arrangements. Kansas City had an array of sandlot and semipro clubs. Several teams organized in 1922 as the Negro Twilight League, with the Monarchs' Secretary Gilmore as president. The *Call* hailed this effort and hoped

that the Twilight League would be the training ground for Monarchs players and umpires. Many of the teams represented local industries: the Leeds Black Oilers, Wilson Packing, the City Ice Company, the Rock Island Railroad, the Santa Fe Scouts, Lilley Motors, the Missouri Pacific Freights, the Kansas City Call, and the 18th Street Merchants. Other youngsters formed neighborhood clubs and adopted traditional names for their teams—Royals, Crowns, Athletics, Red Sox, Black Stars, and Tigers.[58] The Monarchs trained at Paradeway Park at 17th and the Paseo, in the heart of the black community, playing against the strongest of these semipro teams. When Wilkinson saw an opponent with promise, he paid them a few dollars and gave them a chance to break into the line-up. Newt Allen, Frank Duncan, Eddie Dwight, Rube Currie, Roy Johnson, and Allen Bryant all started on Kansas City's sandlots. Newt Allen, who played second base for the Monarchs for twenty-eight years, started as a "canvas puller" and ice boy at the American Association Park when the Monarchs organized in 1920. He practiced with the team, pulled the canvas (tarp) over the field, and in return received two or three balls from the grounds keeper, for games with his neighborhood friends.[59] Young Frank Duncan tried out for the job of bat boy simply "to get into the park."[60] Chet Brewer remembered having sat up in a tree outside the left-field grandstand at Muehlebach Stadium watching Bullet Joe Rogan pitch: " 'Boy,' I said, 'I sure would like to get a chance to play down in there.' But I never dreamed I would."[61]

When traveling, Wilkinson had a knack for spotting ability in the Monarchs' opponents. The Monarchs frequently went to Texas for spring training. These southern forays not only limbered the team up for the long summer but also gave Wilkinson a chance to scout new talent. Leroy Taylor, Hallie Harding, L. D. Livingston, Henry Milton, Hilton Smith, and Pat Patterson developed on the diamonds of Wiley College and Prairie View College in the Lone Star State.[62] While barnstorming, Wilkinson continued to evaluate the opposing players. He signed Hilton Smith after seeing him pitch for the Bismarck, North Dakota, team. Wilkinson also encouraged team members to recommend prospects from the winter leagues in California and Cuba. In particular, Wilkinson signed Jackie Robinson on the advice of Hilton Smith.[63]

New recruits started playing against weaker teams in exhibition games which did not affect league standings. This gave Wilkinson a chance to see them play under pressure and a chance to rest his regulars. At some point, Wilkinson would make his choice: an offer to play with the Monarchs, an offer to play with the All Nations or another semipro team for "seasoning," or a railroad ticket home.[64]

While there was no organized farm-club system, Wilkinson had connections that enabled him to "season" promising young talent. In the early 1920s the All Nations served as the Monarchs' farm club. As he formed the Monarchs, Wilkinson apparently reorganized the All Nations team and based it in Omaha, Nebraska. Many Monarchs, such as Newt Allen and Willie Bobo, spent a rookie year with that team, and some veteran Monarchs, who could no longer sustain the league pace, retired to the All Nations—for their names still drew a crowd in small towns. The All Nations allowed Wilkinson to reduce the Monarchs squad and at the same time to keep "strings on the surplus material."[65] The All Nations served another function; when manager Sam Crawford had discipline problems, he could send offenders to the All Nations for the remainder of the season.[66] The All Nations closed the 1923 season with 117 wins and only 14 losses. By 1924, however, sportswriters reported that the All Nations had disbanded as a result of the raids made between the eastern and midwestern teams.[67]

Wilkinson also maintained a close affiliation with Robert Gilkerson's Union Giants—"the shady diamond gladiators from Illinois," as one reporter described them.[68] This team traveled around the Midwest, playing almost two hundred games a year; but because they had no league affiliation, they were considered semipro. Gilkerson's team appears to have filled the same role that the All Nations did before it disbanded. Several Monarchs started with Gilkerson—Hurly McNair, Cristobel Torrienti, Chet Brewer, George Giles, Eddie Dwight, T. J. Young, Rube Currie, Doolittle Young, and Fred DeWitt. Wilkinson seasoned his new recruits with Gilkerson, in return for the latter's promising players. When Wilkinson released players to Gilkerson's team (so that

The Monarchs in practice, about 1932. From the left: an unidentified player, Q. J. Gilmore, T. Y. Baird, J. L. Wilkinson, Carroll Mothel. Courtesy of Kansas State Historical Society.

he could stay within the NNL limit), the players still were considered the "property" of the Monarchs.[69]

During the 1930s and 1940s, Wilkinson worked out a farm-club arrangement with Winfield Welch's Acme Giants of Shreveport, Louisiana. (Later, Welch became manager of the Birmingham Black Barons and the Harlem Globetrotters.) Wilkinson spotted Buck O'Neil and Willard Brown while the Monarchs were barnstorming against the Acme Giants in spring training.[70]

Because of finances and league restrictions about the size of the roster, new players had to prove themselves quickly on the field and in the dugout. Joe Greene, a Monarchs' catcher during the war years, recalled:

They say we had a "syndicate" there. We admitted it too. We wanted certain guys on the ball club, and if one man wasn't the right kind of guy, five or six of us on the ball team had ways and means of getting him off the team. And he knew it. The team wasn't going to join him, he's going to join the team. He's got to weave himself into the team.[71]

The Monarchs usually started spring training with twenty to thirty men, and sportswriters chronicled the "merry scramble among last year's regulars and the new men to gain a place on the old payroll."[72] The old players did not help the new ones very much, for as pitcher Bill Drake explained, "They couldn't afford to tell you something, they'd only push themselves out of a job."[73] Team tradition demanded that veteran players receive respect. Manager Joe Rogan advised rookies to "await your opportunity." He suggested that they make friends with the older players and in a "nice and quiet way let them know you're anxious to make good but realize you have lots to learn." Rogan assured rookies that "if you

Schmelzer's Sporting Goods Store, which had earlier sponsored the All Nations team, outfitted the Monarchs during the 1920s. *Kansas City Call,* 27 April 1928.

deal of cooperation.[75] The good relationship between the players, managers, and Wilkinson was one of the Monarchs' strengths. Newspaper stories on spring training generally described the players as being in "fine spirits"—not haggling and holding out for more money, as did players on so many other teams.[76]

Every player bought his own glove and shoes, which he carried in a "suit roll" along with his bats and uniforms. Wilkinson bought the uniforms—usually three sets. He liked a variety of colors. At various times the team was outfitted in suits of gray with maroon striping, gray pinstripes, white with maroon trim (saved for home games), black and white, blue, and gray with navy trim. The uniforms usually had Monarchs across the chest and KC on the sleeves.[77]

In the early 1920s the Monarchs—"chief Wilkinson's warriors"—trained locally. They played exhibition games in April against Kansas City semipro teams, the All Nations, semipro teams in Kansas, or a team of prisoners at the federal penitentiary in Leavenworth, Kansas. When the rookies left to play in nearby Kansas towns, the veteran Monarchs would sometimes assemble at the home park for a weekend series.[78]

By the mid 1920s the Monarchs joined other black teams for spring training in the southern states. As soon as players reported to the team, they were in barnstorming games. Catcher Roy Campanella said of his ten years in the Negro Leagues: "No sooner did you pull on your uniform and crack a sweat than you were in a game, playing before paying customers. *Play* yourself into shape."[79] The Monarchs liked Hot Springs, Arkansas; Houston and San Antonio, Texas; and Shreveport, Louisiana, as places to prepare for the long season. As the 1920s came to a close and times became tougher, however, few teams chose to spend a month

act like a gentleman, he will be glad to help you."[74] Some rookies found it difficult to defer to the veterans; they wanted respect for their abilities too. "Internal strife and petty jealousies" of this sort hurt the Monarchs in the early 1920s, but by the end of the decade, sportswriter A. D. Williams reported that the Monarchs showed a good

The Monarchs took their spring training in Hot Springs, Arkansas, in 1928. Courtesy of Black Archives of Mid-America.

in the Sun Belt. In 1929 only the Monarchs could afford the treat.[80]

Whatever the financial highs and lows, the Monarchs never lacked challengers when they began their barnstorming season. It seemed that nearly everyone had a baseball club. Teams organized in post-office leagues, YMCA leagues, church leagues, Sunday School leagues, industrial leagues, and railroad leagues. Blacks, no less than whites, fell victim to the baseball craze of the 1920s.

A problem that all teams shared concerned the acquisition of competent umpires. This issue became an immediate stumbling block for the newly organized Negro National League. At first the home team arranged for the umpires and paid them. For league games, black teams used only two umpires—one at first base and one behind the plate. "A Third man," thought the sportswriter for the *Call*, "is a valuable asset, and would undoubtedly be used as a

regular thing, except that the cost does not offset the benefit derived."[81] For exhibition games the teams employed one umpire, who stood behind the pitcher. Many owners hired umpires from the white International League for NNL games. In some cities, such as Chicago, local umpires formed a union. When the park management informed the union about a game, the organization sent men to cover it. For exhibition games the umpire was often chosen from the fans in the grandstand.[82] Whatever the local arrangements, fans felt that umpires favored the team that was paying them. Pitcher Doolittle Young gave details of one experience with hometown umpires:

> I don't know where I wasn't sweating unless it was my eyes. The umpire—he stood behind me, he wasn't behind the catcher—and every time I got ready to pitch, he'd holler, "Ball!" And I said, "Just wait til I throw the ball and then you can call it a ball. Now the next one you call a ball, I'm going to get on you." I drawed back to throw and he called a ball and I reached down and got a double

handful of sand and put it down his collar, and he took me out of the game. I was sure glad cause it was hot out there.[83]

Rube Foster and Fay Young led a three-year campaign to get the league to pay for umpires. More importantly, Foster and Young argued for "umpires of color," so as to strengthen the race's control of its own enterprise. Young wrote:

> It isn't necessary for us to sit by the thousands watching eighteen men perform in the national pastime, using every bit of strategy and brain work, to have it all spoiled by thinking it is impossible to have any other man officiating but pale faces. Give us a change.[84]

By the beginning of the 1923 season the NNL had signed six black men (mostly former players) to umpire league games. With careful scheduling, the league arranged to have two of these umpires at each game for the next three years.[85]

Fans and the press initially received black umpires with enthusiasm. A white sportswriter reported that "Negro umpires, used for the first time . . . handled the game in big league style, their decisions were good and fair."[86] But the attitude soon changed. There were repeated charges of incompetence, as well as numerous incidents when players and managers physically attacked umpires over a decision. Fans expressed their dislike with "pop bottle showers." A black umpire, one friend of the game commented, had to be restrained—"something like a Pullman porter, no matter how bad you are treated and misused by the fans, you must not lose your head."[87] Sportswriters lamented the fact that the majority of black fans did not consider black men capable of umpiring games. League officials

revealed their own opinions by paying black umpires $25 for work in the World Series or East-West games, at a time when white umpires were receiving $43 for umpiring in the same games.[88]

This lack of confidence in black umpires was just one example of the problem that black leaders often faced in trying to establish their own communities. Businessmen, newspaper editors, and clergymen stressed that patronage of black businesses was a moral obligation for the advancement of the race. Yet they continually found black customers favoring white enterprises. The result, complained one minister, was that "all of that money goes into the white man's pocket and then out of our neighborhoods. It is used to buy white men cars and homes, and their wives mink coats and servants. Our money is being used by the white man to pay us for being his cook, his valet, and his washerwoman."[89] Leaders decried this inferiority complex as a hangover from slave reasoning: "The Negro people, as a whole are suspicious of their own leaders. They hesitate to patronize their doctors and dentists or to purchase supplies from Negro stores. This lack of confidence is a relic of slavery days, when the Negro was forced to look upon his race as inferior."[90]

By the late 1920s the idea of league umpires was abandoned. In addition to the problem of lack of confidence, president Rube Foster seemed to become an irrational boss. He apparently suffered a mental illness that ultimately forced his departure from baseball in 1926. Foster fired four umpires in late summer 1925 and refused to pay them the money that was stipulated in their contracts. Unwilling to endure Foster's unpredictable behavior, the remaining two umpires quit.[91]

Financial instability was another factor.

NNL officials had promised to give the umpires a 15 percent raise in their $142 monthly salary in 1924 and 20 percent in 1925. The umpires not only failed to receive the increases, but by 1927 the league could not afford to hire umpires at all. The owners decided that each team would again employ its own men to work in that city only. Black umpires continued to predominate. Wilkinson frequently used former NNL umpires Bert Gholston and Robert Boone; later he hired former players Hurly McNair, Bullet Rogan, and Frank Duncan to officiate at Monarchs games. Although the owners occasionally tried to reestablish a league umpire staff, their efforts were never successful.[92]

Beyond the problems with umpires, the NNL owners had to come to some agreement about clubs that were not members of the league. Foster advocated that all black clubs—from the East, the West, or the South and pro or semipro—should belong to one organization, namely, the National Association of Colored Professional Base Ball Clubs. In his plan, teams like the Homestead Grays, Gilkerson's Union Giants, and members of the Southern League would serve as farm clubs for the NNL. They would sell their best players to the major black teams according to the model already established in white baseball. The plan came closest to reality when the Texas-Oklahoma-Louisiana (TOL) League formed in 1929. Under the leadership of the Monarchs' secretary, Q. J. Gilmore, the TOL League asked for such an agreement at the annual NNL meeting in 1930. Since the NNL teams had already lost several players to the TOL League, the owners welcomed the idea. But the TOL League folded before the plans could be finalized.[93]

The Southern League (SL), which was modeled after the NNL in 1920, operated sporadically through the 1940s. In 1927 the NNL officials adopted plans for making the SL teams associate members of the NNL. Associate members had their schedules booked by the NNL, but games against these teams did not figure in the league standings. The scheme also included provisions for buying and trading players and a protective clause stating that all exhibition games in either territory had to be played against league teams. Associate members enjoyed full schedules and league protection for only half the cost of a full membership. But some SL owners resented the restrictions, and some could not afford even a $500 membership; so the plan came to little. Because Jim Crow laws prevented black teams from competing against white opponents in their home territory, the SL clubs never experienced the financial stability of the northern teams. Although the SL teams did not officially constitute a farm system, the NNL scooped up their best players quickly. With teams in the main black population centers, the SL continued to be a fertile training ground for the NNL and provided an important link between the North and the South. Depending on their financial situation, Memphis, Birmingham, and St. Louis seesawed between the NNL and the SL.[94]

The real hope that NNL owners had for the SL was that it would form a stronger link between the Midwest and the South and would make the eastern teams see the folly of operating separately. But the eastern teams continued independently, largely as the result of a feud between Foster and Ed Bolden, the owner of the Hilldale, Pennsylvania, club. In 1922 Bolden withdrew from the NNL because all but two NNL teams refused to make the long, expensive trip to Pennsylvania. The NNL officials did not figure the Hilldale team into the league

standings, and Bolden felt cheated. When Bolden withdrew, Foster refused to return Bolden's thousand dollars of good-faith money. Although there was a provision in the NNL constitution that required the forfeiture of good-faith money if a team withdrew, Bolden was angry because some associate members had not made such deposits in the first place. Bolden accused Foster of running the league for his own benefit. Foster claimed that the money was advance compensation for the player raids that Bolden announced he would make.[95]

The black press predicted Bolden's regret over being an outlaw from the NNL. Instead, Bolden became the organizing force for the Mutual Association of Eastern Colored Baseball Clubs and the Eastern Colored League (ECL). This second major league was organized in Philadelphia on 12 December 1923, with Bolden serving as chairman of the commission. The six-team

Ed Bolden withdrew from the NNL in 1922 and organized the rival Eastern Colored League. Bolden, on the far right, with the commissioners of the 1924 World Series. Courtesy of Craig Davidson.

league consisted of Ed Bolden's Hilldale club; Nat Strong's Brooklyn Royal Giants; Thomas Jackson's New York Bacharach Giants; James Keenan's New York Lincoln Giants; Alex Pompez's Havana Cuban Stars; and Charles Spedden's Baltimore Black Sox.[96]

Foster opposed the formation of another league on several counts, but the real point of contention was the predominance of white owners in the ECL. Four of the six were white, leaving Bolden and Pompez with little influence. From the beginning, despite Bolden's organizational efforts, black sportswriters insisted that white booking agent Nat Strong "was the league and ran the league," because he did the booking for five of the six ECL clubs.[97] Foster, though he knew that the two races could do business together—Wilkinson's good standing in the NNL was a case in point—said: "There can be no such thing as [a black baseball league] with four or five of the directors white any more than you can call a street car a steamship. There would be a league all right, but the name would have to be changed."[98]

In 1924 the two leagues reached a strained peace, reportedly with the aid of Commissioner Kenesaw Mountain Landis. Officials agreed that Pittsburgh and Buffalo would be the dividing line between eastern and western territory. NNL owners also agreed to let the eastern teams keep players who had jumped their contracts, but the owners demanded that they be reimbursed for lost advance money. Relations were friendly enough to permit a Negro World Series at the end of the 1924 season, but the harmony was tested yearly over territory, player raids, salaries, and player contracts.[99]

A standard contract evolved in the Negro leagues, which included a reserve clause binding a player to the same team for the following year. All players theoretically signed a contract, but with many the agreement was verbal. Pat Patterson explained: "Each year back in those days you'd put your services out for hire; you'd write to three or four teams. The one that would give you the best salary would be the one that you'd go to."[100] Monarchs' shortstop Jesse Williams elaborated:

> The year we *really* signed contracts was after the year when Jackie [Robinson] came to the Monarchs and after he had signed with organized baseball. And then the contracts that we signed were the same kind of contracts that they signed in the major leagues—after Jackie. But

[before] more or less it was just word of mouth, you're on your honor, with a written letter [from the owner].[101]

Even players who did sign often felt no compulsion to honor the reserve clause, and they freely sought the highest offer. The eastern teams generally were more affluent, since they had larger black populations from which to draw crowds; and they began to raise salaries "to a point," said midwestern owners, "where they abandoned all sense of reason."[102] NNL magnates continued to pay what they considered living wages, but eastern sportswriters criticized them for offering only "starvation wages."[103] The NNL lost eighteen players to the ECL during the first two years. Finally, in an effort to keep balance among the teams, the NNL and the ECL established a payroll limit of $3,000 a month during the 1926 season. Throughout the 1920s the average black player earned from $135 to $175 a month during the six-month season. In comparison, workers in meat-packing plants made about $80 a month. Club owners bragged that even their lowest salary was comparable to that made by a post-office clerk, a schoolteacher, or the sportswriter who reported their games.[104] As a reflection of the status of blacks in the nation's economic hierarchy, black major leaguers earned less than one-fifth of the salary demanded by their white counterparts. Players in the black major leagues made about as much as a white Class B minor-league player.[105] Even so, NNL and ECL owners struggled to balance their ledger books, and the "raiding war" of 1925 caused most of them to go into debt. The NNL officials angrily denounced the ECL as an outlaw organization.[106]

Another problem that the Negro leagues faced was that only one team owner held the deed for his own playing field. Gus Greenlee, owner of the Pittsburg Crawfords, built Greenlee Field in 1932 with $100,000 earned in the numbers racket. But the rest of the owners could not afford this luxury. In the mid 1920s the NNL discussed a "sinking fund," which would finance loans for the purchase of parks. Each owner was to deposit $5,000 and a percentage of his gate receipts. The plan never materialized, because most owners could not afford the initial investment.[107] Negro-league owners at first leased minor-league or city parks; then later, when their economic clout was stronger, they rented major-league stadiums. Many of the city parks were so small that extra chairs had to be placed on the field in front of the grandstands. Without a fence to check their zeal, spectators often rushed onto the field to argue over a decision.

The major drawback to the leased parks, however, was that the black teams had to schedule around the white team's calendar. Each NNL team played about two hundred games a season. Ideally, half of these were against league teams; the rest were barnstorming matches. Although the NNL had a hundred-game schedule, conflicts with park owners for playing dates meant that most teams did not complete it. In 1922, for example, the champion Chicago American Giants played fifty-two league games; the second-place Kansas City Monarchs played seventy-four, while the last-place Cleveland Tate Stars played only forty-six. In addition, some owners simply refused to take to the road for long, unprofitable league trips. Gate receipts were divided so that the home team kept 45 percent, the visitors received 35 percent, 15 percent went for stadium rental, and 5 percent went to the league for operating expenses. But league custom allowed visiting teams to ask for a guarantee of expenses. If crowds were small, 35

**DON'TS FOR NEWCOMERS**

Don't hang out windows
Don't promenade on the boulevards in your hog-killing clothes
Don't walk the streets swearing at the top of your voice.
Don't try to be funny with strangers.
Don't indulge in hugging contests on the grass plots of the boulevards.
Don't try to browbeat anybody on street cars, or in public places.
Don't forget that you are a citizen and as such are expected to be an active force for decency and welfare.
Don't clean your finger nails and pick your nose on the street.
Don't flirt with the grocer, especially if your hair is still chunky and full of bed lint.
Don't sit out on the front steps in bare feet and undershirt.
Don't drink moonshine, especially before going joy-riding.
Don't try to be "bad"; you'll get too much encouragement.
Don't throw garbage and trash out front or rear windows.
Don't forget to bathe—have somebody remind you.
Don't glory in your ignorance and dirt.
Don't forget that you can be disgusting as easily as anybody else.
Don't play off the job and sleep on the job.
Don't go shopping in the Loop wearing your overalls or dress aprons.
Don't discuss your or other persons' personal affairs over the telephone.
Don't forget to memorize "Please" and "Thank you."
Don't brag.
Don't stand on corners and insult women who pass!
Don't spit on the sidewalks, on the floor, or in waste paper baskets. Use gutters and cuspidors.
Don't be a grouch.
Don't be a four-flusher.
Don't be silly.
Don't send your children to school half fed and half dressed.
Don't let your children run you.
Don't make friends.
Don't try to be a fool—it's too easy to succeed.
Don't lounge on the boulevard in overalls.
Don't forget to change clothes before leaving stockyards.
Don't ride on the motor bus unless you are dressed properly.

The black press tried to ease rural blacks' adjustment to urban life by publishing advice about acceptable behavior. *Chicago Defender,* 14 July 1923.

percent might not be enough. The home team then had to reimburse the visiting club. Owners could not see any logic in having Wilkinson, for example, pay a thousand dollars of travel expenses for the Birmingham Black Barons when the gross receipts from three or four games might be only $400. To encourage more complete schedules, Wilkinson proposed a scheme in 1927 whereby all teams would share equally in the cost of league travel. The system worked for a couple of seasons, but some teams were going into debt just to finish the schedule. Birmingham and Memphis lacked large enough black populations to support NNL teams, and they dropped out of the league because of the travel expenses.[108]

"Respectability" was a constant concern among northern blacks, in general, and the baseball leagues in particular. During the early twentieth century, as the patterns of white discrimination crystallized, older black residents in the northern cities tended to believe that the deterioration of race relations was caused by the black masses who brought their peasant ways from the South. Rather than condemning white racism for the poverty and squalor of the overcrowded tenements, these blacks blamed the victims for the crime. The rural habits of the newcomers infuriated the older blacks, who complained that uncleanliness, slovenly dress, and loud talk would only diminish the status of the whole race in the eyes of the white majority. According to this way of thinking, race relations could be improved if blacks would adopt white middle-class standards. Booker T. Washington tried to convince his followers that full citizenship rights could be gained only after blacks had demonstrated their hard work and thrift. Black editorials urged their readers to "be efficient" and "strive and succeed." The *Chicago Defender* issued a list of twenty-six "Don'ts for Newcomers" as a guide for public behavior. The *Cleveland Advocate* implored its readers: "Let us one and all think 'the color of snow.' We have been thinking black for a long while."[109]

This striving for respectability was accentuated in the Negro leagues. Black ballplayers not only had to establish their league as being equal to the white major leagues; they also had to gain acceptance within the black community.

In the wake of the Black Sox scandal, Rube Foster contended that baseball's problem was that in their "narrow ignorance," leading people all over the country believed the game was fit only for the "sporting element" and not for their children.[110] To dispel this belief, black baseball leaders urged players to "link up with people of good names and standing in the communities"—the class of people "without which no business can survive."[111] But Chet Brewer, who began a long pitching career with the Monarchs in 1925, has recalled

how difficult this was to do in the early years:

> I can't say that we were really accepted because we had some ball players that were a bit uncouth, and so they classed all of us the same. They'd come out there and cheer for us, but they didn't invite us to the homes—a lot of them didn't because we weren't their peers. They didn't know us though. They didn't know that some of us had gone to college, that some of us taught school. A lot of the fans didn't know that. They only knew the bad side of the players.[112]

Like white baseball, the Negro leagues actively recruited college players. It was a reciprocal relationship: educated players added to the propriety of the game. Parents were reassured that an athletic son could finish his degree during the winters. For George Sweatt, playing with the Monarchs meant earning tuition money for medical school. College students—as the *Pittsburgh Courier* pointed out—found baseball more dignified "than dish washing, hotel work, dining car and Pullman porter services," the usual summer jobs.[113] By 1923, black umpire Tom Johnson felt that Rube Foster and the NNL had elevated baseball "from the gutter to such a position of cleanliness and respect that even our modest college graduates can point with pride to the fact that he is a ball player instead of as conditions were ten years ago, when ball players were looked upon as uncouth and ungentlemanly persons."[114]

In their efforts to make the game and their teams respectable, owners and sportswriters concentrated on the personal appearance and conduct of the players. Cumberland ("Cum") Posey, owner of the Homestead Grays, instructed his players that "ordinary people making the same money

as ball players mix with everybody, dress neatly but moderately, and are moderate in all things. Baseball players should do the same thing."[115] Stylish dressing became part of the image of professional ballplayers. Second baseman Othello ("Chico") Renfroe relished the memory of initiating new players. When Wilkinson recruited players from small towns, he bought them a new suit of clothes. Renfroe commented: "You know, guys who didn't even know what a suit of clothes was. But I tell you, those guys could step out of those club houses Sunday sharp as a tack."[116] The Monarchs were known as good dressers, especially third baseman Newt Joseph and first baseman Buck O'Neil. Veteran Monarchs strictly enforced the ideas about "proper" dress, which usually meant a suit for travel. Pitcher Allen ("Lefty") Bryant remembered being "called down" by the older players during his rookie season with the team:

Matlaw's Clothing Store, at Eighteenth and Vine, stayed open extra hours when the Monarchs were in town. Courtesy of Black Archives of Mid-America.

Most kids—18, 19, 20 years old—they figured people don't know who they are unless they have on their ball jacket. And that's not right. Because Monarchs never wore ball jackets—we just didn't do that. You wore them on the bus, but when you got off, you left them. A couple of times, I was called down. We were in a little town and I thought I was real keen and I put my jacket on and walked down the street. They told me, "Go on and put on a sports jacket and don't wear that jacket up and down the street. We just don't do those things."[117]

Owners were also concerned about making a good impression on the field. Gilmore, for one, was glad that the leagues were past the days when no two members of the same team dressed alike. By 1924 every team in the NNL had two or more complete sets of uniforms, with sweaters.[118] The New York Bacharachs, to whom some people conceded the reputation for being the best-dressed team in the league, carried four sets of uniforms when they traveled. The *Call* sportswriter noted with approval that the NNL adopted regulation uniforms for umpires in 1927: "They together with the players will try to excell in appearance."[119]

Conduct on and off the field seemed to be a larger problem than cleanliness and personal appearance. The black elite pointed to rowdy behavior in public as the one trait that was most likely to embarrass the race and disgrace its members in the eyes of whites. Rube Foster charged that "colored baseball players are harder to handle than the white player. It seems to be characteristic of our race to act according to the size of attendance, the larger the attendance, the worst [*sic*] our actions."[120] Rowdy actions sometimes included drinking and cursing. "I have seen players walk off the playing field," objected one owner, "to take a drink of bootleg whiskey from the bottle of some rowdy fan, and they use profane language in front of the grandstands, where the fans may hear it."[121] When attendance began to drop, owners and sportswriters were quick to say that "roughneck ball, the scurvy of the diamond," was killing the game.[122]

The game itself was rough at this time. Buck O'Neil remarked: "They've made rules now that keep you from getting too hard. But before, any way they could get you out of there, they would get you out of there."[123] Some players filed their spikes to injure opposing basemen in a slide. Newt Allen, who was often fined because of his quick temper, needed eighteen stitches in his leg when Dave Malarcher slid under a tag.

"Years later," Allen recalled, "I gave into my feelings [of revenge]. I caught him in a double play—he was on first, the ball was hit, the shortstop threw the ball to me, and in throwing the ball to first base, I threw right at his head."[124] Pitchers, too, threw at batters. Doolittle Young has freely admitted: "I threw at anybody. Keeps 'em loose. Now after the ball game's over, we're all good friends again."[125] Black ballplayers' enthusiasm for the game sometimes exploded into fights with umpires and members of the opposing teams, especially when some rivalry had developed or some honor was at stake. Othello Renfroe, a Monarchs infielder, explained:

> Very seldom you played a ball game—a really close ball game—two teams fighting for a pennant or for second place or something—you didn't have a fight. The game was just that heated. The manager didn't want you out there if you didn't have some fight in you. You'd fight your own teammates if they were loafing.[126]

Though Kansas City was not without its offenders, the Monarchs seemed to have a better-than-average reputation for conduct on the field. Sports critic Fay Young decided that Chicago suffered small crowds because fights often delayed the games and drove fans away. "Kansas City always has a good crowd," he noted approvingly, "because the fans know there is going to be a nip and tuck, a hard fought game with each team giving its best."[127] Wilkinson allowed the least possible fighting among his players; the local paper, at least, was convinced that Wilkinson's slogan for his team was "Treat him right, but beat him."[128] Owners stressed that even though the players considered themselves stars and expected crowds to turn out "regardless of the class of ball they play," fans would stop attending unless they saw a "clean and gentlemanly game of ball."[129] The league tried to control fighting by imposing fines of from $5 to $50 and suspensions of from five days to a month without pay. But some owners complained that the fines were issued arbitrarily. The Negro leagues lacked the domineering but impartial authority of a Judge Landis. President Foster financially backed several team owners; in return, he had their support for his league decisions. Fighting continued to plague the game.[130]

Owners saw off-the-field conduct as being equally vital to the image and future of black baseball. One critic said the main reason attendance was declining was "that the players don't care enough for the game to stay in condition. The most they care for is the 1st and 15th of the month when pay day rolls around."[131] Sportswriters attributed the players' poor physical condition and performance to their "drinking and all night carousing."[132] Like his white counterparts, many a black ballplayer found it difficult to be a celebrity. As A. G. Mills, president of the National League, saw it: "The occupation of a ball player is full of life and excitement. Each player is the hero of a certain circle of admirers, and he often finds hero-worship an expensive luxury."[133] Another observer warned: "Sometimes it ruins an athlete to put his picture in the paper."[134] In an age in which the vast majority of Americans never

ventured beyond their home states, traveling ballplayers were glamorous and worldly figures. But the owners protested that fans did not realize what an injustice their all-night entertainments did to the players and to the league: "No one wants to pay to see a ball game and know that the star was out getting brimful of synthetic gin or corn licker [sic] or any other kind of poison the night previous to the big game."[135] Some owners suggested fines for players who drank in public after midnight or were seen in cabarets after 1 A.M. One eastern writer protested that if club owners in both leagues suspended all heavy drinkers, they would not have enough players to supply one league. But he warned, if they did not release them, they would not have enough fans left in "the now emptying parks" to support even one club.[136]

Despite all the attendant problems, the establishment of the Negro leagues was a victory. Working within segregation in the Booker T. Washington tradition, black owners created a successful business that employed about five hundred people. To a large extent they rid the game of white dominance; perhaps 75 percent of the income flowed back into the black community. They established baseball as a profession for blacks, as a parallel institution to the white major leagues. The Negro leagues were a source of pride, a model of achievement.

# THREE

## Monarchs of All They Survey

"To come to Kansas City on a Saturday night was just like trying to walk through Harlem when there's a parade. It was really something to see. Everybody that was everybody was at 18th and Vine."—Jesse Fisher

Eighteenth and Vine was the heart of the black community in Kansas City. The city was wide open under political boss Tom Pendergast, and as in many other urban areas, the vice district was allowed to develop in the black neighborhood. Prohibition simply ceased to be enforced; there were no felony convictions for the use or sale of alcohol in Kansas City during the entire period. Jazz trumpeter Booker T. Washington has recalled that "every cubby hole, every store front had gambling in it. Crap tables, black jack."[1] Open gambling and drinking provided for a raucous cabaret life that supported a lively jazz scene. The Subway, the Sunset, the Panama Club, and the Reno were only a few of the more than fifty clubs lining Twelfth and Eighteenth streets. According to musicians who lived and worked there from 1925 until World War II, Kansas City was "one long twenty-year jam session."[2] Legendary saloon keeper Milton Morris agreed: "Kansas City was swinging. Nobody slept—they were afraid they'd miss something."[3]

Despite the seeming glamour of this fabled district, black Kansas Citians held a second-class status. By 1920 the black population had stabilized at about 10 percent of the city's total, and the white majority insisted on rigid segregation. From Ninth Street south to Twenty-eighth and from Troost east to Indiana Street, Kansas City's blacks created a network of businesses, social organizations, fraternal groups, and churches. Yet the black section of Kansas City was, as the local black newspaper

Bennie Moten's jazz orchestra dominated the lively musical scene in Kansas City during the 1920s. Courtesy of Kansas City Museum.

Blacks formed a cohesive community south and east of downtown Kansas City. Homer Roberts was the only black car dealer in the country during the early 1920s. Courtesy of Black Economic Union of Greater Kansas City.

bitterly announced, "the home of the Swill Center, and the flyblown food, of cellar homes and leaky plumbing, of fire traps and tenement homes."[4] The wards in which blacks lived had the highest percentage of rental housing and the lowest of resident-owned housing in the city. The illiteracy rate there was ten times higher; the death rate was twice as high as for white Kansas Citians. Twice as many black women had to work, and black children, on the average, left school a full two years earlier than white students—presumably working to help support the family. The city's economic boundaries were as rigid as the physical boundaries imposed on the black neighbor-

hood. Less than a quarter of the industries in Kansas City hired blacks at all. Most black men labored in the meat-packing plants or in personal-service jobs.[5]

In this world of economic and social discrimination, the life of a traveling professional baseball player was very alluring: comparatively good salaries, celebrity status within the community, and the chance to travel widely. Jesse ("Kingfish") Fisher—who tried out with the Monarchs, but didn't make the team—explained: "The onliest thing the average kid wanted to be was a baseball player. You traveled a whole lot. You got to see parts of the country, of the world, that you wouldn't see otherwise."[6]

Rural immigrants often found their hopes of a better life dashed in the reality of the northern ghettos. Courtesy of Kansas City Public Library, Missouri Valley Room.

"Now I started at the bottom, and I stays right there, don't seem like I'm gonna get nowhere." Economic discrimination made these lines from a blues song true for many black Kansas Citians. Courtesy of Kansas City Public Library, Missouri Valley Room.

And for black youngsters in the Midwest and the Southwest, the Monarchs were tops. "It was the ambition of every black boy to be a Monarch, just as it was for every white boy to become a Yankee," contended Monarchs shortstop Jesse Williams. "That was the tradition back then. You didn't play ball till you became a Monarch."[7] And in segregated America, ace pitcher Hilton Smith knew that "when you got with the Monarchs, you were as high as you could go."[8]

While the NNL tried to enforce high standards of conduct, the Monarchs themselves also had an image that they tried to maintain. John ("Buck") O'Neil, first base-

man, has defined those standards:

Actually not only the management but the ball players would hand-pick the guys that they thought was good enough physically and good enough morally to play. We would see that it would happen. A Monarch never had a fight on the street. A Monarch never cut anybody. You couldn't shoot craps on our bus, in our hotel, with our manager. Some of the ball clubs could do this, but to be a Monarch you couldn't. Not and let the manager know. This was the Kansas City Monarchs![9]

There were those who went so far as to say that the Monarchs showed "deportment on and off the field which would do honor to the most exacting conventional English family."[10] While the *Kansas City Call* conceded that black baseball players used to be a "rough and ready lot with a well earned reputation for general allround rowdyism," by mid decade the image of the Monarchs at least was different. Players

Professional ballplayers were heroes in a community crushed by segregation. The Monarchs in 1934. Standing, from the left: Sam Bankhead, T. J. Young, George Giles, Turkey Stearnes, Frank Duncan, Moocha Harris, Carroll Mothel, Cool Papa Bell, Newt Allen, Willie Wells, J. L. Wilkinson. Kneeling, from the left: Chet Brewer, Newt Joseph, Bullet Joe Rogan, Charles Beverly. Courtesy of Kansas State Historical Society, Topeka.

were often asked to speak at gatherings of clubs such as the Young Men's Progressive Club or the Twilight City League.[11]

Players knew that a good reputation was also important in the struggle for integration. "Everybody tried to prove that they were good fellows, they were nice," said Buck O'Neil. "We all knew that the only way to open that door—you had to be on your best behavior."[12]

Despite their clean-cut image, the Monarchs were also part of the night life in Kansas City. There was a close friendship between many of the ballplayers and the jazz musicians. Kansas City was the west-

"Probably on the corner of 18th and Vine there, that's the most celebrated street in Kansas City, and all over the world, you can hear about 18th and Vine," commented musician Charles Goodwin. Courtesy of Black Archives of Mid-America.

ernmost stop for both the NNL and the Theatre Owners Booking Association, the black response to discrimination in vaudeville. As traveling entertainers, both groups were celebrities within their communities. Pitcher Chet Brewer remembered that "when we were in the city, we'd go see them on stage, and when we'd play, they'd come to the ball park."[13] And clarinetist Lawrence Denton once said of the Monarchs: "Whenever they come to town, we'd always play for them—send a band out there. A fifteen piece band."[14] One fan said knowingly of the Monarchs: "Don't let them kid you. They were right smack in the middle of everything that was going on."[15] And without question, a lot was going on in Kansas City then. Bartender Kingfish Fisher

recalled: "Wasn't nothing but vice in this town back in them days. [The Monarchs] was in between vice and what we called Society. Society on one side, vice on the other. Sometimes they would come together."[16]

When the Monarchs were in town, players who did not have homes in the city stayed at Street's Hotel, as did their opponents. This fifty-room hotel, located at Eighteenth and Vine, was considered the best west of Chicago. "Everybody that came to Kansas City stopped at the Street's Hotel," explained manager Guy Davis. "Jack Johnson, Ray Robinson, Stepin Fetchit, Joe Louis—I met 'em all."[17] On Saturday night when the Monarchs were in town, fans formed a "carpet" at the famous intersection. Everyone wanted to meet the players, for as pitcher Doolittle Young explained, it was "novel to see a man who did nothing but play ball and didn't have to sweep floors."[18]

Men gathered to discuss their baseball

team at several places, most of which sold tickets for the games—the Monarch Billiard Parlor, Stark's News Stand, Barber and Burt's Billiard Parlor, Panama Taxi Stand, Street's Hotel, and McCampbell and Hueston's Drug Store. And after a game, sportswriter Fay Young reported,

> nowhere in the circuit of the league are the fans so partial as here [in Kansas City]. As I write this story there are crowds gathered here and there on East 18th St. playing the game over and telling what should and what shouldn't have been done.[19]

The Monarchs were popular with women too. Guy Davis, manager of Street's Hotel, laid out his general rule: "Women follow a uniform—whether it's a soldier, musician, ballplayer. They would come in in a uniform, women would be looking them up—players didn't have to look the women up. They'd come out in their finery, come out there to meet them."[20] The flattery from female admirers was not always welcome, as star infielder Newt Allen explained:

> It's hard—you know, you're playing, making good plays and you have admirers sitting up there in the stands. You don't even know them. Ball game's over, go to your hotel and get telephone calls asking for you—you don't even know who it is.[21]

Many of the Monarchs were married while they were with the team, but the siren call of strange women did not seem to be a problem for them. The team often traveled for three weeks or more without returning to Kansas City. If the team was playing a series in a large city, players sometimes had their wives join them, but the wives almost never traveled with the team during the regular season. (Perhaps the only exception was when Georgia Dwight traveled with

Eddie for a two-week honeymoon following their marriage in 1930.) Married players always spoke of the "understanding" a man and his wife had to have. "One thing about playing ball—you can't play ball and think about what your wife's doing at home. You just had to count on her and you be the man that you should be," Newt Allen reasoned. "It's a hard life. There has to be an understanding between you and your wife—a good understanding."[22] Confidant Jesse Fisher dismissed the matter: "As long as they sent money back home, wasn't no problem."[23] And for the most part, the wives did accept their lot—described by one as being "widows for two or three weeks at a time."[24] The long separations and the flattering attention that both partners received understandably caused strains in some marriages however.[25]

For the players who were not married, the "wild life" was part of the attraction of being a ballplayer. Older players sometimes cautioned a young man when he was getting out of line; Wilkinson fined or fired those who preferred parties over a good game. "It's a known fact that an athlete has a flock of strangers around him," said Lefty Bryant. "I wasn't stern enough to throw it out the window like it should be—I had to follow it up. That didn't go over too good with the ball club either. I was too wild."[26] The *Kansas City Call*'s sportswriter upbraided both the partying fans and players:

> The fans do not complain of lost games when the team is right and working, but the last few weeks have demonstrated that while they're perfectly willing to be seen on 12th Street and its neighboring territory all night with a ball player, they are *NOT* willing to go the next day and watch that same player perform.

He argued that the Monarchs might look like a baseball team, but "in reality it is a mutual admiration and sympathetic organization, with the fan-friends of the players holding honorary membership."[27]

The Monarchs games were great social gatherings as well as sporting events. Stepin Fetchit and Count Basie attended whenever they were in Kansas City. Basie explained that he went to Monarchs games on Sunday afternoons "because that was where everybody was going on a Sunday afternoon."[28] Most fans did not attend in casual clothes. "They wore their finery!" asserted Buck O'Neil. "You know, today you go to the ball game casual. You've never seen anything like this. They'd have their fur stoles on and their hats on—just like they left church. They could leave church and come to the ball game."[29] Jesse Fisher, "Kingfish" in the black community, elaborated on the idea of the glamour of the game:

> I tell you, women used to fry their hair. Used to get up early in the morning if the Monarchs were coming to town, like on a Friday . . . they'd be frying their hair on Monday to be ready. You could smell hair burning for a week—straightening that hair, getting ready for them Monarchs, with those great, big, pretty hats on. You couldn't get into the ball park then. It was something to see.[30]

Local merchants took full advantage of the occasion. One advertised: "The Monarchs Are Here! The opening game of the Monarchs is always a Fashion Parade and of course you will want to look your best. At our store . . . you get those pretty clothes."[31] Men also dressed up in straw hats, patent leather shoes, and suits. Reporter A. D. Williams quipped, "A dude is a person who wears a coat in the bleachers."[32]

The Monarchs were known for their staunch fans and large crowds. During the

The *Kansas City Call*, 27 April 1923. One *Call* sportswriter later reported: "The grandstand was a riot of colors. Why not? Everybody dresses up for the Monarchs."

1920s, weekday games drew a loyal four or five hundred, and Sunday games regularly attracted from two to five thousand spectators. Even though they had a league-wide reputation for drawing big crowds, as early as 1922 some local critics were crabbing about small attendance. Poor crowds, they argued, would never entice the big eastern clubs to the edge of the prairie. By 1925, attendance in Kansas City and all league cities was, in fact, a serious problem. With increased costs for players' salaries, travel, and advertising, Wilkinson found that he needed four or five thousand fans at each Sunday game to break even—and the Monarchs were not drawing that many. Even counting the crowds at the Negro World Series in 1924, the gate had fallen off by 50 percent. In the early 1920s many white fans attended black ball games. The *Indianapolis Freeman*'s sportswriter noted that whites received black baseball in his city as enthusiastically as in Chicago: "The white people turn out in large numbers; in fact, at one game, by actual count, we had 3,000 whites and 2,500 colored."[33] In the early years of the NNL, Kansas City followed suit with the black/white mix being almost 50-50 at Monarchs games. The *Call* reporter contended that whites attended Monarchs games because the Blues, Kansas City's American Association entry, had a poor team. When the Blues won the Junior World Series in 1923, white followers abandoned the Monarchs. By 1926 the *Kansas City Call* estimated that only one in ten of the tickets to Monarchs games were purchased by whites. And when regular radio broadcasts brought major-league games into the home, minor-league as well as black teams lost a significant portion of their patronage. Still, the Blues drew almost five times as many fans for weekend games as did the Monarchs. Even though the *Indianapolis Freeman* optimistically declared that "prosperity has put the dollars into circulation, and the plain fan has his share of the dollars," the fact was that most of Kansas City's thirty thousand blacks did not have the discretionary income or the leisure so that they could frequent baseball games.[34]

In response to the declining attendance, sportswriters urged civic groups to buy blocks of seats, asked women to take advantage of the free ladies' night, and publicized Knothole Day, when children fifteen and under were admitted free. Wilkinson tried to expand the publicity. Secretary Gilmore bragged that in the "old days," teams had used only handbills to advertise their games. Local merchants continued to proudly display game placards in their store windows; but by 1924, streetcars, daily newspapers, and weeklies also carried announcements of the upcoming contests. By 1926 Wilkinson was scheduling fewer games in Kansas City, and he cut the price of a box-seat ticket from $1.10 to $.75, the lowest in the league. Sports editor A. D. Williams urged readers to show their support for the team: "Banquets and star parties are all right, but an increased volume of business at the turnstile of the old ball lot means more money in each player's pocket when the season is over."[35]

The community responded by forming a Booster Club, a popular idea with many teams. Kansas City's Booster Club was the most active and enduring in the league. A couple of lines by a local sportswriter could have been used as their rallying cry: "Nonsupport of the team will do more than anything to ruin it. Don't do so much street corner managing—put the old hammer away and boost for a change."[36]

The Booster Club in the early 1920s was a loose amalgam of neighborhood fans, including the 12th Street Rooters, the Vine Street Rooters, the 18th Street Rooters, the Kansas City (Kansas) Rooters, and the North End Fans Association. The Boosters' only activity in the early years was organizing the parade for the opening game. This yearly procession started at 12:30 in the heart of the black district and crisscrossed the streets to the park for the two o'clock first pitch.

By mid decade the Booster Club was a popular civic organization in the black community. Monarchs' secretary Gilmore had revived Kansas City's Elks Club in 1918, and this group formed the nucleus of the Booster Club, with the Elks Rest known as "the home of the Monarch's Booster Club." In addition to Gilmore, the Boosters had the support of many prominent men: Chester A. Franklin, editor of the *Kansas City Call;* Dr. Howard Smith, superintendent of General Hospital No. 2; T. B. Watkins, a mortician and civic leader; Felix Payne, a politician and night-club owner; Dr. J. Edward Perry, founder of Perry Sanitarium; and Frank Cromwell, mayor of Kansas City, Missouri. Robert Sweeney, a

Monarchs Boosters T. B. Watkins, Felix Payne, and Q. J. Gilmore at opening-day ceremonies. The *Call* announced on the front page: "Saturday, May 25, 1928, has been duly set aside as being 'no good' for any other purpose than that of journeying to Muehlebach Park and taking part in the grand opening ceremonies of the Monarchs. Be there!" Courtesy of Phil Dixon, Dixon Paper Company.

civic leader and the publicity director for the Boosters, remarked on the Monarchs' standing in the community: "You had some of the most sophisticated ball players and then you had some of the more rowdy kind. There was a stratification of Negroes just like in the white race. Water will seek its level. I couldn't say the Monarchs were considered leaders in the black community, but I'll say some of the people that were identified with the Monarchs stood very well in the community."[37] About twenty businesses supported the Monarchs through the

Booster Club, including a few white merchants who had their shops in the black neighborhood—such as tailors Eisen and Meyer, Matlaw's clothing store, Fox's Tavern, and the Lincoln Theatre. The rest of the hundred or so members were ordinary fans. Buck O'Neil characterized the group this way, "Black merchants, different organizations, fraternal organizations, deacons, and everybody—everybody!"[38] Wilkinson showed his appreciation for the community support by playing a number of games as benefits for various organizations. The Negro National Business League, the Red Cross, the NAACP, the Salvation Army, as well as churches, hospitals, and youth organizations, received the proceeds from these games.[39]

The Boosters organized the opening-day festivities every year. The parade grew until by mid decade the line-up included a

The Elks band marched in the opening-game parade each year. Reuben Street's Hotel was for many years a focal point of the area. Courtesy of Kansas City Museum.

Western University Band at Muehlebach Stadium, 1925. Western University, in Kansas City, Kansas, attracted budding musicians from the Midwest. Jazz trumpeter Booker McDaniels recalled: "We used to play at the old Muehlebach Stadium. Every time . . . the Monarchs . . . would have a grand opening on the opening ball game, we would play there." Courtesy of Kansas City Museum.

motorcycle police escort; decorated cars for the owners of the opposing teams; a car for Gilmore, manager Bullet Joe Rogan, and Dr. Howard Smith; a car for visiting newspapermen; the Elks band; the 2nd Regiment band; Western University's band; the ball clubs of the Negro Twilight City League; the Lincoln High School cadets; cars for the players; and cars for fans. The 1923 parade featured a truck "filled with tooters of jazz sounds," playing nothing but "Good-Bye Tootsie." "If Tootsie isn't gone," wrote a reviewer, "she'll never get away because the band played her good-bye all through the town."[40] The Lincoln High School cadets raised the flag at the stadium during the opening ceremonies. Judge Crittenden Clark (the only black judge in Missouri), the mayor of Kansas City, Missouri, or the mayor of Kansas City, Kansas, threw out the first pitch. High-school bands, the Elks band, Western University's band, or sometimes jazz groups led by George Lee or Bennie Moten gave concerts before and during the opening game.

This ritualistic season opener usually drew the largest crowd. The NNL teams frequently vied for a loving cup in a contest for the largest attendance at an opening game. People came from all over the state, and the mayor traditionally gave city employees a half-day holiday so that they could greet the team. Three times in the 1920s the *Kansas City Call* alerted readers that "moving pictures" would be taken of the parade,

The 1920s was an economically propitious time for
building theaters exclusively for black entertainment
and black audiences. The house orchestra posed in
front of the Lincoln Theatre at Eighteenth and Lydia in
1927. Courtesy of Kansas City Museum.

the opening ceremonies, and the game.
These films were shown the following week
at the Lincoln Theatre in the black neighborhood.[41]

The Boosters also sponsored banquets to
honor the team. Pitcher Hilton Smith
recalled: "We were invited—doctors,
preachers and all of them would give us a
banquet on Monday or Friday when we
came into town."[42] These dinners were held
at the Entertainers Cafe, Street's Hotel, or
the Elks Hall. Although the dinners were
usually restricted to the Monarchs players,
Boosters, and local umpires, a dinner in
1924 brought both Negro World Series
teams, the commissioners, and visiting
newspapermen together in the banquet
hall.[43]

The Boosters' membership fees supported

other activities. They printed pennant decals
for car windows and sponsored trips to
Chicago for hotly contested series. In 1925
the Boosters gave each player a gold
baseball charm in honor of their league
championship. Buck O'Neil, who joined the
Monarchs in 1938, recalled: "The old
champs wore the little balls on their watch
chains. Oh, how I envied them!"[44] Understanding that the Monarchs were celebrities
within the community, the Boosters sponsored events at which the fans could meet
them. In 1929, for example, the Boosters
held a grand ball at Paseo Hall, an
exclusively black dance hall that could
accommodate three thousand dancers.
Hailed as the "First Annual Kansas City
Monarchs Home Coming Dance and
Frolic," the party gave fans a chance to see
"the Boys Do the 'Home Run Strut'" and
to hear Chauncey Downs and his Rinky
Dinks "blow those 'Hateful Monarchs
Blues.'"[45]

Merchants and ministers actively sup-

First K.C. Monarchs Annual

NEGRO NATIONAL LEAGUE

Monarch Home Coming

# DANCE and FROLIC

— The Season's Sensation —

— $250 in Prizes —

Eddie "Sheik" Gardner  Famous C. C. Pyle cross country runner, who was forced out of the race on account of a pulled tendon will pull the lucky number tickets.

9:00 Until ?   **Paseo Hall**   15th Street and The Paseo

## THURSDAY, MAY 23rd

Dance ○ Stomp ○ Frolic!

to the melodious strains of

CHAUNCEY DOWNS AND HIS **Rinky Dinks**

THE entire Monarch baseball club will be on hand to share in this mammoth welcome. Would you know the ball players in their street attire? See if you can pick them out among the crowd. Do you know all the new players of the team? Meet the new ones along with the old timers. Know the men who make the Monarchs—MONARCHS of the league.

Some are married. Some are not; some not quite—but all fine fellows and worth meeting. All will be there—with and without. Can they dance? Well, yes, "and how!" Stomp to your hearts' content with the Monarchs.

| All Tickets Numbered | $250 in Prizes! | FREE 50 Single Tickets |
|---|---|---|
| All tickets will be numbered, thus assuring all an equal chance to win one of these worthwhile prizes. Keep the stub with the number on it. You may win a season ticket. | 4 Baseball Season Tickets -- FREE! Four Full Season tickets will be given to the holders of the lucky number tickets. Each ticket is worth $50.00. Think of it—a season ticket for the price of admission to the Frolic 50c. Four people will get these tickets and you have an equal chance to win one of these $50 tickets and see all the games at Muehlebach Field FREE during the 1929 season. Keep your numbered ticket stub and win a ticket | To be sent to the owner there will be free single admission—good for single game—at time during the season—to the free & complete servicing in ball. Thursday evening May 23. Be there on time and get your ticket—FREE. |

HEAR THE RINKY DINKS BLOW THOSE "HATEFUL" MONARCHS BLUES

See the Boys do that "Home Run Strut"—They're Hot!

Fall in line behind Rogan and his gang in the big Grand March

Sponsored by the

BASEBALL BOOSTERS' CLUB OF GREATER KANSAS CITY

DOORS OPEN 8:30 P. M.                    ADMISSION 50 CENT

The *Kansas City Call,* 17 May 1929.

ported these local heroes and helped to establish them as role models. The Elbon and Lincoln theaters advertised the games, flashed the players' pictures up on the screen, and sponsored theater parties for the Monarchs and their visiting opponents. The Ministerial Alliance solicited gifts from store owners as prizes for various achievements by the players—the first home run of the season, the most stolen bases, the pitcher who won the most games.[46]

Because the church was a primary association for most blacks and because the ministers were generally the most educated

and consequently the most respected members of the community, the ministers' support helped to secure the Monarchs' status. Missouri was an early proponent of Sunday sports, and laws preventing them were rarely enforced. The Reverend T. H. Ewing of the Vine Street Baptist Church was one of the few black ministers in Kansas City who opposed Sunday amusements. In contrast, the Reverend A. E. Rankin organized the Ministerial Alliance's solicitation of gifts from businessmen for the Monarchs. Player John O'Neil recalled: "I think this started them actually here letting church out by one o'clock—so you can go see the Monarchs. The preachers here would preach sermons for the Monarchs . . . they would preach baseball sermons. And after we'd leave and the people would all go to the ball park."[47] Wilkinson cultivated the favor of Kansas City ministers by giving them free passes and by occasionally playing exhibition games as benefits for local churches. He also allowed the Baptist churches to hold hour-long "Unity Services" at the stadium after a game had ended. Outside Kansas City, too, the ministers recognized the inspiration a successful black man could offer their congregations. "The thing that moved me the most," confided Lefty Bryant, "was little towns that you'd go into, on Sundays if the Monarchs were there, they would invite the team down to be introduced and say a few words—about how to become an athlete, what to do while you're an athlete, and who to trust when you're an athlete—and there's only one person to trust—that's the man upstairs."[48]

While the Boosters were the backbone of support for the Monarchs, Wilkinson did not rely on them entirely for good attendance. He mounted numerous efforts of his own to arouse enthusiasm for the game. One device was described as a "hell's on fire" publicity

Chauncey Downs and his Rinky Dinks played for the Monarchs Home Coming Dance and Frolic. Courtesy of Black Archives of Mid-America.

campaign—constantly filling the papers with news of the team. Wilkinson, the traveling secretary, or sometimes Gilmore's wife, Alberta, sent articles to thirty-six black and white newspapers across the nation. Wilkinson also offered prizes to any fan who guessed the score of the opening game, the line-up, and the manager; those who loaned a car for the Boosters' opening-day parade received free admission. Wilkinson and other club owners recognized the changing role of women after World War I. They courted these potential fans with ladies' days—when women passed the turnstile free or at half price. "Fannettes" turned out in large numbers for the Monarchs; about two thousand women attended a Tuesday ladies' night in 1923. When prices were reduced in 1926, the management appealed to women by advertising that box seats cost little more

than general admission: "If you fannettes want to display new hats and dresses this summer, you can do so at an added expense of only $.15."[49] Wilkinson used women ushers in 1922—hoping both that the fair sex would be an attraction for male fans and that women would help to elevate the tone of the crowd. The major leagues, too, had early clung to the gallant but naïve notion that women would keep order in the grandstands. *Sporting News* declared that "the presence of the fair sex . . . not only adds beauty to the scene, but . . . has a good effect on the crowd." Men, they hoped, would be less excited about the final score and "more choice in their selection of adjectives."[50]

The crowds at Negro-league baseball games were loud and lively in support of the home team. The ball-park behavior of many of the newly arrived southerners, however, sometimes offended the sensibilities of middle-class blacks. They saw this boisterous "rowdyism" (including everything from drinking and gambling to harassing the umpires, throwing seat cushions, and fighting) as an embarrassment for the race. Sportswriters led a vigorous campaign to improve stadium behavior and to expel rowdyism—''the sinister shadow . . . the dangerous running mate of Negro baseball.''[51]

Although prohibition lasted from 1919 until 1933, liquor was part of the stadium scene. Fans brought it in hip flasks and sold it under the stands. It was as easy to obtain, said one player, as yelling for the peanut vendor. The *Kansas City Call* criticized the men—''and they don't all come from 12th Street or the Avenue''—who flaunted ''their money, their mouths, and their ability to obtain corn liquor'' because they thought it was ''safe and clever.''[52] Sportswriters urged the ''corn bibbers'' to let it age until after the game.

Gambling, like drinking, directly violated city ordinances, but it continued full pace nonetheless. Together they led to so many fights among fans that Muehlebach threatened to discontinue the Monarchs' lease on his stadium. A. D. Williams, writing in the *Kansas City Call,* chastised the offenders: ''If the boys who can't afford to lose will stop betting, we'll get along fine this season, without any post game, pool-hall criticisms, which are carried over till the next game and then aired out in the grandstand.''[53]

Gamblers might lay a direct wager on the outcome of the game, or they might bet on it indirectly by using box scores or batting averages to pick a number for the numbers game. As much an institution as the church in the black community, this illegal lottery was a protected business under the benevolent patronage of political machines. In Kansas City the charismatic night-club owner and Booster Club member Felix Payne controlled the numbers operation in

return for his influence in delivering black votes for Pendergast. The poorest chased hopes of riches by betting pennies that their chosen number would coincide with the last three numbers of the stock-exchange report. Besides using box scores and batting averages, bettors also picked numbers based on their dreams, as interpreted by several popular ''dream books.'' *The Lucky Star Dream Book* interpreted baseball dreams favorably: ''To dream that you play this game denotes safety of your affairs and a happy reunion among your neighbors. Bet 100.'' *The Success Dream Book* advised readers: ''To dream of playing baseball is a sign that you will live to a good old age, and then die happily. Bet 945. To see others play this game is a sign of peace and satisfaction. Bet 567.''[54]

Black leaders feared that besides being a threat to the Monarchs' lease on Muehlebach Stadium, ball-park rowdyism would hinder advances in race relations. Sports editor A. D. Williams sadly related how a stockholder for the white Kansas City Blues had told him that the difference between the two races was that ''you folks don't show proper respect for the presence of your women folk.'' Williams warned that whites would use the rowdyism to bolster their argument ''They're all bad.''[55]

The Monarchs played in the American Association Park, home of the white minor-league team, the Kansas City Blues, from 1920 until 1922. Owned by George Tebeau, this stadium was a single-deck wooden structure with a thirty-foot screen in right field. Tebeau and George Muehlebach, a brewer who owned the Blues, had a disagreement in 1922. Local black sportswriters hoped that if a fight between the two were to force Muehlebach to build a new stadium, the Monarchs could continue their lease with Tebeau for the park at Nineteenth and Olive and thus have a field of their own. Muehlebach did, in fact, build his own stadium in 1923, but Wilkinson alone could not afford to pay Tebeau's operating expenses. Wilkinson then made an agreement with Muehlebach for use of his new field. Muehlebach's stadium, located in the black community at Twenty-second and Brooklyn, was regarded as one of the best in the white minor leagues. It boasted an electric scoreboard and seated about sixteen thousand, exclusive of the bleacher seats, which were seldom used because of the poor view.[56]

Because contracts between Wilkinson and Muehlebach are not extant, details of the rental are not known. But during this negotiation period, Wilkinson incorporated the Kansas City Monarchs Baseball and Amusement Company with $20,000 capital stock. Incorporation was a safeguard so that he would not be held personally liable in case of a default.[57] Park owners generally charged from 15 to 25 percent of the total gate receipts, although some charged a flat fee. The Cuban Stars, for example, paid four thousand dollars a year for the use of Cincinnati's Redland Park. Owner Karl Finke claimed 20 percent of the gross receipts until this amount was paid. In return, he furnished four police officers at weekday games and ten on Sundays. Finke also provided tickets, ticket agents, and groundsmen. Some park owners provided concessionaires. Some park owners denied the black teams the use of the clubhouses, but Muehlebach granted the Monarchs full use of the stadium facilities.[58]

Kansas City blacks held that the only difference between Kansas City and the Deep South, with respect to race relations, was that in Kansas City, blacks could ride the streetcars. Movie houses, restaurants, hotels, tennis courts, and swimming pools were all tightly segregated.[59] Segregation of

the fans at the ball parks seemed to depend on the social convictions of the owner. Tebeau forced blacks to sit in the upper fourteen rows of seats or in the wooden grandstands—even when black teams were using the field. When Muehlebach built his stadium, seating was segregated when the Blues played, but the dividing signs were removed for Monarchs games. Former Chicago Cubs catcher Johnny Kling purchased the Blues and the stadium in the mid 1930s, and he refused to segregate the Blues games. When brewer Jacob Ruppert purchased the park for his New York Yankees organization in 1938, he again divided the races when the Blues played. The *Kansas City Call*'s sportswriter wrote a scathing attack on Ruppert's policy. He contended that blacks supported Ruppert's team, bought his beer, and therefore deserved to be treated equally in the park.[60]

This protest against Ruppert's attempt to humiliate Kansas City blacks was typical of the role that black sportswriters created for themselves. They reported the results of games and were active in the league organization, but their activities stretched beyond the sporting realm. The sportswriters—and the black press in general—worked along with churches and the YMCAs in trying to help the peasant southerners adapt to city ways. The black newspapers helped to ease the transition by publishing job opportunities, train schedules, and available housing. The sportswriters tried to ease the discrimination by prescribing public behavior for players and fans that the white middle-class would find acceptable. As a corollary, sportswriters vigorously worked for full citizenship for blacks. They hoped that baseball could be a common meeting ground where whites would accept them as peers. When the two races intermingled in Muehlebach Stadium, the *Kansas City Call*'s writer was quick to point out that "there they were, the humble Negroes and the superior whites, all losing their relative social position in the interest of a very good game of ball."[61] Finally, baseball gave sportswriters a chance regularly to assert the race's worth. The sports world furnished many examples of achievements, which offered a direct challenge to the notion of black inferiority.

Though most black newspapers remained local voices, some had a regional circulation, and a few had a national impact. Begun in 1919, the weekly *Kansas City Call* had a circulation of more than twenty-five thousand in the 1920s and became an important influence throughout the Southwest. The *Call* carried detailed stories of the Monarchs and gave readers comprehensive articles on NNL operations. The white *Kansas City Star* did not report on all Monarchs games, but its coverage of them tended to be unbiased and complete with box scores. It did not report any league activities, and in fact, viewed the NNL as only a "booking agency."[62]

The *Chicago Defender* and the *Pittsburgh Courier,* two nationally known papers that were located in hotbeds for black baseball, provided the black community with much of its baseball knowledge. But coverage of games was uneven at best. Each spring during the 1920s, sportswriters were enthusiastic about the upcoming season. The *Kansas City Call* even promised to install a ticker so as to have the game results more quickly. It also assured fans that the results of away games would be broadcast on the Star and Sweeney radio stations. Before summer was very far advanced, however, both fans and sportswriters became frustrated. Fans blamed the newspapers for withholding scores and batting averages. Sportswriters, in turn, blamed the league

and the owners. The reporters said the owners did not have the good business sense to realize the importance of statistics and media exposure:

> Owners will put out large amounts of money for uniforms, automobiles and buses, pay high salaries to managers and business agents. They will equip the team properly and provide transportation facilities, hire men to direct strategy and men to collect their share of the money, but the majority will not spend 60¢ or a dollar for a score book. Owners . . . are deaf, dumb and blind to the fact that status is based on records of performance, good or bad.[63]

Sportswriters also accused owners of withholding news of losses until they could report offsetting victories, which made it impossible to keep a running tally. For one season the NNL sent a reporter, Harry Sinclair, around the circuit to keep information flowing. The job was abolished the following year, however, because owners did not think the money for it was well spent. For a while the NNL tried fining teams that failed to report league scores, but this failed miserably. At the end of each season, team standings were disputed, and statistics on individual players were nearly impossible to validate. Surviving records are of little help. Team rosters changed during the course of each year. Because players were such well-known members of the community, scorekeepers often failed to record first names, or they would use nicknames, and spellings of last names varied. The sale of a team always caused problems in making comparisons. For example, when the Toledo Stars moved to Milwaukee in 1923, they assumed Milwaukee's previous percentages.[64]

This is not to say that there were no

*Left:* "Bullet Joe" Rogan, who is generally regarded as the best fielding pitcher in Negro baseball history. Courtesy of Black Archives of Mid-America.

*Center:* With his slight build and quick moves, Newt Allen earned the nickname "Colt." A consistent hitter from either side of the plate, he played for the Monarchs for more than twenty years. Courtesy of John Holway.

*Right:* Newt Joseph, Newt Allen's roommate, was known as one of the best dressers in the Negro leagues. Courtesy of John Holway.

estimates of individual players' ability. A. D. Williams from the *Call* or Ernest Mehl from the *Kansas City Star* often kept score for the Monarchs home games. When they were on the road, the Monarchs usually designated a player to keep score, most often a pitcher who was off for that game. If it were an important game—a play-off, World Series, or East-West Game—the league would appoint a scorer from the local newspaper office. Incomplete but impressive statistics have been culled from those records.

Wilbur ("Bullet Joe") Rogan, for example, started his professional career with the Monarchs in 1920 at the age of thirty. In 1924 he led the Negro leagues with a 19 and 10 season record and then won two more games in the World Series. Generally, players who saw them both have ranked Rogan above Leroy ("Satchel") Paige. Paige had only his fast ball, but Rogan was noted for being a smart pitcher. Chet Brewer remembered that "Rogan could throw the ball by you and he had one of the greatest curves too."[65] Even more incredibly, Rogan finished the 1924 season with a .450 batting average. Paige once said of Bullet Joe: "He was the onliest pitcher I ever saw, I ever heard of in my life, was pitching and hitting in the clean-up place. He was a chunky little guy, but he could throw hard."[66]

Some players kept track of their own achievements. For example, right-hander Hilton Smith justifiably boasted of thirty wins and one loss in 1941. But most players could not say what their batting average or earned-run average was. Players were keenly aware of their opponents' strengths and weaknesses, and ultimately, reputations rest on the evaluations of the men they played against. Newt Allen was regarded by many as the best second baseman in the Negro leagues. Teammate Bill Drake said fondly: "He wouldn't even look at first base on the pivot. He'd throw the ball to first under his left arm."[67] Pitcher and teammate Chet Brewer regarded Dobie Moore as being perhaps the greatest shortstop ever: "He could come up and hit the ball out of the park. That to my mind made him the best shortstop. Willie Wells was as great a fielder, but he didn't have the strong arm or the power Moore had. Moore was the best I saw all around."[68] With Newt Allen at second, they formed an impenetrable infield. Allen recalled: "In the World Series against Philadelphia in 1924, we made six double plays in one game. Two of them came in the 8th and 9th innings. The last one ended the ball game with what would have been the winning run crossing the plate."[69]

Buck Leonard, a powerful hitter for the Homestead Grays, admired Monarchs catcher Joe Greene: "He was big, strong, had a great arm. He couldn't hit a curve ball, but he could hit a fast ball four miles."[70] Third baseman Newt Joseph was described by his roommate Newt Allen as a "great signal catcher. He'd watch everybody on the other ball club . . . and in three innings, if there was any kind of sign, he'd have one or two of them."[71] Joseph's reputation also included his lively chatter: "Newt Joseph, the little noise box down on third, is the life of the team. Without Newt in the game it might appear like a funeral."[72]

Despite the lack of accurate statistics in the sports pages, the black press gave the teams exposure far beyond their hometowns. With a conglomeration of hyperbole, tongue-in-cheek humor, and endless similes, sportswriters such as Fay Young, Wendell Smith, Ric Roberts, and A. D. Williams made the Negro leaguers heroes across the nation. As fans became familiar with the legendary feats of players in the other league, they demanded a World Series to determine the champion. By 1924 the bitter feud between the NNL and the Eastern Colored League over the player raids, contracts, and territory had been mediated, with both Secretary Gilmore and the *Pittsburgh Courier* taking credit for negotiating the settlement. This tenuous peace allowed a commission of two men from each league to plan the series that seemed to herald financial stability for the sport.

In the first Negro World Series, the Kansas City Monarchs of the NNL defeated the ECL champions, Hilldale of Darby, Pennsylvania. The World Series games were played in Philadelphia, Baltimore, Kansas City, and Chicago. Originally, Commissioner Rube Foster scheduled Kansas City for only the last games, if they were needed. He claimed that Muehlebach Stadium was too difficult to reserve because of the many civic groups and high schools that wanted to use it. Evidently, Kansas Citians suspected Foster's motives, for when they

The Monarchs and the Hilldale club, lined up before the fifth game of the 1924 World Series in Kansas City's Muehlebach Stadium. Courtesy of Robert Peterson.

"yelled about Chicago's getting the cream," the commissioners conceded that the crucial fifth, sixth, and seventh games could be played at the home of the western champions.[73] When the exciting games finally took place, army men from Ft. Leavenworth, Kansas, and businessmen from many towns joined the crowd of more than fifteen thousand fans who saw the games in Kansas City.

But the games at Muehlebach only tied the series (one contest was called because of darkness), and both teams headed for Chicago. A stiff, cold wind held the crowd down to only twenty-five hundred for the decisive tenth game. Manager/pitcher José Mendez had been advised by his doctor to sit out the rest of the season following surgery, but the thirty-seven-year-old Cuban decided to go for the victory himself. After eight innings, neither side had scored. Just as fans were settling in for extra innings, five hits, a walk, a sacrifice, and daring base running put five Monarchs across the plate. José Mendez, the "Black Diamond," captured a two-hit shutout, and the Monarchs snagged the title of "World's Colored Champions."

After the victory, Kansas City night-club owner Piney Brown sponsored a party at the Sunset Inn, Chicago's "biggest and best amusement palace," for the Monarchs,

# K. C. MONARCHS

## BASE BALL CLUB OF KANSAS CITY, MO.

For years the Monarchs used this World Series flag to advertise their games. Courtesy of Gladys Wilkinson Catron.

sportswriters, and visiting Kansas City fans. The triumphant Monarchs relished an evening of food, drinks, dancing, and a musical show by Billie Young, Blanche Calloway, and Amon Davis. The *Call*'s sportswriter quipped: "Let no hint of how long the party continued, nor the condition of the guests on leaving escape. Just remember that it happened in Chicago—and guess the rest!"[74]

The treasurer's tally sheet showed that the idea of a Negro World Series was a good one. Almost forty-six thousand fans bought tickets, paying $1.10 for general admission and $1.65 for box seats. The gate receipts amounted to over $52,000. After expenses, the commissioners distributed more than $23,000. Kansas City took a winner's 42 percent—or about $9,800. Wilkinson took half and divided the rest among his sixteen players ($308 each). Hilldale received only 28 percent as loser— about $6,500—which was also divided 50/50 between owner and players. Each of Hill-

dale's seventeen regular players received $193. The four commissioners (including Dr. Howard Smith of Kansas City) divided 10 percent of the profits, while each of the second-place teams in the two leagues received 6 percent, and the third-place teams, 4 percent.[75]

Beginning in 1925 the NNL divided its season into fifty-game halves. The winners of each half staged a play-off, and the Monarchs again faced Hilldale in the October contest. This time Hilldale won, five games to one. Hilldale gloated over their victory and issued a memoriam for the Monarchs:

In loving memory of the Kansas City Monarchs, infant prodigy of the United National League and only child of J. L. Wilkinson, who held the title of World

Champions of the diamond until its sudden and violent death at the hands (and bats) of the Clan of Darby, better known as Hilldale, pets of the Eastern league of the baseball war sector. Kansas City departed this life at the tender age of one year, after being crowned "King."[76]

Two changes in the operation were made. All of the games were played in Kansas City and Philadelphia, and the 1925 World Series Commission was composed of the presidents of the NNL and the ECL and the owners of the opposing teams; the owners had been excluded in 1924. The 1925 series was a financial failure. Only twenty thousand supporters turned out for the games, half of the previous year's total, and the receipts before expenses were only $21,000. By the time the commissioners had paid the bills, they had less than $6,000 to distribute. Kansas City's share was again divided 50/50; each of the fourteen players took home $57.64 for twelve days of work. A reporter pointed out the obvious: "Now figure out how much a day and see if the world series is worth while under the present system."[77] Since the players had gone off salary as of the first of October, the World Series was a bitter disappointment. One disgruntled Kansas City player said, "We could have made more in two games barnstorming than we'll get out of the whole series."[78]

In the 1926 Negro World Series, the Chicago American Giants beat the Atlantic City Bacharach Giants in nine games. The Monarchs, having finished second in the NNL, received 6 percent of the net—or $443—to divide among the players. The fifteen who had played the full season received $25 each; the two who had played half the season split a share, as did secretary Gilmore and trainer Jewbaby. The Chicago American Giants also won the 1927 series. The Monarchs, finishing fourth, did not share in the winnings.[79]

By 1926 Fay Young of the *Chicago Defender* had declared the World Series an unprofitable joke, played for the benefit of the commissioners. But the World Series only magnified the underlying problem of the Negro leagues: dependence on an impoverished people who had too little discretionary money and too little leisure time. Wilkinson suggested making the series more profitable by alternating between an eastern and a western city every other year to reduce travel costs and by having only the participants in the series share in the profits. But the Negro World Series was dropped from 1927 until 1942.[80]

After the official season had ended in September, many teams took to the road for a month of barnstorming. Barnstorming—before, during, and after the season—was the common bond among black ballplayers. The league gave a structure to black baseball, but more than half of the two hundred games that the Monarchs played each season were against nonleague teams. With more than 90 percent of American blacks still living in the South, black ball teams were forced to leave the ghettos of northern cities in search of another crowd and another payday among rural Americans.

The Monarchs barnstormed mostly in the Midwest. Gilmore reported that fifty-two Chambers of Commerce had written to him on behalf of challenging teams in 1922. In Missouri the Monarchs might tour through Marshall, Sedalia, Booneville, Jefferson City, Joplin, and Springfield. They often played in Clinton as part of its Emancipation Day celebrations. Organized in 1922, the Western League of Colored Baseball Clubs had teams in Oklahoma City, Tulsa, Topeka, Independence (Kansas), Wichita, Kansas

The Monarchs barnstormed across the Midwest in this "parlor bus," which allowed them to reach small towns not on the railroad route. Carroll Mothel, left, shakes hands with Turkey Stearnes. Courtesy of Kansas State Historical Society, Topeka.

City (Kansas), Omaha, and St. Joseph. This league provided a yearly route for the barnstorming Monarchs.[81] Traveling through Missouri, Kansas, Nebraska, Iowa, Arkansas, Texas, and Oklahoma, they also played local—usually white—teams in towns that were not large enough to support a professional team. They competed against the strong independent teams that Black Sox players Buck Weaver, Swede Risberg, and Happy Felsch had put together in the Upper Midwest. As Georgia Dwight put it: "Back there in the boondocks they were not concerned with the terrible thing they had pulled in the World Series. They were only concerned that they were some darned good ball players."[82] As the Monarchs ventured further south, social customs sometimes prohibited their playing against white teams.

In 1928 Clarksville, Arkansas, and Pitcher, Oklahoma, were the only southern cities that allowed the Monarchs to compete against their white clubs. But Texas and Oklahoma, in particular, had a lively tradition of black baseball and offered many competitors.

At a time when major-league teams were concentrated on the East Coast and before television brought the national pastime into rural Americans' living rooms, the arrival of a professional ball team was quite an event. Businesses and schools closed, and the townspeople held parades and dinners to honor the barnstorming team. When the Monarchs arrived in Dallas for an exhibition game, the *Call*'s sportswriter exclaimed, "One would have thought a circus was in town as the streets of the Negro district were crowded to see the Big Leaguers arrive."[83] As the Monarchs' reputation spread throughout the region, white Americans as well as blacks anxiously laid down their dollars to see them. Monarchs' games in rural communities typically drew two thousand fans—even if they knew the local nine was no match for the traveling professionals. When the Monarchs took on the Houston Black Buffalos, champions of the Texas-Oklahoma-Louisiana League, special trains brought eleven thousand baseball-hungry Texans in from all over the state. The black citizens of Houston formed a housing committee to care for the out-of-town fans.[84]

Sportswriter Paul Fisher captured the excitement that was typical in midwestern towns when the Monarchs arrived:

Consider one of those great and wonderful days. It is a warm, yellow September Sunday in the late 1920s, barely noon, ordinarily a time when there is little motion in Pittsburg, Kansas. Today the town is in ferment. Broadway, the main street, streams with traffic, all bound north to the fairgrounds. The Fords and Essexes, the Chevies and Darts, the Buicks and Hupmobiles growl along, bumper to bumper, many bearing Missouri, Oklahoma, or Arkansas tags.

The pedestrian traffic swings along the walk thickly. Some fathers carrying picnic baskets in one hand, support young sons on the opposite shoulder. Strangely, there are no bicycles.

Then, abruptly at Fourth Street, the traffic breaks. A moment passes. Into the vacuum an army of boys and girls come sweeping and planing on their bikes, the vanguard for the Monarch bus carrying the team. The players had dressed a block down the street at the Y with its showers and lockers, essential for all the fried chicken, hams, picalilli, cakes, pies, and other edibles the townsmen will present through the day to the Monarchs.

At the fairgrounds, scores of little boys and girls stand shyly on the plot of grass where the bus unloads. Each of the 16 Monarchs picks his thralls. Each one goes marching off toward the field with this little girl carrying his sunglasses, this small Negro boy with his baseball shoes, these blond brothers with his two bats, this barefoot Italian lad with his glove. Frank Duncan resembles a Pied Piper, since it requires a small battalion to carry his vast array of catching equipment. Rogan, the old soldier of the 25th Infantry, who usually marches with quick steps, comes last, accommodating his steps slowly to two tough little Irish kids, who are choked with their good fortune, each holding one of Rogan's hands just like little old sissies.[85]

Barnstorming rounded out the season's schedule and, at the end of the summer, provided extra money in the players'

pockets for winter. Players went off salary in mid September, and then they barnstormed on what they termed a "cooperative," or "cold," basis: after expenses, the owner and the players split their share of the gate receipts 50/50. Owners and managers tried to second-guess their opponents in making the financial agreements. Shortstop Bill Yancey explained the reasoning that was used:

> If they want to give you a guarantee, you want a percentage; if they want to give you a percentage, you want a guarantee. Because when they want to give you a big guarantee, they *know* they're going to make it. And when they're not sure they're going to make it, they want you to take a percentage, so you want a guarantee.[86]

When the Monarchs barnstormed against local teams, they could expect at least 53 percent of the gate and hoped for as much as 80 or 90 percent.[87]

Very seldom did the Monarchs experience discrimination from the players in these interracial contests. Racial strife was minimal, because prejudiced players usually just refused to take the field. Buck O'Neil explained: "He might say, 'I ain't going to play with that nigger' and he wouldn't go. But if he would come to play, he wouldn't say that. We never had no friction whatsoever."[88] Newt Allen concurred: "Ball players—white and black—have a lot of respect for each other. They know they can play ball, and they know they're going to play with them or against them. You hear a lot of harsh words from the grandstand, but very seldom find prejudiced ball players."[89] The harsh words from the crowds sometimes became more than a man could bear. On a barnstorming tour in Texas, infielder Pat Patterson went up in the grandstand and punched a man because of his constant name-calling. Wilkinson fined Patterson $50. "He was right for fining me," Patterson recalled. "He explained to me, 'That's our policy—you just don't bite the hand that feeds you. Those people are paying their money to come out here and see you play ball.' "[90] And for barnstorming black teams, the paying customer could say what he pleased.

After the game the prejudice was sometimes expressed in humiliating gestures. Second baseman Roy Johnson described the discrimination that prompted him to quit the team, "People yell and clap for you while you're playing, but afterward you can't even get a sandwich."[91] And sometimes this petty segregation pushed a man's limits too. Once in Michigan, after the team had already ordered, the owner told the players that they couldn't eat inside his restaurant. It was one indignity too many. Newt Allen recalled: "We just all walked out—we left them with fifty some hamburgers on the grill. It was one of those times when you even the score."[92]

Wilkinson tried to avoid these unpleasant incidents as much as possible. Working with Harry Peebles, of the Semi-Pro Baseball Association, or later with promoter Abe Saperstein, Wilkinson developed a circuit of friendly communities that the Monarchs visited yearly. "We trained and played all through the South," said Buck O'Neil, "but we didn't get cut too much because we knew the places to go. The only time it would cut you would be this—we'd go to say a filling station to get gas and the guy would lock the restroom. After traveling so long, we knew the stations to stop to get gas so we would have these things."[93]

To ease the problem of overnight accommodations, the Monarchs at first traveled in a private sleeping car. The conveyance permitted them, like Wilkinson's All Nations team earlier, to eat and sleep on the train and thus avoid racial episodes. When playing in a large city, the Monarchs stayed in black hotels, though most of them were denigrated as "flop houses." The players preferred staying in private residences where black families took in boarders. "Ball players had been traveling in those same towns for years and years," Lefty Bryant recalled with a smile. "And they know those people just like sisters and brothers. And the people look forward to them coming, and they just made a routine of going there. Lucky me, I met my wife that way in Little Rock."[94] For barnstorming trips to towns that did not have railroad connections, the Monarchs traveled in three cars. As the schedule expanded and travel costs increased, Wilkinson abandoned the Pullman car and bought a bus. Purchased in 1926, this "parlor bus of the latest type" featured semireclining seats for twenty-one and a luggage rack on top. The bus cost about $9,000, but it gave the team tremendous visibility and saved Wilkinson a great deal in travel expenses.[95] When the Monarchs left for a barnstorming tour through Kansas and Nebraska in 1926, they were wearing overalls, and they packed tents, cooking utensils, and fishing poles. Some team members later remembered the trips as "the time of their lives . . . joyriding in a big deluxe bus, fishing, shooting jack rabbits, swimming, and playing just enough baseball to win games and keep in condition."[96] Though the chance to travel was often the biggest attraction, the months of flea-bitten hotels, tents pitched outside town, or long nights riding in a bus chipped away at the glamour of being a ballplayer. Pitcher Chet Brewer wearily summed it up: "We'd just eat and ride and play. That was the size of it. It wasn't easy street."[97]

In the 1920s, white major and minor leaguers were not paid very well either, and they were easily induced to barnstorm

Bullet Joe Rogan "holds up" his teammates on a barnstorming tour in 1931. Upper row, from the left: Newt Allen, T. J. Young, Goo Goo Livingston, Carroll Mothel. Lower row, from the left: Newt Joseph, Moocha Harris, Hallie Harding, Frank Duncan, Andy Cooper. Courtesy of Phil Dixon, Dixon Paper Company.

against their black counterparts. In 1922 the Monarchs beat Babe Ruth's All Stars in both games of a doubleheader in Kansas City. But the series that was most often recounted, the victory most cherished by the Monarchs, was the one against the Kansas City Blues. In 1921 the Monarchs challenged the Blues to a city championship, which the Monarchs lost, five games to three. In October 1922 the Monarchs again challenged these American Association leaders. Despite the crisp autumn weather, more than twelve thousand Kansas Citians turned out for the series. With a line-up that included Newt Allen, Frank Duncan, Newt Joseph, Dobie Moore, and Bullet Joe

**--BASEBALL!!--**
# BABE RUTH & BOB MEUSEL
### Playing with an All Star Team
--- vs ---
## Kansas City Monarchs
### SUNDAY, OCT. 22. 1 o'clock Sharp
This will be the first game of a double header participated in by Ruth and Mensel.
THE LAST CHANCE TO SEE THE MONARCHS AND THE FIRST CHANCE TO SEE THE GREAT BABE.

The *Kansas City Call,* 20 October 1922.

Rogan, the Monarchs defeated the white minor leaguers, five games to one. The *Kansas City Star* at first treated the series lightly, but after the fourth game, the *Call* reported, "The sentiment has veered slightly, however, and the Blues fans are 'blue' in spirit as well as in name."[98] When the series ended, the *Star* congratulated the winners: "The Monarchs outplayed the Blues in five of the sextet of exhibitions and

# HERE at LAST!

# BASEBALL

### For Kansas City Championship

## Kansas City Monarchs
### v.s.
## Kansas City Blues

### AT ASSOCIATION PARK

#### Nine Game Series, Beginning

## Friday, Oct 6th-7th-8th

Continued on Oct. 14, 15, 16, 17, 18, 19th.

## Tickets on Sale Now!

The *Kansas City Call*, 27 September 1922. The Monarchs captured the city championship after defeating the Blues five out of six games.

so are entitled to their full share of tribute and glory."[99] The Monarchs became the first black team to win a city championship from an intact class-A team. The *Kansas City Call* proudly proclaimed the victory with a front-page story and picture. Black sportswriter A. D. Williams asserted:

> The series has done more to boost Negro-organized baseball in this town with the white fans than anything else could have done. While they have always attended in large numbers, still the games they saw were regular league games and they have generally believed that it was an inferior grade of ball. But their eyes are open now to the fact that it isn't lack of ability that keeps Negro ball players off the big time—it's color.[100]

Commissioner Landis realized this, too, and he contrived even more strenuously to keep the teams separate. Landis saw the black Detroit Stars win three games from the St. Louis Browns, the black American

Giants break even with the Detroit Tigers, and black Hilldale win six out of seven against white league teams. He argued that major- and minor-league players failed to keep in condition after their season ended and that such losses hurt the reputation of white organized baseball. He ruled that any postseason games would have to be against "all-star" aggregates. Landis knew he could not stop white major and minor leaguers from competing against the black athletes, but he tried to diffuse the meaning of the contests. Whatever the public explanations, black players and fans understood Landis's ulterior motive. Cool Papa Bell, who played twenty-five summers in the Negro leagues, expressed the common sentiment: "They was keeping blacks out of the Major Leagues, and if we could beat 'em, why not let 'em play? So they would let 'em play as All-Star teams, and if we beat 'em, we hadn't beat no big league team."[101]

Black players pointed with pride to their many victories over the white all-star teams. The many interracial contests confirmed what the black players already knew. Chet Brewer said confidently, "At that time I knew if given a chance, we could play in the major leagues, 'cause all those fellows were top major leaguers."[102] These games also gave the ballplayers a chance to make a direct comparison of their talents. A comparison of batting averages, runs batted in, or other statistics had little meaning. Records for black teams were too incomplete, the caliber of competing teams varied too widely, and the differences in life styles were too pronounced. The Negro leaguers generally agreed that their level of play was consistently equal to Triple A teams, the highest minor league in white baseball. Black teams, out of economic necessity, did not have the depth of second-string players that major leagues could afford to carry.

Black players admitted that over the course of the summer a white team might "outgeneral" them. But in the short series, black players were confident that they could outguess and outplay their white opponents. For many blacks, these contests took on a symbolic meaning as well. Unable to compete freely as individuals, the black masses took a vicarious pleasure in seeing these athletic heroes beat the white man at his own game. These contests offered a chance to vindicate the injustices that the social system leveled. Pat Patterson eloquently explained: "I guess we tried probably harder than they did, because we had something to prove. We usually would beat them because of that. They were just out there to get their money. We had something to prove. In the end we proved that a ball player is a ball player."[103]

The *Kansas City Call* knew that the October barnstorming "helped the boys eat in the winter," but as soon as the season ended, most ballplayers had to find a winter job.[104] Some players, such as pitcher Bill Drake, hoped to find a "chick" to help them through the winter: "Back in those days you couldn't get a ball player to work in the winter. You wanted to find someone to take care of you. And that's what you needed, because you sure weren't making enough in the summer."[105] George Sweatt, the only man to play in all of the first four Negro World Series, taught school in Coffeyville, Kansas, after the season ended. Leroy Taylor, Hallie Harding, and L. D. Livingston used their summer wages to pay for college tuition. Most players wintered in Kansas City, their adopted home. George Carr and Newt Joseph, for example, drove cabs. The most ardent fans survived the offseason at Stark's Shining Parlor, known as "a popular place for both players and fans, situated as it was, near the baseball

headquarters.[106] The Winter Hot Stove League met at Stark's every afternoon, and according to some who remembered, "many hard games were replayed there during the winter."[107] Players and fans also gathered at Fox's Tavern, Newt Joseph's taxi stand, the Elks Club, and various barbershops.

The very best athletes usually opted for year-round ball playing. Even before the organization of the Negro leagues, two hotels in Palm Beach, Florida—the Poinciana and the Breakers—sponsored black baseball teams as entertainment for their wealthy guests. Teams from these two hotels played a couple of games each week. The players were not required to do any other work for their monthly salaries, although some worked as bellhops or waiters in order to earn extra money. Rube Foster's Chicago American Giants represented the Poinciana Hotel for years.[108]

Beginning in the 1920s, businessman Joe Pironne organized the four-team Southern California Winter League in Los Angeles. Pironne signed as many white major leaguers as possible (these included Babe Ruth, Lou Gehrig, and Mickey Cochran) for three of the teams and lured the best black ballplayers for the fourth team. This black team was known as the Los Angeles Stars, the Los Angeles White Sox, or the Philadelphia Royal Giants. Lonnie Goodwin, manager of the ECL Philadelphia Royal Giants, contacted players in the black leagues for this winter team. When he contacted Joe Rogan, this ace pitcher brought many of his Monarch teammates with him to California. In 1926 the team went to California almost intact. The winter league opened its season in late October and played until March. Players received about fifty dollars a month plus expenses.

In 1927 Lonnie Goodwin organized a trip to Japan for the black winter-league team.

The Royal Giants posed in Jingu Stadium in Tokyo. Top row, from the left: Johnny Reddle, Biz Mackey, Rap Dixon, Frank Duncan, Lonnie Goodwin, Andy Cooper, Hoss Walker, an unidentified player. Front row, from left: Neal Pullen, Joe Green, an unidentified player, G. Irie (translator), Evence, Bob Fagan, Cade. Courtesy of Phil Dixon, Dixon Paper Company.

Several Monarchs planned to go, but only catcher Frank Duncan actually joined the other NNL and ECL players as they sailed from San Pedro, California, in March. Billed as the Philadelphia Royal Giants, this team played in Japan, China, the Philippines, Australia, and Hawaii. When the team returned in June, some NNL officials wanted to punish the players with a five-year suspension. Clearly the players would have simply gone to the ECL. Under the circumstances, the NNL owners decided on a thirty-day suspension and a two-hundred-dollar fine.[109]

Cuba also became a favorite wintering spot for the Negro leaguers. Near the turn of the century, American blacks had discovered Cuba as a baseball haven. Rube Foster's American Giants and C. I. Taylor's Indianapolis ABCs toured Cuba in the

Tokyo's Mayor Nishikubo threw out the first pitch for a game on 1 April 1927. Andy Cooper is in the background. Courtesy of Phil Dixon, Dixon Paper Company.

1910s, following the major-league pattern. Cuban officials actively recruited the best black and white American ballplayers for the winter leagues. Many Cuban players earned spots on United States teams, although the American caste system usually forced them into the black leagues. The "coal black Cuban" José Mendez pitched for the Monarchs for years, and the NNL posted a $10,000 bond with the Immigration Service of the U.S. Department of Labor so that the Havana Cuban Stars could play in their league.[110]

Beginning in 1923, several Monarchs went to Cuba and Mexico to play winter ball. Again, money was part of the attraction. A good pitcher in 1924 made about $225 a month in the Negro leagues; he could pick up an additional $125 a month during the winter in Cuba. Part of the lure was the chance to continue their lives as celebrities. Latin fans were fanatical about baseball. Once when Newt Joseph hit a crucial home run, Cuban fans "went wild with joy" and showed their appreciation with a case of beer, a box of cigars, a shirt and tie, money, and a barbequed pig.[111] Another part of the Latin attraction was the chance to compete with the major leaguers on the same teams for similar salaries. Here, truly, they could measure their abilities and compete as equals.

By 1929, however, the Cuban leagues had fallen on hard times, and the second half of the season was canceled. When Newt Joseph and Frank Duncan returned to

Kansas City, they wrote a series of articles about Cuba for the *Call*. Some of their comments were light-hearted. They complained that the women looked good until they smiled—and then revealed few or no teeth. They agreed with the sportswriter who jested that "the bunch who go to Cuba will probably have choked themselves to death trying to say 'gimme a beer' in Spanish!"[112] Like all tourists, they complained about the food, which was based heavily on rice and bananas. To Duncan and Joseph, this made "home seem like a heaven." Other comments reflected on the decline of the Cuban leagues. When attendance fell off, the Cuban owners eliminated accident insurance for the players. It was conceivable that a player could be injured, receive no remuneration, and be stuck in Cuba. But the saddest comments concerned the increasing racial prejudice. In the early 1920s Duncan and Joseph reported they had been treated with respect. By 1929 the prejudice and discrimination resembled that in the United States. The players blamed the American tourists for bringing intolerance to the island.[113]

In the American Midwest or south of the border, the Monarchs established a reputation as being one of the outstanding ball teams in the country. For black Kansas Citians crushed by harsh discrimination, the Monarchs became a community focus. And with their victories against white opponents, they were a challenge to the assumptions made by segregation itself.

# FOUR

## Hard Times

"The Depression didn't mean too much in the Negro vicinity because we'd had a depression all our lives."—Jesse Fisher

Even before the stock market crashed in 1929, the fragile structure of the Negro leagues had already collapsed. Changing franchises, financial instability, scheduling problems, inability to enforce league rulings, and the poorest attendance in league history were the "deep, dull, ominous rumblings in the ranks of Negro baseball" that sportswriters sensed in their 1929 prediction that the NNL was doomed.[1] None of these problems were new; they were inherent in an organization based on an economically oppressed population. But the visionary Rube Foster had alleviated the obstacles to some extent by advancing money to players in the winter, investing in league clubs in several cities, loaning money to teams who suffered a bout of bad weather, and forcing major-league owners to deal with the black teams as a league. When Foster was hospitalized for mental problems in 1926, Dr. G. B. Key, vice-president of the NNL and coowner of the St. Louis Stars, assumed Foster's position. The following year, owners elected a Kansas City native, Judge William C. Hueston, as president. But the growing economic woes of the 1920s magnified the Negro leagues' difficulties. The ECL crumbled in 1928. And when Rube Foster died in December 1930, the *Kansas City Call*'s sportswriter concluded that "when Foster died, Negro baseball as a league died."[2]

The NNL limped along through the short 1930 season, but Wilkinson complained of "losing a bunch of coin" and then withdrew from the league at the end of summer. The

"Symbol of Departed Glory"

K.C.
Monarchs
NEGRO
NATIONAL
LEAGUE

The *Kansas City Call*, 22 May 1931.

Wilkinson's innovative portable lighting system was the
Monarchs' lifesaver during the Great Depression.
Courtesy of Gladys Wilkinson Catron.

black press declared that the league was dead without Kansas City: "Fans knew they were going to see a baseball game when Kansas City came to town. Say 'Kansas City Monarchs' and the fans poured through the turnstile. Now there aren't any Monarchs this year."[3] President Hueston insisted that the league would operate in 1931, but a string of disasters sealed its fate. The St. Louis Stars' park was sold to the city, leaving that team without a home field. Detroit's stadium burned. Then, without the Monarchs and the Chicago American Giants (who had ceased to operate after Foster's death because of legal problems with his estate), the NNL could not afford to post bond for the Cuban Giants. When President Hueston finally announced that the league would not operate in 1932, the *Call*'s reporter asked, "Is Judge Hueston trying to kid the gentle baseball public or is he trying to kid himself?"[4] For two years the league had existed in name only.

Wilkinson and the Monarchs had little to lose in withdrawing from the league. The other owners knew that Kansas City was not as dependent on the league as they were. Cum Posey, owner of the Homestead Grays, said that the Monarchs and Grays had "nothing to fear in 1931, as both clubs could play a schedule of 160 games and not meet a colored club, but the other clubs cannot wait too long" to organize another league.[5]

Wilkinson's safety net during the harsh years of the Great Depression was his portable lighting system. Wilkinson was heralded as the "father of night baseball," but, in fact, the first night game occurred on 2 September 1880, less than one year after Thomas Edison had perfected his remarkable electric light. Teams from two Boston department stores played this game in Hull, Massachusetts. Though the game went a full

A 1930 night game in Muehlebach Stadium. The white canvas fence around the outfield aided the hitters' depth perception. Courtesy of Gladys Wilkinson Catron.

nine innings, baseball was not the real purpose of the event—it was a demonstration of electricity. Several other teams experimented with lights in the late nineteenth and early twentieth centuries. Wilkinson's All Nations tried a night game with gas lights near Des Moines in 1920. But baseball authorities recognize the game between teams from Salem and Lynne, Massachusets, on 24 June 1927, as having been the first organized night game. Even though Wilkinson may not have been the first, he resurrected the idea and made it a popular solution to declining attendance.[6]

In 1929 Wilkinson commissioned the Giant Manufacturing Company of Omaha, Nebraska, to build a portable lighting system. Wilkinson's lighting equipment consisted of telescoping poles, which elevated lights forty-five to fifty feet above the playing field. Each pole supported six floodlights measuring four feet across. The poles were fastened on a pivot to truck beds

and were raised by means of a derrick. Wilkinson positioned the trucks along the foul lines, behind a six-foot canvas fence that stretched around the outfield. If playing in a stadium, he placed a "battery of lights" on the roof of the grandstand; otherwise, another truck was parked behind home plate. The whole system took about two hours to assemble. After the game was over, mechanics would lower the poles to the sides of the trucks and pack the reflectors on the truck beds. A 250-horsepower motor powered a 100-kilowatt generator which provided the electricity. This motor was reportedly as "large as a Ford car"; it had triple ignition and a triple carburetor system that used fifteen gallons of gasoline every hour. The generator was set up in center field; one player recalled that "it made so

Wilkinson used this photograph on his promotional posters. The bus on the far left had been revamped as the power plant. Courtesy of Gladys Wilkinson Catron.

much noise you couldn't hear.''[7] To make road travel as efficient as possible, Wilkinson revamped the players' bus so as to accommodate the motor and generator, and the players traveled in a car which they christened ''Dr. Yak.''

The whole system cost between fifty and one hundred thousand dollars. Wilkinson's wife operated an antique shop, but the family had no other source of income. Wilkinson's son remembered that his family ''mortgaged everything they had that would mortgage and probably went a little beyond that in order to get the lighting started.''[8] Wilkinson forfeited the Monarchs' charter of incorporation at this time, and he found it necessary to take a partner. Thomas Y. Baird was born in Arkansas and had played semipro baseball until an accident while he was working on the Rock Island Railroad left him crippled. He then operated a billiard parlor in Kansas City, Kansas. Baird took a chance with Wilkinson on the lighting system, apparently as an equal coowner.[9]

Wilkinson and Baird tried raising ticket

prices to pay for the lighting equipment— from sixty to seventy-five cents, then from seventy-five cents to one dollar. But the worsening economic situation quickly forced them to cut prices even lower than before. Fans were then able to see a night game for as little as twenty-five cents. Risky as the idea may have seemed to some at the time, the lights proved to be the Monarchs' salvation during the depression.

The Monarchs started the 1930 season with an early spring game in Lawrence, Kansas—which was perhaps the first game played with the portable lights. Then they barnstormed through Independence and Arkansas City, Kansas, and Crescent, Tonkawa, Oklahoma City, Okmulgee, and Enid, Oklahoma, in April and early May. The *Kansas City Call* accepted night base-ball rather nonchalantly. Early in the 1930 season the *Call* ran its only front-page article about the lighting system—and that was to note how the lights kept the zoo animals awake in Independence, Kansas. But the *Defender* announced that the first night game in Chicago would be ''the most spectacular event in all baseball history.''[10]

People came from miles around to marvel at the electric curiosity. The team and the lights brought between three and

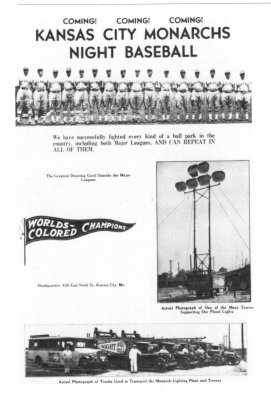

COMING! COMING! COMING!

# KANSAS CITY MONARCHS NIGHT BASEBALL

We have successfully lighted every kind of a ball park in the country, including both Major Leagues, AND CAN REPEAT IN ALL OF THEM.

The Greatest Drawing Card Outside the Major Leagues

WORLDS COLORED CHAMPIONS

Headquarters 420 East Ninth St., Kansas City, Mo.

Actual Photograph of One of the Many Towers Supporting Our Flood Lights

Actual Photograph of Trucks Used to Transport the Monarch Lighting Plant and Towers

Wilkinson advertised the Monarchs and their lights as "The Greatest Drawing Card Outside the Major Leagues." Courtesy of Gladys Wilkinson Catron.

twelve thousand spectators to every game. One reporter noted, "When one considers the fact that really good Sunday games usually attract only about three thousand, it can be said with some accuracy that the night ball idea has caught the fancy of the fans."[11] Pitcher Chet Brewer put it simply, "You never saw so many people."[12]

Players were not quite so taken with the idea of playing under lights. Earlier baseball games at night had been marred by compromises—teams had used bigger and softer balls, played on smaller fields, and committed many errors. Local sportswriters boasted that Wilkinson's lights made "the field as light as day and playing even easier than in the sunlight as it will not reflect in the faces of the players."[13] Coowner Baird assured fans that hitters would be able to see curve balls break better than in daylight. Some players were willing to agree for the sake of the crowds, but others admitted that the lights were not much better than candles, dimming as the generator coughed and sputtered. The Monarchs' lighting system required a slight alteration in the rules, namely a limit on the number of bases the batter could take on a ball that was hit high in the darkness. "Whenever a fly ball went above the lights, you couldn't see it," chuckled one player. "You just looked up and prayed, dear Lord, bring it here."[14] Another flaw was that outfielders had to avoid running into poles or tripping over the wires that ran through the outfield to the generator. Some players complained of eye strain, and some fans worried that players would be "beaned." Despite these small problems, the system was a success. The sportswriter for the *Kansas City Call* praised the technology: "The Monarchs will probably do to baseball this year, what talkies have done to the movies."[15]

Sportswriters quickly recognized what lights and night games would mean to the black leagues. A local supporter reassured readers: "Believe it or not—there's method in the supposed madness of friend Wilkinson. There's one thing about him—he knows his baseball . . . and the highway to dollars."[16] Those who were employed during the day could now attend baseball games after work. The lights also softened the financial losses that were often suffered as a result of rainouts, by giving the team more playing time. Gus Greenlee, owner of the black Pittsburgh Crawfords, had installed lights in Greenlee Field by 1933, and most minor leagues soon thereafter placed arc-light systems in their stadiums. After the owners of the American Association Park in Indianapolis invested in a lighting system, they opened the facility to the local black

The House of David team rented Wilkinson's lighting system for the early summer months. Courtesy of Phil Dixon, Dixon Paper Company.

team with the idea that the rental paid by the black ABCs would help to pay for the lighting system. For the white minor leagues as well as the black leagues, night baseball was a "lifesaver." The president of the white Denver Western League announced that his organization could now forgo the controversial Sunday afternoon games: the Sundays games drew only twelve hundred, while five to six thousand turned out for the night games.[17]

Major-league owners were not so quick to accept the idea of night baseball. Critics held that lights made for an "outdoor vaudeville" and "profaned a great game God meant to go with sunlight." The first major-league night game was not played until 23 May 1935, in Cincinnati. When it was over, Sam Bredon of the St. Louis Cardinals proclaimed what the black players already knew: "It makes every day a Sunday."[18]

During the six years that the Monarchs were not members of a league (1931–37), they played independent ball. Each spring, Wilkinson announced that he would start the

season late, and until then, the players could join other teams if they so wished. Several players scattered around the country to former league teams or to Gilkerson's Union Giants. Some stayed in Kansas City and joined semipro teams such as the Independence ABCs, the Armour Grays, the Kansas City Giants, or the Board of Trade's club. Others, such as Bullet Joe Rogan and John Donaldson, organized barnstorming groups of their own. And some waited for Wilkinson and Baird to find the resources to start a new season.[19]

One of the main ways in which Wilkinson and Baird made enough money to start the season was by leasing their lighting system to the House of David baseball team. The House of David was a religious sect, established in Michigan in 1903. As part of their religious identity, members did not shave their beards or cut their hair. In the public mind, the House of David was best known for its traveling baseball team. In the beginning, all players were members of the sect. As their popularity grew, long hair and beards continued to be their trademark, but baseball ability soon outweighed religious convictions as the criterion for membership on the team. Former Monarchs pitcher

Satchel Paige claimed that James (''Cool Papa'') Bell was so fast ''he would flip the switch and get into bed before the room went dark.'' Courtesy of John Holway.

Doolittle Young had a three-year stint with the House of David.[20]

From 1932 until 1937, Baird functioned as the booking agent for both the Monarchs and the House of David. Under this arrangement the House of David leased the Monarchs' lighting plant for at least the first half of the summer. Wilkinson's brother Lee and his nephew Dwight traveled with the House of David as mechanics for the lighting system. The House of David started its baseball season in May, and when Wilkinson and Baird had saved enough money from the rental of the lights, they would start the Monarchs' season.[21]

Though Wilkinson often started the season late during the 1930s—sometimes as late as August—he was proud of the fact that he fielded a team every year. The black press enthusiastically greeted the announcement that the team was being reorganized. ''It's true, fans!'' cried the *Kansas City Call*'s sportswriter. ''The return of the Monarchs will be welcomed by the local fans, who have been baseball hungry all this season.''[22] Sportswriters urged fans to buy tickets to support the team. Swearing at the team when it lost, standing on the street corners telling the world how great the team was, and giving the players a few gifts on opening day were not enough: ''A patron saint of the highest order, J. Wilkerson [*sic*] . . . believes and swears by his Monarchs and backs it up with what it takes to make a real baseball team—money. If we love our team, let's pay for it.''[23]

When Wilkinson announced that he had enough money to begin, most of his former players would return. And he was able to lure stars such as Cool Papa Bell and Willie Wells to the Monarchs. Their departure from teams in Chicago, Pittsburgh, Indianapolis, Detroit, and Baltimore caused hard feelings among other owners, who complained that the Monarchs waited until the ''flag race is hottest and in many cases undecided'' and then started ''grabbing players.''[24] The *Call*'s sportswriter contended that the players felt a great sense of loyalty to Wilkinson: ''Owner Wilkinson of the Monarchs has stayed in baseball during these stressing times for the sake of the men who have played for him during the more prosperous years.''[25] Probably outweighing their loyalty to Wilkinson, however, was the fact that the Monarchs, because of their lighting system, drew larger crowds—which meant a bigger check on payday. As the depression dragged on, many owners abandoned fixed salaries in favor of a cooperative plan under which the players worked for a percentage of the gate. Wilkinson used

Barnstorming with the House of David in Canada in 1934. Back row, from the left: Bullet Rogan, Newt Joseph, Newt Allen. Standing, from the left: Chet Brewer, Wilkinson, George Giles, Frank Duncan, Carroll Mothel, Sam Crawford, a House of David player, Charles Beverly, Andy Cooper. Kneeling, from the left: Hurley McNair, a House of David player, Eddie Dwight, a House of David player. The car was christened "Dr. Yak." Courtesy of Lee Wilkinson.

this "cold" playing plan from 1932 until 1936.[26]

Once the season had started, the Monarchs played every day and became the most traveled team in baseball. During their nonleague years they played in eighteen states and two foreign countries. Baird scheduled day and night games wherever he could get a crowd, sometimes squeezing in as many as three contests a day. The team had used Saturdays for travel during the 1920s, but the economy of the thirties forced it to abandon this luxury. Although the Monarchs started the season late, they managed to play about one hundred and fifty games each summer. Even in 1935, when they did not start until August, they took to the field eighty times.

While the Monarchs were not in the NNL, fans in league cities always welcomed them, and the crowd was often as much as 45 percent white. Three to six thousand baseball enthusiasts typically turned out for the small number of games in Kansas City. Attendance in other cities was not so large—bottoming out at five hundred for a Labor Day game in Chicago. But the crowds were, as one reporter noted, "as great as any ball team could expect considering the present state of affairs."[27] Most games were played in rural communities, where competition for the entertainment dollar was not so fierce. Wilkinson said experience had taught him that "colored players were better attractions through the sticks and the cactus."[28] The owner of the Sioux Falls, South Dakota, Canaries—where pitcher Swede Risberg finished his career after the Black Sox scandal—recalled that his club lost money playing local teams; but he ended the season with a profit when the Monarchs came through town.[29] Often the Monarchs and the House of David traveled together during the last two months of the summer. The

Newt Allen, T. J. Young, Turkey Stearnes, Eddie Dwight, Carroll Mothel, and Bullet Rogan in Denver, Colorado, 1934. Courtesy of Gladys Wilkinson Catron.

Monarchs would travel across a state, defeating all the local teams that they met. A few days later, the House of David would play through the same towns and again defeat the hometown talent. The Monarchs and the House of David would then return to these same small towns together and would play each other in a well-attended championship game. For at least one summer, former Chicago Cubs star Grover Cleveland Alexander regularly pitched for the House of David against the Monarchs' ace, Satchel Paige.[30]

Racial tensions lessened somewhat during the 1930s, as both races grappled with the Great Depression, and certainly, black baseball benefited from this. The *Call*'s sportswriter remarked that if the depression was the cause for the advances being made— "Oh but! for just a little more of this 'depression.' "[31] In 1933, because so many white semipro clubs had disbanded, southern teams—in order to fill out their schedules— dropped the prohibition against playing black teams. In 1934 the Monarchs became the first black team in the annual *Denver Post* tournament. Sponsored each August by the newspaper, this "little World Series of the West" was the natural outgrowth of the strong minor-league and semipro competition in the Midwest. The invitation to the Monarchs was partially the result of the campaign that was being waged by the black press for full citizenship rights for black Americans. The bottom line, though, was the promoters' recognition that a contest among the best teams in the Midwest had to include the Monarchs. The *Pittsburgh Courier* pronounced the Monarchs team "one of the best ball clubs in America,

National Semi-Pro Champions – 1935

The integrated Bismarck, North Dakota, team after its tournament victory. Back row, from the left: Hilton Smith, two unidentified players, Satchel Paige, an unidentified player, Quincy Trouppe, Double Duty Radcliffe. Courtesy of Gladys Wilkinson Catron.

regardless of race,'' and the promoters knew it would draw a crowd.[32] Black sports commentators declared the invitation ''the most significant announcement in a decade, insofar as Negro baseball is concerned.''[33] At last a black team was competing on a truly equal basis in the United States. Whites would not be able to dismiss the game as a mere exhibition. The eighteen-team contest lasted for two weeks. When it came down to the championship match, the Monarchs faced the House of David. A record-breaking crowd of eleven thousand— ''banked many deep in a semicircle around the playing field''—saw Satchel Paige pitch the House of David to a 2 to 1 victory over the Monarchs and capture the $7,500 prize money for the team.[34]

Ray Dumont, the president of the National Baseball Congress and a close friend

of Wilkinson's, developed a second midwestern classic in 1935—the National Baseball Congress Tournament, which was held annually in Wichita, Kansas, and to which black teams were regularly invited. The integrated Bismarck, North Dakota, team won the first year, with the help of former or future Monarchs Satchel Paige, Hilton Smith, Chet Brewer, and Quincy Trouppe.[35]

Yet another effect of the depression was the increasing willingness of white major leaguers to barnstorm against black teams. Because of Landis's ban on barnstorming with intact teams, two or three white stars would form the nucleus and fill out the roster of their all-star team with other major- or minor-league recruits. The Monarchs played against several such teams throughout the 1930s, most importantly the Dean All-Stars. Dizzy and Daffy Dean were fresh from a World Series victory in 1934 as members of the white St. Louis Cardinals. The Monarchs and the Dean All-Stars played a short barnstorming series in Kansas City, Chicago, Des Moines, and Oklahoma City. In publicizing the October match, the

The Monarchs and the St. Louis Cardinals attracted 6,000 fans for this night game in Oxford, Nebraska. Courtesy of Gladys Wilkinson Catron.

*Call* declared, "Since the Blues fell down into the cellar of the American Association . . . the Kansas City fans, colored and white, are looking for the Monarchs to uphold the baseball prestige of Kansas City by turning back the invaders."[36] These end-of-the-season contests with white major leaguers gave individual Monarchs something of a financial cushion for winter. Tickets for these games were priced higher than those for regular exhibition games—costing as much as seventy-five cents and one dollar. The Dean All-Stars and the Monarchs drew an amazing fourteen to twenty thousand fans per game. The teams divided the net gate receipts so that the winner received 60 percent. The Deans conceded that they made more by barnstorming against the Monarchs—reportedly $14,000 in four days—than they did in World Series play.[37]

In search of a crowd, the Monarchs extended their travel to Canada and Mexico. The Monarchs often teamed up with the House of David for a forty-day coast-to-coast tour of Canada. The *Winnipeg Free Press and Bulletin* reported on a game that

Charles Beverly won for the Monarchs: "The exhibition of baseball the House of David and the Kansas City Monarchs dished up may never be equalled again. You don't see many games that go eleven innings with errorless baseball, and a pitcher knocking at baseball's hall of fame."[38] In late October 1932 the Monarchs made a thirty-day trip to Mexico City for a series of games against the Mexico City Aztecs. With their lighting equipment and their superior brand of baseball, the Monarchs were a great hit with Mexican fans, who christened the team the Steam Rollers. Wilkinson had picked up the Negro leagues' greatest shortstop, Willie Wells, in 1932. Together with second baseman Carroll ("Dink") Mothel, Wilkinson had a combination that one admirer said made "more double plays than a crooked wife."[39] Baseball games in Mexico City usually preceded a bullfight, and the fans, reacting to spectacular plays with bullfighting enthusiasm, usually demanded that the players take "a dozen or so bows" or make a "series of grandiloquent gestures" before retiring to the dugout.[40] Q. J. Gilmore, in a series of articles written for the hometown *Kansas City Call,* bragged that the Monarchs' good conduct on and off the field had been noted by the Mexican press and that the players had been the guests of some of the city's most prominent citizens. He also made special note of the more harmonious race relations: "In Mexico, everyone eats where he pleases. We are treated here just like any other visitor."[41]

The nomadic Monarchs traveled in two buses with trailers. Purchased in 1935, each trailer contained bunks for eight, a shower, and a small kitchen. With their dollar a day "eating money" the players stocked the kitchen with cold cuts, cheese, crackers, sardines, and bread to eat as they traveled from town to town. Playing cards and singing helped to pass the hours on the bus. Buck Leonard, a Hall of Fame member from the Homestead Grays, recalled, "It would kill our worries and our tiredness to sing as we went from one town to another at night."[42] Roy Campanella, who joined the Negro leagues in 1937, commented: "Rarely were we in the same city two days in a row. Mostly we played by day and traveled by night; sometimes we played both day and night and usually in two different cities. . . . Many's the time we never even bothered to take off our uniforms going from one place to another. The bus was our home, dressing room, dining room, and hotel."[43]

During the depression, teams carried a minimum number of men. Players, including pitchers, were in the game for a full nine innings. Hilton Smith later remarked: "We didn't know what it was to relieve. When you went out there, you didn't look at

Bullet Rogan, Carroll Mothel, and Newt Allen stood before a billboard announcing a "sensational event!" Los Famosos Negros Americanos, the Kansas City Monarchs, were hailed in Mexico as "Campeones Mundiales de Color"—"World's Colored Champions." Courtesy of Kansas State Historical Society.

the bullpen, you were expected to go the whole route."[44] The Monarchs had a definite pitching rotation, but playing seven to ten games a week with only three or four pitchers did not allow any of them much rest.

Balls were too expensive to be thrown away quickly, and sometimes they would be "mushy" from several games' wear. Bar owner and Monarchs fan Milton Morris recalled that "if they knocked a ball into the stands, you got a ticket to come into a free game if you gave the ball back."[45] In addition, a pitcher could do almost anything to a ball to gain an advantage over a hitter. The cork-centered ball, which had more resiliency, replaced the rubber-centered ball of the "deadball era" and gave hitters a decided advantage over pitchers. The white

The 1936 Monarchs with their trailer. Standing, from the left: Andy Cooper, Pat Patterson, an unidentified player, Moocha Harris, Floyd Kransen, Henry Milton, Willard Brown, an unidentified player. Bottom row, from the left: Newt Allen, Leroy Taylor, Bullet Rogan, Bob Madison, Eddie Dwight. Courtesy of National Baseball Library, Cooperstown, N.Y.

major leagues at that same time had outlawed all pitches using foreign substances on the ball; but in the Negro leagues, everything was legal: spitballs, emery balls (the ball was roughed up with an abrasive emery cloth to make it jump and dip), cut balls (the pitcher would cut the hide with his fingernail or belt buckle to make the ball sail), mud balls (mud on the seams made the ball sink), and shine balls (with "so much Vaseline on it, it made you blink your eyes on a sunny day"). If an opposing team was known for its hitting strength, a pitcher would lay a dozen balls on ice overnight, which would make the balls so dead that they could not be hit out of the infield.[46]

The barnstorming Monarchs learned to hit all of these types of pitches, and they also learned to cope with hometown umpires. Monarchs' mainstay Newt Allen recalled with a smile: "The hometown umpire would call a strike way out here or way low if he thought you were a good hitter. Our owner told us that's what was happening and not to be arguing about it. Just go up there and if it's close enough to

hit, hit it. And when you did find a pitcher who threw the ball right down the middle, he had less trouble getting us out than the tricky pitcher."[47] White organized baseball was dominated by home-run hitters. But in the Negro leagues, the old style of play— which featured tight pitching duels, bunts, sacrifices, hit-and-run plays, and daring base stealing—continued to flourish.

Hard times and life on the road brought other changes. As gate receipts dropped, teams looked for curiosities to lure fans back to the parks. The portable lighting system buoyed the Monarchs for several years. To diversify the appeal, Wilkinson and many other owners arranged for the 1936 Olympic gold medalist Jesse Owens to barnstorm with the teams. The black hero's challenge to run against "cars, motorcycles, racehorses, and guys from college" assured the black teams a larger take at the gate.[48] Many teams considered that the curiosity of the House of David (long hair, beards, and alleged piety) was worthy of imitation. The Original House of David, the Eastern House of David, the Colored House of David, the Bearded House of David, the Mexican House of David, and the Kansas City House of David all capitalized on the slightly comic appearance of having a man with long hair play baseball. The original religious sect's team added yet another attraction—track star Babe Didrikson, who was billed by the advance man as "the world's greatest girl athlete." Newt Allen admitted that Didrikson was a fair pitcher, but he also said that the Monarchs did not play as hard against her. The newspapers then hailed her as the woman who could silence the bats of the mighty Monarchs, and the teams then drew tremendous crowds in the next town. The Monarchs and the House of David sometimes played donkey ball, in which all players except the pitcher and catcher straddle a beast of burden.[49]

The search for gimmicks to lure fans back to the ball parks brought clowning back into the game. The original Cuban Giants and most nineteenth-century black teams depended on clowning as part of their drawing power. As in the popular minstrel shows, their humor pandered to the white fans' stereotype of a lovable darky, and their performances included a series of songs and stunts before and during the game. The clowning attracted a substantial white audience, but black-baseball purists objected to the show because they considered it degrading to the players and to the game. As early as 1906, player and historian Sol White predicted the end of clowning in black baseball: "Where every man on a team

would do a funny stunt during a game back in the eighties or early nineties, now will be found only one or two on a team who essays to amuse the spectators of the present day."[50] The formation of the leagues professionalized the game during the 1920s, and league teams eliminated clowning from their games. Nat C. Strong, the white booking agent who controlled parks in New York, refused to book comedy teams in the 1920s. "You don't see no major leaguers clowning. Be like major leaguers," Strong advised.[51] But the clowning tradition survived in rural America. For example, Brown's Tennessee Rats, a black club from Holden, Missouri, traveled with a minstrel show, a band, and a carnival. Eddie Dwight's wife recalled that Eddie started with Brown in 1924: "In the morning he helped set up the carnival, then he played baseball, starting at 12 or 1 o'clock. Then they opened up the carnival and he sold games of chance or hotdogs. At night he helped move the scenery on the stages."[52] This comic club was also the training ground for good ballplayers: Monarchs' pitchers Bill Drake and Chet Brewer and outfielder Eddie Dwight all started with the Tennessee Rats.

During the thirties, many good ball clubs found that clowning was a necessary attraction. Showboating heightened the entertainment value of games in which the black teams were clearly superior to their small-town opponents. The comic relief also helped to defuse potential racial confrontations. In the early 1930s a few teams were organized in which baseball was secondary to clowning. The Zulu Cannibals, from Louisville, Kentucky, wore grass skirts and painted their faces. The Miami Clowns became so popular that the other club owners compromised their standards and asked the Clowns to join the Negro leagues.

Opposing hitters said of Satchel Paige's pitching, "You can't hit what you can't see." Courtesy of John Holway.

The Clowns, who were based in Cincinnati and later in Indianapolis, played inferior baseball but drew large crowds because of their minstrel show. The black press worried that the Clowns were merely perpetuating the negative stereotypes that black leaders were fighting to dispel. One sportswriter admonished that "the team has been capitalizing on the slap-stick comedy and the kind of nonsense which many white people like to believe is typical and characteristic of all Negroes."[53] The players, too, resented the popular image that the Clowns created. "If you were black, you was a clown. Because in the movies, the only time you saw a black man he was a comedian or a butler. But didn't nobody clown in our league but the Indianapolis Clowns. We played baseball," asserted Piper Davis, player/manager of the Birmingham Black Barons. "You'd have clubs—Kansas City put on pepper shows before the games started, guys out there handling the ball. Kansas City had the best team at handling the ball. But when it came to clowning, didn't nobody do that but the Indianapolis Clowns."[54]

Legendary pitcher Leroy ("Satchel") Paige came into his prime in this circuslike atmosphere. Paige started his professional career with the Chattanooga Black Lookouts in 1926. By his own count, he pitched with more than one hundred teams in the course of his thirty-year career. Paige had phenomenal control. Never shy in boasting about his talents, Paige remarked: "I was born with control. I have trouble walking guys. Even if the count was 3-2 and the catcher steps out for an intentional walk, I can't help myself. I have to throw a strike."[55] Paige matched his control with terrific speed. Always the master of exaggeration, Paige warned hitters that they would have to bat by sound as they would not be able to see his pitches. Among his repertoire of windups, Paige sported a Model T, a windmill, and a hesitation. He threw "bloopers, loopers, and droopers . . . [a] jump ball, bee ball, screw ball, woobly ball, whipsy-dipsy-do, a hurry-up ball, a nothin' ball and a bat dodger."[56] Whatever the name, Satchel's mainstay was his fast ball. Some hitters called this pitch a pea ball, indicating how small it looked as it whizzed across the plate. Others, such as Connie Johnson, claimed that they couldn't even see his pitches. "I'm sitting up in the stands, looking down at Satchel," Connie Johnson said of the first time he saw Paige pitch. "He started pitching—I couldn't see the ball! Now, I thought he was playing shadow ball—where you're pretending you're throwing the ball, but you wasn't."[57] Several times, Paige struck out twenty-two men in a game with his blazing fast ball. Sportswriters had a heyday. One proclaimed that "Satchel smoked the ball across the platter so fast that the friction thus achieved almost caused the bats . . . to catch afire when by some unforeseen accident the wood became connected with the horsehide."[58]

But it was Paige's showmanship that captured sports-page headlines and the imagination of fans—both black and white—across the nation. In some ways, Paige's image was in keeping with the stereotype that whites had created for blacks during slavery: the shuffling darky, the country coon. Paige's list of crowd pleasers also included some unique wiles, such as letting people guess his real age and various stories about his nickname. He also resurrected some old tricks, such as calling in the outfielders and striking out the next batters—or with variations, such as pointing to the player who would field the next out and pointing to himself for a strike-out. Paige advertised himself as "The World's Greatest Pitcher—Guaranteed to Strike Out the First Nine Men!" Often enough, he did just that. The independent Paige developed a reputation for not showing up at games, for making grand entrances at the stadium, and for wandering off to hunt and fish. Paige created an aura of mystery about his personal life, yet the newspapers were filled with accounts of his extravagant buying sprees, flashy women, guns and cars, and exaggerated tales about his baseball trips to Latin America.[59]

Despite all these added attractions during the 1930s, many black teams did not survive. Those that did were on the edge of bankruptcy and were clamoring for the "safety in numbers" prospect offered by a league organization. The NNL had barely died before the owners attempted to organize another such group. Oddly enough, the impetus came from Cumberland ("Cum") Posey, owner of the Homestead Grays of Pittsburgh. For years, Posey had refused to join either the NNL or the ECL. As an independent owner, Posey ignored player contracts and freely raided both leagues. But with the collapse of so many independent teams, Posey wanted the security of a league schedule. He rallied six owners to join the new East-West League in 1932. The organization started out with grand hopes of scheduling league games every day, but economic conditions forced all of its members back to barnstorming before the end of summer.[60]

In the early thirties, Gus Greenlee put together a team to rival Posey's Homestead Grays. Using a fortune made from Pittsburgh's policy racket, Greenlee signed five future Hall of Famers for his Pittsburgh Crawfords: Satchel Paige, Josh Gibson, Oscar Charleston, Judy Johnson, and Cool Papa Bell. Greenlee then set out to convince his friends who controlled the numbers rackets in eastern cities to invest in teams. Ed Bolden of the Philadelphia Stars, Tom Wilson of the Nashville Elite Giants, Abe and Effa Manley of the Newark Eagles, Alex Pompez of the New York Cubans, Ed Semler of the Black Yankees, and Rufus Jackson, who began to bankroll the Homestead Grays, joined Greenlee in forming the new Negro National League in 1933.[61]

"Back in those days, the only blacks who had money usually were in the numbers business," noted player Pat Patterson.[62] When the depression weakened legitimate black businesses, the policy kings—with their large sums of liquid capital—emerged as leaders in the black community. By also operating successful legal businesses, supporting charities, or helping to advance the race, these policy kings hoped to gain respectability in the black social structure. For Greenlee and his friends, baseball became the route to legitimacy. Cum Posey, who was pressured to accept Rufus Jackson as a partner, justified the gentlemen racketeers' control of the NNL: "Regardless of opinions concerning the owners of the clubs it is helping the Negro Race morally and financially."[63]

Gus Greenlee served as president of the league, but to avoid charges that he favored his own team, Greenlee hired an independent commissioner to arbitrate disputes. W.

Rollo Wilson, a sportswriter for the *Pittsburgh Courier,* and then Ferdinand Morton, a New York City civil-service official, tried to run the league, but the owners succeeded in dominating them with bribes and intimidation. The new league officials cut players' salaries by 20 to 30 percent, reduced the number of men on the team rosters, reduced the price of tickets, shortened the season to about two months, and agreed to play mostly sectional games in order to avoid the long, costly road trips. Many clubs were anxious to join the new league. During the first four years, 1933 to 1936, the new NNL admitted twenty-one teams, but many barely lasted one season. The problem, one analyst complained, was that franchises were granted to "fly-by-night promoters, whose funds barely exceeded the price of a railroad ticket to the meeting."[64] Fly-by-night or not, few owners could afford the $50,000 that Greenlee claimed to have lost in baseball during 1933. With the tremendous losses being suffered in the new NNL, the *Chicago Defender,* once the mouthpiece and leading advocate of a black league, now questioned the wisdom of having such an association. The *Defender* noted that the Kansas City Monarchs "are playing through Nebraska and other western points at a very high rate of profit and laughing merrily as the associated clubs wallow in the confines of a red ledger."[65]

Wilkinson himself had not given up on a league organization. As the only original club owner left from the first NNL, he was thought by some sportswriters and managers to be the logical successor to Rube Foster. "Gentleman Dave" Malarcher, who succeeded Foster as the manager of the Chicago American Giants, said that only Wilkinson had the "good sense and business and baseball acumen and experience and judgement" to follow Foster.[66] As early as

1932 Wilkinson tried to organize several
owners. Part of his plan included moving
the Monarchs to Chicago, where the black
population was three times larger than in
Kansas City. After Foster's death, the
American Giants' franchise and use of the
stadium had been complicated with legal
problems. One fan moaned, "Chicago's ball
park has been dark for months and shows
no signs of coming back to light."[67]
Wilkinson eventually decided against the
Chicago venture because park owners there
were unwilling to lease the stadium for
more than two years, an unacceptably short
term. Rather than join a league, Wilkinson
and the Monarchs took to the road. But the
other owners were anxious to have the
Monarchs in the new NNL. League officials
specially invited Wilkinson to attend all
meetings. Both the new NNL and the
struggling Southern League allowed the
Monarchs to be an associate member while
denying this same privilege to all other
teams. As an associate member, the Monarchs had the benefit of regularly scheduled
games in large cities, without having to pay
full membership dues. The other owners
gained because the Monarchs were a good
drawing card in their communities. Wilkinson kept negotiating. When he called a
meeting in Kansas City in 1934 to discuss a
western organization, sportswriters were
hopeful. "Not since the days of Rube Foster
have the moguls appeared so eager to secure
franchises in any loop," wrote one.[68] But
the owners were unwilling to compromise,
and the meeting came to nothing.

When the barnstorming season ended in
mid October, many Monarchs faced a
desperate winter. In the early years of the
depression, the winter leagues were in as
much disarray as the summer leagues, and
few Monarchs participated in them. Most of
the players took their chances in Kansas
City.

Tom Pendergast, who dominated Kansas City politics
from 1910 until 1938. His local "New Deal" caused
the black vote in Kansas City to shift from 80 percent
Republican in 1922 to 70 percent Democrat in 1932.
Courtesy of Kansas City Museum.

Because of massive construction programs sponsored by political boss Tom
Pendergast, the early years of the depression
were not as bad in Kansas City as they were
elsewhere. City manager Henry McElroy
developed a successful program for giving
work to the unemployed. He put labor-
saving machinery aside and used manpower
instead for the construction of water mains
and sewer systems. Though the federal
government was the source of many jobs,
the Pendergast machine still controlled the
local distribution of the aid through the
Federal Reemployment Service and the Civil
Works Administration. One analyst declared
that "neither business anxiety nor unemployment was among . . . [Kansas City's]
problems. The Pendergast organization, for

better or worse, had steered the city through the depression.''[69]

Nevertheless, unemployment was one of black Kansas City's problems. Pendergast had won favor among blacks during his term as county marshal in the early 1900s. The black *Rising Son* declared: ''Mr. Pendergast's term as marshal established a new era in penal progress. He stood for the Negro as well as the white man.''[70] And his machine continued to provide welfare services for the poor that were not available before the New Deal. Bartender Jesse Fisher put it simply: ''When you feed a hungry man, you expect a hungry man to help you. That's what was happening back in those days.''[71] Black Kansas Citians fared better than blacks in many other cities during the depression. Most notably, the death rate among blacks declined by one-third. But black Kansas Citians received far less than their share of help during the recovery. The National Reemployment Service set up a

Food baskets for the city's poor, in front of Democratic Ward headquarters in 1932. The *Call* asserted, ''It is not how much power T. J. Pendergast has, but what he does with it, that concerns the people.'' Courtesy of Kansas City Museum.

classification system in Kansas City which limited blacks to domestic or personal service, regardless of their qualifications or experience. Black skilled construction workers were excluded from nearly all federal projects. And it was not until the state of Missouri was threatened with the withdrawal of federal money for the Civil Works Administration that blacks were assigned to projects in Jackson County. Almost half of the black women were gainfully employed, in comparison to only one-fifth of white women. Also, like the men, many black women worked in personal-service occupations.[72]

Though a government study showed that employed black families were spending 4 to

5 percent of their total income on recreation, the low-paying jobs that blacks held meant that they had little money for amusements such as Monarchs games. The *Call*'s sportswriter noted regretfully, "With the present depression hurting most everyone, few folks have the money for baseball."[73] In addition, 25 percent of Kansas City's blacks were on welfare by 1935. A ballplayer had little chance of finding winter employment in such an economic climate.

"In those days, the ball players were like musicians," said saxophonist Eddie Barefield. "They didn't make enough money to make a living, and they did everything. They played ball and did everything else on the side, drove cabs and did these things, just to make up for their living."[74] Outfielder Eddie Dwight's situation was typical. His salary was $125, and he earned an extra $25 a month by driving the bus. But after living on the road and sending money home, he had $45.73 coming to him at the end of the 1936 season. Going home to a wife and three children, he was anxious to find work. When he could not, qualifying for welfare assistance was difficult. The caseworker castigated the Dwight family for not having saved more of Eddie's summer earnings. The family survived by gleaning vegetables from the truck gardens in the Fairfax industrial district. Eventually the Dwights received three dollars a week for groceries.[75] For players who did find work, the "everything else" that they did was usually menial, such as shoveling snow or coal or scrubbing saloon floors. Newt Joseph and Frank Duncan maintained their taxi service. And Frank Duncan, who was married to the Kansas City–born blues singer Julia Lee, periodically drove the bus for Bennie Moten's band. The editors of the *Kansas City Call* singled Joseph and Duncan out for praise: "There's something else in life for a

Frank Duncan, a Kansas City native, who joined the Monarchs as catcher in 1922. He was manager of the team when Jackie Robinson signed on in 1945. Courtesy of John Holway.

good ball player to do in the winter besides loafing around, playing cards or going out into the far sunshine to play winter league ball."[76]

In the winter of 1933/34, Tom Young, Chet Brewer, Newt Allen, Carroll Mothel, Andy Cooper, and Bullet Joe Rogan of the Monarchs joined a twelve-man all-star team

Ted Strong was guard and captain for the western unit of the Globetrotters. He was regarded as one of their best ball handlers. Courtesy of Harlem Globetrotters.

that traveled to China, Japan, and the Philippines. Lonnie Goodwin, the promoter and manager of the Philadelphia Royal Giants, organized the three-months' trip. Sailing on the S.S. *President Lincoln,* the team left San Francisco in November. They played for two days in Japan and for a short time in China; then they remained in the Philippines until early February. The black squad played against army teams and clubs from sugar plantations. Goodwin took 60 percent of the team's income, and the remaining 40 percent was divided equally among the players.[77]

Some ballplayers opted for year-round

athletic work by signing on with the barnstorming Harlem Globetrotters. Organized by Abe Saperstein in 1926, the Globetrotters entertained with a comic game of basketball, much as the Indianapolis Clowns played baseball. Clowns' first baseman Goose Tatum, Black Barons' second baseman Piper Davis, and Monarchs' outfielder Ted Strong earned winter money by dazzling crowds to the tune of "Sweet Georgia Brown."[78]

By mid decade the black teams began to pull out of the depression. The Monarchs started the 1934 season with an early spring trip to Texas, and Secretary Gilmore reported having more requests for the team in 1934 than in the previous five years. The following year the NNL members played a complete schedule, the first since 1929. By 1936 many teams ended with a slight profit, though this represented only a small percentage of their recent losses.[79]

One reason that the owners started making a few dollars' profit was the success of an innovation called the East-West Game. In 1933 a collection of sportswriters and owners decided to cash in on the fact that baseball fans constantly "hashed, re-hashed and discussed in barbershops, on street corners, in apartments, buildings, in mills, factories" the relative merits of individual players.[80] The white American and National leagues staged their first annual All Star classic in 1933 as part of Chicago's "Century of Progress" exposition. The black owners called for a similar one-game contest between players from the eastern and western regions to decide "with a bombardment of balls and a barrage of bats" who was best.[81] Hailed by the black press as a "dream game," the East-West contest captured and held public interest as the black World Series of the 1920s had never been able to do. Fay Young, by this time sports editor for the *Kansas City Call,* convinced himself that the idea was "sweeping the country like wildfire!"[82] Fans chose players for the East-West Game through polls. Daily and weekly papers in the black communities across the country ran lists of eligible players and teams. Fans clipped the ballots and mailed them to the league secretaries for tabulation. The line-ups for the East-West games often were heavily loaded with players from Chicago and Pittsburgh, home base for two major black papers. But in 1936 Kansas City captured ten of the seventeen spots on the West's roster.[83]

The balloting attracted much attention. In a two-week period, "old man paying public" selected sixteen to twenty players and a manager for each team. In 1933 the highest vote count for a single player was forty-three thousand. By 1939 some men received as many as five hundred thousand votes. White newspapers paid little attention to black baseball before the East-West games, but by 1935 even the *New York Times* carried the results of the game.[84]

Held every August in Chicago's Co-miskey Park, the East-West Game became a major sports event for black Americans, their own summer ritual as part of the National Pastime. Twenty to fifty thousand fans from all over the country packed the stands. Secretary Gilmore arranged a special trip to Chicago in 1935 so that Kansas Citians could see the Joe Louis–Levinsky fight and the East-West Game. Accounts of the games often made the front page of the papers that had polled the fans. In 1936 the *Chicago Defender* announced the upcoming game on the society page: "Without Satchell [*sic*], the ball game would be well worth attending as all of the major Race players compose the opposing teams, and with Satchell present, baseball takes on the aspect of a social affair."[85] The excitement of the game came through most poignantly in the report filed by the *Kansas City Call*'s reporter after the 1935 game:

> Not since the celebration following the news that the armistice had been signed [ending] the bloody conflict known as the World War has Chicago seen its citizenry go stark mad for a few minutes. Score cards were torn up and hurled into the air. Men tossed away their summer straw hats and women screamed.[86]

A showcase for black talent, the East-West Game provided a financial bonus for owners. Most of the profits from the first two games went to the three men who financed the game: Gus Greenlee (the Pittsburgh Crawfords), Robert A. Cole (the Chicago American Giants), and Tom Wilson (the Nashville Elite Giants). Starting in 1935, half of the profits endowed a players' emergency fund. This fund protected players against defaulted salaries, and it aided owners when they were hit with a string of rainouts. Each club owner in the league also received a share of the profits. This money helped many of them to end the season with a balanced ledger and gave them cash to start the next year. In 1938, for example, the gross receipts were $27,000. Each owner collected $900. The owners of Comiskey Park were said to be the real winners. They retained 20 to 25 percent of the gate receipts for the use of the stadium and made additional charges for the use of the dressing rooms and dugouts. But the black press proudly reported that the East-West Game employed about one hundred and fifty blacks and that three-fourths of the money generated by the game passed into the hands of blacks.[87]

During the 1930s, players received nothing for playing in the East-West Game. A place on the roster was a coveted honor.

The *Pittsburgh Courier*'s announcement for the 1937
East-West Game.

Monarchs shortstop Jesse Williams said, "I'd have to say my biggest thrill was the first time I went to the East-West classic."[88] One sportswriter agreed, "The average colored player has been interested more or less in his salary and what it would be, but now they are all trying to make the East-West classic."[89] But by 1940 the players wanted a financial reward too. Owners argued that the players were on a salary and deserved no bonus. The players complained that the travel money that they received did not even cover their expenses. The West players in 1940 received a gold Elgin watch as a token for their participation in the game, but the issue surfaced again and again.[90]

Trying to capitalize on a good thing, some owners decided to stage a second All-Star Game in New York in 1938. Claiming that fans had not chosen the best players for the Chicago event, the owners arranged for sportswriters to chose the teams for this second match. At the last minute, Robert Jackson, president of the newly formed Negro American League (NAL), refused to sanction the game and fined each player who participated twenty-five dollars. Players protested Jackson's decision, asking if they would be forced to go on WPA or welfare to survive the winter. Both the NNL and the NAL sanctioned a second game in New York in 1939. The West changed the line-up from the Chicago game, but the East used the same team. Only twenty thousand people attended, and thereafter the second East-West Game of the season was discontinued.[91]

Owners in the western states banded together as the Negro American League in 1937, and Wilkinson joined—his first full league membership since dropping from the NNL in 1931. Major Robert Jackson of Chicago and Dr. J. B. Martin of Memphis

alternated as NAL president and commissioner, and Wilkinson served as either vice-president or treasurer.[92] Despite the strong leadership, the leagues found themselves at the mercy of the white booking agents. The major-league park owners guaranteed the agents a monopoly. By being able to reward or punish back teams with playing dates and percentages, the powerful clique of booking agents often had the strongest voice in league affairs. Owners complained of being in "the clutches of the rotten booking system that keeps us busy only four months and leaves us idle when the bookers' parks close on Labor Day."[93] Nat Strong and Ed Gottlieb (who had long been connected with black baseball as owner of the Philadelphia Stars) controlled bookings in the East and claimed 10 percent of the gate receipts of all league games. In the West, sports promoter Abe Saperstein received nothing from league games, but he skimmed 5 percent off receipts of nonleague games that he booked in Chicago. Saperstein not only received 5 percent of the gate receipts for the East-West Game, he also tried to claim $1,100 for publicizing this event. The black sportswriters, rebelling against his domination, formed the American Sports Writers Association at the East-West Game in 1940. The NAL owners then hired Tom Baird, coowner of the Kansas City Monarchs, as their official booking agent, replacing Saperstein.[94]

As with the ECL and NNL before them, the new NNL and NAL argued over player contracts and raids. Some western sportswriters complained that the East raided the West during periods of prosperity, but bargained for peace during hard times. The most unreconcilable difference between the two leagues, however, centered on "the elongated individual, Satchel Paige."[95]

In 1937 Gus Greenlee, owner of the

*Above:* Executives of the Negro American League in 1940. Seated, from the left: Fay Young, *Chicago Defender;* J. L. Wilkinson, Kansas City Monarchs, J. B. Martin, Chicago American Giants; Ernest Wright, Cleveland Buckeyes; Dr. W. S. Martin, Memphis Red Sox. Standing, from the left: Candy Jim Taylor, Chicago American Giants; Syd Pollock, Indianapolis Clowns; Dr. B. B. Martin, Memphis Red Sox; T. Y. Baird, Kansas City Monarchs; Tom Hayes, Birmingham Black Barons; Wilbur Hayes, Cleveland Buckeyes. Courtesy of Ocania Chalk.

*Below:* Trujillo's team, with its manager, in Santo Domingo, 1937. Josh Gibson is standing at the far left; Satchel Paige is sitting on the manager's right; and Cool Papa Bell is sitting in front of the manager. Courtesy of Negro Baseball Hall of History, Ashland, Ky.

Pittsburgh Crawfords, sold Paige to Abe and Effa Manley's Newark Eagles for $5,000. Paige instead jumped to the Dominican Republic for the summer season. He had signed with two Cuban players, Martin Dihigo and Lazaro Salazar, who acted as agents for the dictator of the Dominican Republic, Generalissimo Rafael Trujillo. Wanting to enhance his political reputation by winning the Dominican pennant, Trujillo authorized Paige to negotiate with other members of the Pittsburgh Crawfords. The exodus of black talent to Santo Domingo caused the Crawfords to disband.[96]

Cuba, Puerto Rico, Venezuela, Mexico, Panama, and the Dominican Republic were powerful magnets for the best black ballplayers during the 1930s and 1940s. The Monarchs' Frank Duncan, Chet Brewer, Willard Brown, Hilton Smith, Ted Strong, and Jesse Williams all traveled south of the border. As with Cuba before, the Latin lure was a mixture of money and freedom. In Latin American countries, political power struggles were often played out on the baseball diamond. With backing from United States oil and sugar companies, the owners were willing and able to buy a good team. "Down there they were paying that fabulous salary," marveled shortstop Jesse Williams. The Negro leagues could not compete with the $775, with all expenses paid, for an eight-week season, which Latin American owners offered.[97]

Despite the cultural differences, life in the Latin American countries was more "normal." Black ballplayers did not have to play three games a day; they did not have to sleep in busses as they jounced to another town. On the ball field they played against and with white major leaguers such as Early Wynn, Mickey Owens, Sal Maglie, Max Lanier, Whitey Ford, and Tommy Lasorda. And they competed as equals. Away from

Cool Papa Bell, with his wife, in Havana, Cuba, 1928. Courtesy of Negro Baseball Hall of History, Ashland, Ky.

the ball field they were also treated as equals—eating in the same restaurants, staying at the same fine hotels, and basking in the same hero's glory.

Earlier in the century, blacks had migrated to the northern cities in search of decent wages and freedom. "And by freedom," W. E. B. DuBois explained in 1905, "he means a chance for expansion, amusement, interest, something to make life larger than it has been on the lonely country plantation, or in the Negro quarter of a Southern town."[98] But the North was not the promised land that it seemed to be. "We knew what we couldn't do in the South," said Jesse Williams, "and when you came

North you were surprised because you couldn't do a whole lot of things that you thought you'd be able to do when you got here."[99] For the black ball players, Latin America offered a chance to escape the oppressive racism of the United States—it was another journey for work and freedom. When Willie Wells left the Newark Eagles for Mexico, he poignantly explained that he was not quitting the team; he was quitting the country: "I've found freedom and democracy here, something I never found in the United States. I was branded a Negro in the United States and had to act accordingly. Everything I did, including playing ball was regulated by my color. Well, here . . . I am a man."[100]

Though as black men, the owners may have understood, as businessmen, this exodus enraged them. After Paige led the Dominican flight, the owners retaliated with a three-year suspension. Finding it impossible to enforce the suspension, they reduced the punishment to a nominal fine. The players were unaffected either way. When they returned at the end of the 1937 season, they formed an independent team, Trujillo's All Stars or the Santo Domingo Negro Stars. With the House of David's promoter, Ray Doan, they barnstormed through the Midwest and won the *Denver Post* tournament.

In 1939 Paige again led what owners called a "wholesale jumping of contracts" to foreign countries. The owners again threatened suspension and warned Paige that he would be "the forgotten man" of baseball. The threats carried little weight—this time because the World War II draft was depleting the rosters so quickly that any player was welcomed back with open arms.[101]

When Paige returned to the States, he refused to recognize the deal that Greenlee

had made, which would have sent Paige to Newark, and signed instead with Wilkinson. Wilkinson sent Paige to Wilkinson's traveling farm club, which his brother Lee managed. Since this team played independent ball and was not a member of the NAL, Abe and Effa Manley technically had no recourse through the league. Effa Manley accused Wilkinson of using his brother as a "puppet ruler" for a team that Wilkinson himself actually owned. She charged that Wilkinson was, like the white booking agents or ball-park owners, interested only in money. To keep interleague harmony, the NAL allowed the Manleys to keep two disputed players in return for Paige.[102]

The Satchel Paige whom Wilkinson signed in 1939 was a ballplayer with an arm that was sore and weak from year-round pitching. Paige blamed his miseries on the spicy Mexican food, which his delicate stomach could not handle. The *Kansas City Call*'s sportswriter explained eloquently:

> The great one owned a wing that was as dead as a new bride's biscuit . . . Satch's great flipper just wouldn't work any more. It was at that time that J. L. Wilkerson [sic], owner of the Monarchs, toyed with the idea of employing Satch, who was nursing the once-poisonous paw in pathetic pity.[103]

Thus began the lifelong friendship between the two men.

Wilkinson signed Paige to his traveling team and named it Satchel Paige's All Stars. Paige recalled: "I'd been dead. Now I was alive again. I didn't have my arm, but I didn't even think of that. I had me a piece of work."[104] This traveling team served as the Monarchs' farm club. The team mostly consisted of young recruits in need of "seasoning," but a few older players, such as Newt Joseph, George Giles, and Cool

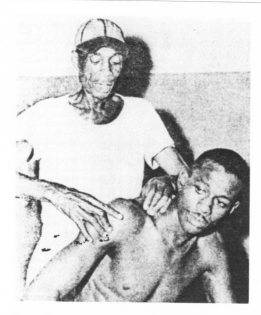

Frank ("Jewbaby") Floyd, the Monarchs' trainer for thirty years, claimed the credit for restoring Paige's pitching arm. Courtesy of John Holway.

Hilton Smith, who was born in Giddings, Texas, played in the Texas Negro League before joining the Bismarck, North Dakota, team, where Wilkinson spotted him. Smith suggested that Wilkinson give Jackie Robinson a try. Courtesy of Black Archives of Mid-America.

Papa Bell (known as the fastest man in the Negro leagues), also retired to this team. Paige respected Wilkinson for hiring ballplayers who were past their prime. According to Paige, Wilkinson said: "They can still do some good. And they've done a lot for the Negro leagues and made us all some money, so I'm just trying to pay them back a little."[105] Wilkinson also knew that the older players were still an attraction at the box office.

With Paige as coach, the roving club played several NAL and NNL teams, barnstormed through the Northwest, and played in the California winter league. Paige led his own battle for equality with his barnstorming team. Jack Marshall of the Chicago American Giants recalled: "When Satchel Paige had his all-stars they wouldn't play in a town if they couldn't lodge there. Wilkinson owned the ball club, and if Satchel Paige couldn't sleep where they played or eat where they played, they wouldn't play there. He'd just tell the

Chamber of Commerce, no soap. They were warned beforehand, so they didn't have any trouble; the Chamber of Commerce made the arrangements."[106] Kansas City fans considered this team to be the "little brothers" or "little cousins" of the Monarchs. At the end of the season, Kansas Citians enjoyed a Missouri dream game in which the Monarchs consistently defeated Paige's team.[107]

When Paige signed on with the Monarchs, Wilkinson assigned Jewbaby as his personal trainer. Jewbaby, reported the *Pittsburgh Courier*, "cuddles and babys that bronze slingshot Satchel carries around on the right side of his anatomy for an arm."[108] Though Paige had been told by several doctors that he would never pitch again, by 1941 he had regained strength in his arm and had moved up to the Monarchs' main team. Probably the only man who suffered from Paige's recovery was pitcher Hilton Smith. College-educated and a former teacher, Smith, by several accounts, was as good or better than Paige. Fellow pitcher Lefty Bryant confessed: "Hilton never got the credit he deserved. We never told him, but Hilton was the best pitcher we had, including Satchel."[109] Buck O'Neil concurred: "From 1940 to 1946 Hilton Smith might have been the greatest pitcher in the world."[110] Smith opened most Sunday games, especially in Kansas City, for fourteen years and saved many games that Paige started. Yet Paige had the flair that reporters noticed, and the headlines on the sports page almost always read "Satchel and the Monarchs Win Again!"

Magnanimously, Smith never resented the publicity that Paige received. But Smith did delight in telling about a doubleheader against the Chicago American Giants in 1941. "The Mills Brothers were real strong and they were Satchel's favorites," Smith recounted. "We were all in Detroit and they came out to see us play. There were thirty-five or forty thousand people out there. Satchel pitched the first ball game and beat 'em 7-4. I pitched the second game and shut 'em out 5-0. They got on Satchel, said, 'Lord, we came out to see the wrong man. This youngster's the one we should see.' "[111] Satchel realized the inequity and tried to make amends during the 1942 World Series against the Homestead Grays. He approached Smith and said: "You're always saving games for me. Tonight let me relieve you."[112]

Paige angered many owners, league officials, and managers with his disregard for contracts. "You talk about hard times and gray hairs," sighed one owner who worked with Satchel.[113] A sportswriter declared that he was "as undependable as a pair of second-hand suspenders."[114] Players sometimes resented the amount of publicity that Paige commanded, but they also had to admit that Paige kept the black leagues alive. Whenever a team had financial troubles, the owner would borrow the nomadic Paige for a game. Teammate Othello Renfroe observed: "There's not a Negro baseball player will say anything against Satchel, because he kept our league going. Anytime a team got in trouble, it sent for Satchel to pitch. So you're talking about your bread and butter when you talk about Satchel."[115]

Although the depression and the Monarch's constant traveling had silenced the Boosters during the early 1930s, they rallied again after the team joined the NAL in 1937. Fay Young rejoiced at this resurgence of spirit: "It looked like old times on East 18th Street, for the past few days as baseball players and baseball fans gathered in little knots to talk about the coming season."[116] Twelve to fourteen thousand fans turned out for the opening games, and Kansas City again dominated the contest for largest attendance.

The Boosters tried all manner of ways in which to restore in local fans what one called "that wild enthusiasm that subsided during the early days of the depression."[117] In addition to the traditional opening-day parade, the Boosters planned a homecoming dance, to introduce the players to the fans, and stag parties for members of the opposing teams at the Elks Rest. As in the 1920s, this 200-member club solicited prizes for "firsts"—the first home run, the first out, and even the first error. Local merchants donated socks, ties, caps, straw hats, flannel trousers, razors, dozens of eggs,

T. B. Watkins throws out the first pitch for a Monarchs game in 1935. A mortician and influential civic leader, Watkins was a stalwart Monarchs Booster for years. Courtesy of Black Archives of Mid-America.

Mary Jo Weaver was crowned Miss Kansas City Monarch in 1940. Courtesy of Mary Jo (''Josette'') Weaver Owens.

flour, and ham.[118] One summer they sponsored a jitterbug contest between the games of a doubleheader, with $35 as first prize. Jazz musicians Harlan Leonard, George Lee, Ernie Williams, and Bill Martin formed swing bands for this contest and for the opening-day celebrations.[119]

The Booster Club's ''Miss Monarch'' bathing beauty contest attracted the most attention. The original idea for a beauty contest envisioned league-wide competition. Each city would select a woman to represent its team; the city with the largest attendance at a designated game would then host the contest to choose Miss Negro American League from among the teams' representatives. Kansas City chose a queen, but the other league cities never selected her competitors. Each woman who entered the Kansas City contest found a business to sponsor her. Beauty shops, theaters, drug-

stores, gas stations, taxi companies, grocery stores, taverns, barbershops, cafes, hotels, insurance companies, and clothing stores—about an equal number of black and of white—paid the five-dollar entry fee. In return, the woman wore the store's color and a ribbon with the sponsor's name on it. More than thirty women sought the title of Miss Monarch in each of the two years that the Boosters held the contest. The women paraded from the dugout one by one to a podium at home plate, where they removed their beach robes. Applause from the crowd of fifteen thousand and a committee of judges (which included Mrs. Felix Payne and women from the *New York Amsterdam News* and the white *Kansas City Journal*) selected the winner. Mrs. Muriel Hawkins won in 1939 and received $25. Mary Jo Weaver recalled that she and her mother kept her entry in the 1940 contest a secret from her father. When Mary Jo convinced Gold Crown Liquors to be her sponsor, she then spray-painted her swimsuit gold. She laughed as she remembered removing her beach robe that summer afternoon: ''And all this gold! When the sun hit it! Some of them had on red and white suits, but mine came out gold metallic! That's probably why I won.'' Her father was in the stands that afternoon. ''He didn't even know I was in the contest till he saw me walk across the stage,'' she continued. ''When they called my name, he jumped up, 'That's my child!' '' The eighteen-year-old beauty received a loving cup, red roses, and $50.[120] Mary Jo Weaver was the last Miss Kansas City chosen in such a contest. In 1942 the *Kansas City Call*'s sports editor selected Bettylue Cespedes to represent the ''spirit of Baseball.'' Gone were the swimsuits, the applause, and the smiles. Bettylue Cespedes's somber photograph was said to ''stress the seriousness'' of the war situation.[121]

The depression sent the Monarchs on the road, scuffling for a crowd and a payday. The reception that they received revealed a country with racial attitudes in a state of flux. The inclusion of blacks in the New Deal programs, the growing exasperation of northern liberals with the South, and the increasing militancy of blacks were weakening the rigid patterns of discrimination. As all-star aggregates, black teams barnstormed against the best white major leaguers in the United States and in Latin America. The popular East-West Game became a major sporting event for black America and confirmed for all fans that some of the best baseball in the country was being played in the Negro leagues.

# FIVE

## Double Victory

"If he's good enough for the navy, he's good enough for the majors."—*Pittsburgh Courier*

**A** total effort, such as World War II was, affected every aspect of American life. The irony for black baseball was that the wartime economy allowed the leagues to prosper as never before—but the war effort also spurred integration and the end of the Negro leagues.

The military draft began to affect black baseball right after the attack on Pearl Harbor. More than one million blacks, including at least fourteen Monarchs, marched away to defend a democracy that repressed them. Some black teams that had carried eighteen players in 1941 were reduced to nine men by 1944, with pitchers finding relief only by rotating to other positions. Players who were past their prime and unseasoned youngsters filled the fast-emptying rosters. NAL owners at first ruled that soldiers on furlough and workers in defense plants could not play on league teams, but as Uncle Sam called more of the young men away, the owners relented.[1]

Baseball suffered a manpower shortage also because of the Mexican fever, which was started by Jorge Pasquel. A millionaire, Pasquel lured clusters of major and Negro leaguers south of the border. These included Josh Gibson, Willie Wells, Buck Leonard, Ray Dandridge, and the Monarchs' Jesse Williams, William ("Bonnie") Serrell, Joe Greene, and Booker McDaniels. Pasquel's influence was such that when Quincy Trouppe and Theolic Smith were denied a draft exemption so that they could play baseball in Mexico, Pasquel arranged for the loan of 80,000 Mexican workers to fill the

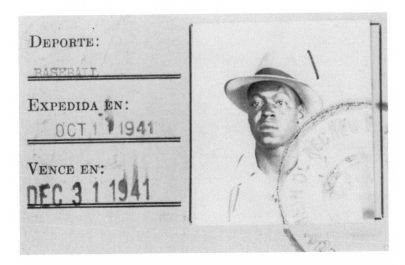

manpower shortage in return for these two ballplayers.[2]

The Office of Defense Transportation (ODT) ordered the twelve black teams to quit using their buses in 1943. The order to use "existing facilities" did not affect the eastern NNL teams as much as it did the midwestern NAL clubs. In the East, as one observer noted, trains "run almost on street car schedules and distances are short."[3] The

*Above:* Joe Greene's passport to Mexico, 1941. Courtesy of Phil Dixon, Dixon Paper Company.

*Below:* T. Y. Baird, Chester A. Franklin, and J. L. Wilkinson urged the Office of Defense Transportation to let the Negro leagues continue to use their buses. Courtesy of Kansas City Public Library, Missouri Valley Room.

NAL teams were more spread out geograph-
ically—from Kansas City, St. Louis, and
Chicago to Memphis, Jacksonville, and
Birmingham. The NAL owners appealed the
ODT order, arguing that social custom
banned blacks from public accommodations
and that without buses, black teams would
not be able to schedule enough games to
break even. Chester A. Franklin, the activist
editor of the *Kansas City Call,* organized a
petition drive and mailed the signed requests
to the director of the ODT. Franklin's cover
letter charged: ''Negro baseball is an
integral part of the national game which
President Roosevelt wishes continued for its
morale values to fighters and workers.
Baseball has been the chief summer entertainment of many of the signers of this
petition. Let Negro baseball live.''[4] Wilkinson, Baird, and Franklin also reminded the
government that the Monarchs had produced
$30,000 in taxes during the previous year.
Black teams started the 1943 season traveling by train, but the ODT granted them an
exemption midway through the season. The
Monarchs were then back on the road in
their bus, the Blue Goose.[5]

Gas rationing forced teams to abandon
spring training in the South and to play
much-reduced schedules. In the peak seasons of the 1920s, the black squads had
become accustomed to the one-hundred-
game league schedules. In 1943 the NAL
ruled that teams needed to play only thirty
games in order to qualify for the Negro
World Series. In 1945 the ODT further
reduced the mileage allowance for each
team by 25 percent. The Monarchs opened
their season on May 6 and closed it on July
4. In addition, the government restricted the
number of night games, both for the
conservation of electric power and for
security in the face of potential air attacks.[6]

Despite all these problems, the stepped-

up production for the war meant that black
baseball flourished. Thousands of black and
white Americans poured into the cities in
search of jobs. At the beginning of the war,
black workers not only were ignored; they
were, in fact, barred from jobs in defense
plants. The number of unemployed whites
dropped by 16 percent, while the rate for
blacks held steady at 22 percent. In March
1942, thirteen thousand black Kansas Citians
gathered at Municipal Auditorium to protest
the discriminatory practices of the war
industries. Protests like this around the
nation helped to speed the implementation of
President Roosevelt's Fair Employment
Practices Committee. As a result, blacks
were able to enter plants and to obtain jobs
that had previously been closed to them, and
''the steady, heavy jingle of sawbucks''
began to fill black pockets as well as white
ones.[7]

Wilkinson was quick to use patriotism in
promoting Monarchs games. ''We know that
baseball is essential,'' he declared, ''and
we're going to play for war workers, both
day and night games and on Sundays and
weekdays.''[8] He adjusted game times to
accommodate the swing-shift workers in the
defense plants, and he gave free admission
to soldiers in uniforms. Before the war, only
special games had attracted crowds of more
than ten thousand, but with wartime prosperity, and perhaps because of a psychological need to participate in something
American, owners ''ranted and raved'' if
ordinary games did not draw that many.
Throughout the war, the Monarchs drew
better than any other team in the league—
averaging six or seven thousand and sometimes drawing as many as thirty to forty
thousand fans when Satchel Paige was
pitching. Equal numbers of black and white
fans filled the stadium. Buck O'Neil explained: ''They were out of the South and

they didn't know too much about the North, no place to go and they just *flocked* to the ball games. During the war years we just packed 'em in those ball parks.''[9] Advertisements in the *Kansas City Call* for the opening welcome took on a patriotic theme. Scott's Theatre, for example, showed Uncle Sam batting, with the caption: ''Here's Wishing Victory to the Monarchs!'' And the Boosters, under the direction of Arthur Toney and Robert Sweeney, sold war bonds and stamps at the games. The United States Treasury Department's posters took on baseball imagery, urging ''Strike out the Axis! Invest 10% of Your Income in War Bonds.'' The Monarchs also played a yearly benefit for the war-relief fund or the Red Cross.[10]

The Monarchs games consistently outdrew those played by the white Kansas City Blues. Purchased as a farm club for the far-flung Yankees organization in 1937, the Blues paraded the likes of Yogi Berra, Hank Bauer, and Mickey Mantle before their fans. The Blues won the American Association pennant in 1939, 1940, 1942, and 1947. But attendance throughout the white leagues sagged, especially among minor-league teams. Promising young talent was quickly called away to New York, and the centralized nature of the game meant that Kansas City did not ''own'' the team as before.[11]

But the black community embraced the Monarchs. Mary Jo Weaver, Miss Monarch in 1940, asserted, ''I don't think there was a black person in Kansas City that would miss a game.''[12] The Monarchs had been a dominant team since their beginning, but from the late thirties on, they were a powerhouse.

Although the Negro leaguers lacked formal training and started spring training in front of paying customers, they studied the game. ''We went to school on a team,'' Newt Allen asserted. ''When we were riding on the bus or when we used to ride on the train, we would sit up and talk about how we're going to pitch to this guy or how we got to watch this man.''[13] But the players were in agreement that the discussions *after* the game set them apart. ''That was one thing we did here [on the Monarchs] that majors never did,'' remembered pitcher Connie Johnson, who signed with the Chicago White Sox. ''They never did talk about the game. The game's over, that's it. Whether you win or lose, we were talking about the game—what happened, what we could have did, what we didn't do. We called it a skull session.''[14]

The skull sessions seemed to pay off. Fielding from Willard Brown, Newt Allen, Buck O'Neil, Turkey Stearnes, Ted Strong, Joe Greene, Jesse Williams, Bonnie Serrell, and Hank Thompson made the Monarchs nearly invincible. But the combination of pitchers probably left the fielders with little to do. In 1942 the Monarchs boasted some of the finest hurlers in the game: Satchel Paige, Hilton Smith, Connie Johnson, Lefty LaMarque, Jack Matchett, and Booker McDaniels. A sportswriter jested that the infielders ''have come close to getting arrested for loitering'' and were begging ''to throw a few out so the boss could see they were still worthy of their hire.''[15] The Monarchs won the NAL pennant in 1937, 1939, 1940, 1941, 1942, 1946, and 1950. Few fans were surprised when the Monarchs also won the Negro World Series pennant in 1942. Only when the war forced the Monarchs to compete with only nine men did they fall behind. One fan lamented in 1944, ''The cellar-dragging Kansas City Monarchs . . . have advertised for two wells—one to weep in and one to wish on.''[16]

The Monarchs' 1942 pitching staff, from the left:
Hilton Smith, Jack Matchett, Booker McDaniels, Jim
LaMarque, Connie Johnson, and Satchel Paige. Cour-
tesy of National Baseball Library, Cooperstown, N.Y.

Increased attendance meant higher salaries for the players. During the depression,
salaries had dropped to around $125 or $150
a month. The war economy assured even
average players of $300 to $500 a month, a
salary that had been enjoyed only by stars
earlier. Stars could now demand as much as
$1,000 a month. As always, Satchel Paige
was in a class by himself—making between
$30,000 and $40,000 a year. When asked
how ballplayers' wages compared with what
other workers were making, Lefty Bryant
replied, "Definitely, definitely made more
being a ball player, because I considered
myself what you would call a white collar
job. You could go down to the oil field and
work all day and get about $50 a week. And
I was making [$300 a month] for fun.
That's what it was. Baseball for me was
fun."[17]

From 1942 to 1946 the owners cleared

about $25,000 each season. Wilkinson, with
Satchel Paige as an attraction, grossed close
to $100,000 and probably closed the sum-
mer with a larger profit than did other
teams. The money came so fast and so easy,
they called it an era of "wonderful nonsense."[18] Because the number of good
players nearly always exceeded the number
of places on the roster, owners were able to
dominate the game. Monarchs' pitcher Lefty
Bryant explained the sentiment among the
players: "Everyone was exploited—that's in
the majors and every place else. Their idea
is to save as much money as possible on ball
players—to pay only what they have to. I
mean, if you're good and you can go some
place else to get a job, he'll have to come
up to your standards. But I don't think that
Wilkinson exploited us; he didn't do us that
way. He was liberal with his money, but he
wasn't gracious with it. But he paid you
what he felt you were worth, not what you
thought you were worth," he added with a
chuckle, "but what he thought you were
worth and what you were worth to the ball
team."[19]

The issue of exploitation boiled up at the annual East-West classic. Always a summer favorite, the East-West Game drew tremendous crowds during the war years. In 1942 almost forty-eight thousand fans watched the East defeat the West squad 5 to 2. Noting the profits that the owners were making, players even more stridently pushed for a share. In 1942 they came close to revolting. The West squad issued an ultimatum that unless the owners paid the team members for participating, they would boycott the game. The black press sympathized. In condemning the owners for not sharing the wealth with the players, one reporter remarked that he now understood "why Negro baseballers regard their owners as Shylocks and chiselers."[20] The owners finally decided to give each player in the East-West Game $50 plus expenses. This did not satisfy Satchel Paige, who demanded a percentage of the total gate receipts. He reasoned, "Without me, that East-West game wouldn't draw two-thirds the people it would if I was playing."[21] Wilkinson took extra money from his own pocket in order temporarily to pacify Paige. The next year, fans again voted Paige a membership on the West squad, and Paige again demanded extra money. The NNL owners claimed that they could not be bullied, but since Paige was advertised to pitch, the NAL owners paid him $800 for a three-inning appearance. Bullied they had been, and even sportwrtiers who were sympathetic to the players criticized Paige for being so self-centered. It seemed unfair, said one, that "Paige has been stuffing his pockets with bills, [while] these other players have been 'scuffling along.' "[22] Back on the squad in 1944, Paige asked for more money. This time the owners did refuse, saying that fans had complained when Paige had received more than men who had played the whole

game. Paige then announced that all profits should be donated to the Army-Navy Relief Fund. The owners retaliated by declaring Paige ineligible for this annual all-star game.[23]

While Paige grabbed headlines, other players struggled for greater equality. Learning that Paige had earned $800 for three innings of work, the East squad (with Paige's prompting) threatened to strike in 1943. They asked for, and ultimately received, $200 per player. Out West, the NAL players asked for $100 each. In 1945 the owners settled on $100 plus expenses for each player who participated. All managers and coaches received $300. The clubs each divided $300 among their players who were not selected to compete. In comparison, the owners were splitting about half of the gross receipts; each owner collected about $3,500.[24]

As the East-West Game became more popular, league officials decided that "the sentiment of fans . . . swayed them in their voting" and that many good players were being ignored. In 1944, league presidents Dr. J. B. Martin and Tom Wilson decided to select the teams on the basis of individual batting and fielding averages. Over the years, the selection group expanded to include managers and owners, but for as long as the East-West games were played, fans regained control over the roster only twice.[25] In 1945 the ODT canceled the white All Star Game and threatened to cancel the East-West Game. Only after black owners convinced the government officials that most of their fans came from the Chicago area did the government rescind the ban.

The new stability also prompted owners to revive the Negro World Series in 1942, the first championship contest to be held since 1927. The 1942 series pitted the

**Official Score Card    10 cents**

LEROY (Satchel) PAIGE

A scorecard from 1942 World Series: Kansas City Monarchs vs. Homestead Grays. Courtesy of Craig Davidson.

The success of the barnstorming tour between Paige's and Feller's All Stars prompted Commissioner Landis to ban future contests. Paige joined Feller on the Cleveland Indians in 1948. Courtesy of John Holway.

Kansas City Monarchs of the NAL against their supreme rivals, the Homestead Grays of the NNL. The Grays, even with the batting of Josh Gibson and Buck Leonard, were defeated in the first three games. The eastern aggregate then borrowed players Monte Irvin and Leon Day for the fourth game. Hilton Smith, who watched from the bull pen, remembered that Wilkinson played the game under protest, but he did not want to turn away a paying crowd. Satchel Paige pitched the full nine innings for the Monarchs, but was defeated 5 to 2 by ace pitcher Leon Day. The Monarchs won the pennant in the next game. These arguments

over disputed games and borrowed players led the owners, in the following year, to demand a $1,000 deposit of "good faith" and to create a three-man arbitration commission.[26] In 1946 the Negro World Series competitors abandoned trains and began flying from one cheering crowd to another. The Negro World Series continued to be played throughout the 1940s, but it never gained the prestige of the East-West Game. Some sportswriters derided it as a "farce" when the owners stretched the series from seven to nine games and then to two weeks of glorified barnstorming.[27]

After the season ended, Satchel Paige again rounded up a group of all-stars to compete against the white major leaguers. In the 1940s Bob Feller replaced Dizzy Dean as the main attraction for the white stars. As in the regular season, Paige captured the headlines, but Hilton Smith won the games for the Negro leaguers. Smith remembered a

Satchel Paige's All Stars posed with their Flying Tiger, 1946. From the left: Hilton Smith, Monarchs; Howard Easterling, Homestead Grays; Barney Brown, Philadelphia Stars; Sam Jethroe, Cleveland Buckeyes; Gentry Jessup, Chicago American Giants; Hank Thompson, Monarchs; Max Manning, Newark Eagles; Othello Renfro, Monarchs; Refus Lewis, Newark Eagles; Gene Benson, Philadelphia Stars; Buck O'Neil, Monarchs; Frank Duncan, Monarchs; Artie Wilson, Birmingham Black Barons; Quincy Trouppe, Cleveland Buckeyes. On the steps, Dizzy Dismukes, the All Stars' business manager. Paige is in the doorway, with his valet. Courtesy of Phil Dixon, Dixon Paper Company.

1941 game in St. Louis against Feller's All-Stars as one of the greatest thrills of his career. The white major leaguers ran Paige off the mound after two innings. Reliever Smith, who won thirty games and lost only one that year, struck out twelve and allowed just one hit.[28] In 1946 the Paige/Feller all-stars crossed the nation in two Flying Tiger aircraft left over from the war. The teams played thirty-two games in twenty-six days and drew over four hundred thousand fans. When the barnstorming players made more than the World Series competitors—and posed a threat to white organized baseball—Commissioner Landis banned the barnstorming tours until after the series was over. The *Call*'s sportswriter took a jab at Landis's decision: "Can't have the Negro ball player showing up the whites, y'know."[29]

After the barnstorming tour, Feller's All-Stars and many of the best black ballplayers headed for Los Angeles. The black stars became Chet Brewer's Kansas City Royals in the California winter league. If Cab Calloway or Lionel Hampton happened to show up at the stadium, Brewer would quickly put him in uniform and let him coach the team, to the delight of the fans and entertainers. Hilton Smith was playing

The 1945 Monarchs. Top row, from the left: Jesse Williams, George Walker, Booker McDaniels, Jim LaMarque, two unidentified players, Lee Moody, Hilton Smith, Ensloe Wylie. Bottom row, from the left: an unidentified player, John Scott, Jackie Robinson, Othello Renfroe, an unidentified player, Herb Souell, two unidentified players. Courtesy of National Baseball Library, Cooperstown, N.Y.

with the Kansas City Royals when Jackie Robinson asked Smith to intervene with Wilkinson to get Jackie a job with the Monarchs.[30]

As early as spring 1940, black newspapers had carried reports of ''Jitterbug'' Jackie Robinson's athletic prowess at the University of California in Los Angeles, where he lettered in football, track, and baseball. Robinson joined the army in 1942; when he was discharged in the fall of 1944 as a lieutenant, he approached Hilton Smith about playing with the Monarchs. On Smith's advice, Wilkinson invited Robinson to join the team in spring training in Houston. When Wilkinson signed Robinson in March 1945, the *Chicago Defender*'s sportswriter announced that ''the Kansas City Monarchs slipped one over on the other owners when they signed Jackie Robinson.''[31] Veteran Monarch Newt Allen evaluated Robinson for Wilkinson: ''He's a very smart ball player, but he can't play short-

stop—he can't throw from the hole. Try him at second base.''[32] But when regular shortstop Jesse Williams hurt his arm, Robinson won the position. By the time spring training broke, Robinson's name was already ''magic in sportsdom,'' and major-league scouts watched his game closely.

The Negro leaguers were well aware that pressure was building for integration of the sport. Before World War II, integration held few economic benefits for the white major leagues. More than 75 percent of black Americans still lived in the South, and the major-league teams were clustered in the North. Sam Lacy, sports editor for the *Baltimore Afro-American,* explained: ''Black patronage was negligible, so they didn't feel that it was worthwhile to appease these black customers and run the risk of the white customers who were in the majority of the population.''[33] But the black population in the northern states had increased by 50 percent during the 1940s. While attendance floundered in the white leagues, black fans poured into the stadiums to watch Negro League games. As early as 1933 some black sportswriters had envisaged the East-West Game as the opening wedge for integration. They reasoned that if two black teams consistently could draw upwards of twenty thousand fans, white owners could not afford to ignore the potential income. The 1944 East-West Game attracted 46,247 fans—compared to only 29,589 who attended the white All Star contest. Larry MacPhail, owner of the Yankees and the Blues, reluctantly admitted that the Monarchs were outdrawing his Kansas City farm club. Owners also carefully watched barnstorming games between black and major-league teams. Satchel Paige and the Monarchs defeated an all-star major-league squad in Wrigley Field before a crowd of thirty thousand on the same day that only nineteen thousand witnessed a game between the Chicago White Sox and the St. Louis Browns. After Satchel Paige was hailed in articles in the *Saturday Evening Post, Time,* and *Life* magazines, the white baseball public was anxious to see the man described by Dizzy Dean: "That skinny old Satchel Paige with those long arms is my idea of the pitcher with the greatest stuff I ever saw."[34] White and black sportswriters alike urged major-league owners to trade their mediocre players for spectacular black talent as a boost to declining attendance. "I think Rickey was looking at the crowds," Hilton Smith summed up. "Major league baseball just wasn't drawing and we were just drawing tremendous."[35] Another player agreed that integration would be an economic decision; it would happen, he quipped, when "black and white makes green."[36] The black press advised readers that they could hurry this along by using their economic clout and avoiding ball parks with segregated teams and seating. With the same reasoning used in the "Don't buy where you can't work" campaign, sportswriters warned: "So long as we help fill the ball yards—nothing will ever happen. Every time we lay down our dollar we are telling these owners that we are satisfied."[37]

The United States war propaganda also brought America's race problems into sharp focus. The United States war message stressed above all else the abhorrence of Hitler's racial bigotry and his bogus theories about racial supremacy. Increasingly, whites had to confront the hyprocrisy of their domestic practices in relation to their war aims. Some black Americans questioned whether they should be fighting Nazi racism while enduring white racism at home. The *Kansas City Call*'s sportswriter asked the piercing question, "Are colored servicemen fighting for a 'separate' democracy?"[38] The NAACP and the black press reaffirmed the loyalty of black Americans. They took up slogans that encouraged a positive attitude toward the war but that also urged that an end be put to discrimination. The *Chicago Defender* exhorted readers, "Remember Pearl Harbor and Sikeston, too"—in reference to the lynching of a young black man in Sikeston, Missouri, in 1941. The *Pittsburgh Courier*'s "Double V"—victory at home and victory abroad—was widely adopted. The number of blacks who openly opposed participating in the war effort was small. Most blacks felt that the war provided them with a chance to prove that they were first-class citizens. By accepting the duties and responsibilities, they hoped to be better able to demand the rights of full citizenship.

In addition, blacks were becoming more vociferous in their protests against the injustices of the system. In 1937, Kansas City blacks won a court case for daily use of the municipal golf course, and a staff member of the *Kansas City Call* (where NAACP president Roy Wilkins had been editor) sued for admission to the University of Missouri's School of Journalism. That same year the "Citizen's Movement" organized in the city, with the aim of getting "a square deal for the Negro."[39] Becoming

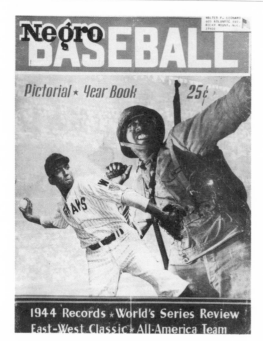

**Ne̊gro BASEBALL**

Pictorial ★ Year Book                    25¢

1944 Records ★ World's Series Review
East-West Classic ★ All-America Team

Many blacks hoped that their participation in the war
effort would win for them first-class citizenship. Roy
Wilkins, president of the NAACP, asked, "If we make
war to save democracy in Europe and Southeast Asia,
why not act to save and guarantee democracy in our
own race relations?" Courtesy of Art Carter.

increasingly frustrated with the restrictions
on their participation in the armed services
and defense plants, black leaders called for
a March on Washington in 1941. During the
summer of 1943 the Congress of Racial
Equality (CORE) reinforced the efforts to
abolish racial discrimination.[40]

Analogous currents rippled through baseball. When Roosevelt encouraged the major-
league teams to continue during the war as a
morale booster, a black sportswriter questioned the consequences of this for black
Americans:

I doubt that the morale of approximately
thirteen million Negroes will be helped if
the Government gives baseball the
"green light" and the owners in the
majors continue to bar qualified black

players simply because they are
black. . . . It's going to be difficult for
big league baseball, which discriminates
and segregates with a bold viciousness, to
"sell" thirteen million Negroes that this
particular "American" enterprise is
something worth fighting for.[41]

When Roosevelt issued his "work or
fight" order, demanding that all men either
join the service or take jobs in defense
plants, major-league owners changed their
schedules so that many players could work
in the plants by day and play for the team
on Sundays and evenings. White organized
baseball sent over four thousand men to the
service. Black players hoped that shortages
caused by the draft would negate the
gentleman's agreement that barred them
from the major leagues. Said one reporter,
"The major league will be hit hard—so hard
that the door might be forced open to let the
Negro ball players get in."[42] The one-armed
Pete Gray with the St. Louis Browns
became the symbol of wartime sacrifices—
but to black Americans, he also symbolized
the bigotry of the national pastime that
ignored their talents.

White owners were also well aware of
the pressure that was building for integration. In 1938 Clark Griffith, owner of the
Washington Senators, admitted, "There are
few big league magnates who are not aware
of the fact that the time is not far off when
colored players will take their places beside
those of the other races in the major
leagues."[43]

A small coterie of white sportswriters
needled the baseball establishment about
integration. Westbrook Pegler of the *Chicago Tribune* took up the cause in 1931; he
was later joined by Shirley Povich of the
*Washington Post,* Dan Parker of the *New
York Daily Mirror,* Dave Egan of the *Boston*

*Record,* and Jimmy Powers of the *New York Daily News.* In 1938 Powers began a campaign for the inclusion of black stars in the Hall of Fame. The *Chicago Defender* praised Powers for his fair-mindedness: "Certainly he is a guy you and I should love. Of all the scribes known to major in the art of calling a spade a spade, Powers alone stands out as a fellow who believes in giving credit where 'tis due and particularly if said credit is due one of us."[44]

The American Communist Party also actively supported the integration struggle. In the late 1930s the *Daily Worker* campaigned with the Brooklyn Federation of the National Negro Congress in appealing to the Dodgers for integration. When the Dodgers' manager, Leo Durocher, was rejected by the armed services because of an ear problem, the International Workers suggested that his best contribution to the war effort and national unity would be hiring a black player for the Brooklyn team.[45] The Communists sponsored resolutions calling for the end of segregation; organized petition drives at the East-West games, urging the inclusion of blacks in organized baseball; and picketed Yankee Stadium on opening day. The Communist Party aroused public awareness, but the black players and the press rejected the party's help. They did not want to cast their lot with a radical group and risk even greater hardships. When asked why they did not protest discrimination in baseball, the Homestead Gray's Buck Leonard spoke for his colleagues, "We're out here to play ball, we're not out here to demonstrate or anything like that."[46] Wendell Smith claimed that "the Communists did more to delay the entrance of Negroes in big league baseball than any other single factor."[47] The *Daily Worker* claimed to have done a series of interviews with white managers and players about using blacks in the major

leagues. Actually, Smith conducted the interviews, and the *Daily Worker* reprinted them. Smith wanted the record corrected: "Someday an ambitious historian might want to put the story in our kids' school books. Our history is twisted around enough as it is. It would be a tragedy to . . . louse up our sports history too."[48]

Rumors swirled through the black community during the early 1940s. One integration plan called for bringing an intact black team into the majors. The Monarchs—established as a winning combination and a tremendous drawing card—were mentioned most often. Joe Bostic of the *Harlem People's Voice,* Sam Lacy of the *Baltimore Afro-American,* and Frank Young of the *Chicago Defender,* but most importantly Wendell Smith of the *Pittsburgh Courier,* struggled for equality for the stars on their sports pages. Josh Gibson, Satchel Paige, Willie Wells, Leon Day, Roy Campanella, Chet Brewer, Sam Bankhead, Howard Easterling, and Nate Moreland were among the stars whom the sportswriters promoted for tryouts with major-league teams. The anxiously awaited tryouts always ended in disappointment for the players and the sportswriters. Apparently no white owner had the courage to disturb the status quo.[49]

When Brooklyn manager Leo Durocher announced that he would gladly employ blacks if it were not for the commissioner's opposition, Landis ludicrously insisted that blacks were not banned: "Negroes are not barred from organized baseball by the commissioner. . . . There is no rule in organized baseball prohibiting their participation."[50] Yet when promoter Bill Veeck mentioned to Landis that he was planning to buy the lackluster Phillies and to stock the team with black talent, the franchise was quickly sold to someone else.[51]

If owners had been using Landis as a

After a rookie year with the Kansas City Monarchs, Jackie Robinson signed a contract with the Brooklyn Dodgers, thus breaking baseball's color barrier at last. In 1949 Jackie Robinson and Commissioner A. B. ("Happy") Chandler shake hands while teammate Don Newcombe looks on. Courtesy of Bettman Archive.

scapegoat for their intransigence, his death in the fall of 1944 removed any official obstacles to integration. The owners probably expected that their new commissioner would be an opponent of integration as well. But Kentucky's former governor A. B. ("Happy") Chandler publicly announced: "I'm for the four freedoms. If a black boy can make it on Okinawa and Guadalcanal, hell, he can make it in baseball."[52]

The black press rejoiced at this breakthrough and stepped up their efforts. White politicians, especially in Boston and New York, also took up the issue of integration. Boston liberals threatened to team up with the traditional opponents of Sunday baseball unless blacks were given a chance. Wendell Smith chose Jackie Robinson, Marvin Williams, and Sam Jethroe for the Red Sox work out. Once again the baseball establishment stalled, and nothing happened.[53]

After the passage of the Fair Employment Practices Committee law in New York State in 1945, sportswriters urged blacks to apply the new statute prohibiting segregation in employment to professional baseball. Joe Bostic embarrassed Branch Rickey into watching Terris McDuffie and Dave ("Showboat") Thomas try out. The *Daily Worker* sent a photographer and a reporter to cover the event. Rickey was furious at having his hand forced, so he dismissed the pair after a short workout. McDuffie, who was thirty-four, and Thomas, who was thirty-nine, were both probably past their prime, and Bostic admitted that he had done it largely for publicity: "It was the psychological breaking of the conspiracy of silence."[54]

New York's mayor, Fiorello La Guardia,

appointed a committee to study how integration in baseball might be brought about. He appointed Larry MacPhail, the owner of the New York Yankees, and Branch Rickey, president of the Brooklyn Dodgers, to represent the two major leagues on the study commission. The group issued its report in late October 1945. They argued that black baseball met a need among rural communities and that signing blacks to the major leagues might destroy black teams. But they concluded that if black teams were not disturbed, "the practice which arose because of an evil" would be perpetuated indefinitely and that organized baseball had a responsibility to take "postive, aggressive action" to end segregation.[55] Their report was academic, however, because Branch Rickey had signed Jackie Robinson to a contract with the Brooklyn Dodgers' farm club earlier that week.

According to the traditional account, Rickey tried to disguise his intentions of signing a black athlete by pretending to organize another black league, the United States League (USL), with Gus Greenlee in the spring of 1945. Rickey pretended to be scouting black talent for the Brooklyn Brown Dodgers, which would supposedly be his entry in the new league. Black sportswriters and owners resented Rickey's involvement with the USL. They thought his motive was to dominate the black leagues and to stave off integration. Fay Young roared: "We want Negroes in the major leagues if they have to crawl to get there. . . . Rickey is no Abraham Lincoln or Franklin D. Roosevelt, and we won't accept him as dictator of Negro baseball. Hitler and Mussolini are dead! We need no American dictator!"[56]

But the owners soon found that Rickey's USL posed little threat. Abe Saperstein refused to book for the new league owners,

and they were unable to get adequate playing sites or enough fan support. Rickey withdrew from the foundering league after two months.[57]

Another interpretation of Rickey's motives offers a different twist on the USL: perhaps Rickey intended for the USL to be viable competition for the NAL and the NNL, and only when the USL failed did he give serious thought to direct integration. Bill Veeck believed that Rickey wanted a share in the profits that the New York Yankees and the Giants were receiving by renting their stadiums to black clubs. Having the Brooklyn Brown Dodgers play in Ebbets Field would give him the 20 percent gate receipts that were being enjoyed by many other major-league teams. When the USL failed, Veeck explained, "Jackie wanted a three-year contract with the Brown Dodgers. Rickey had three more years of Robinson. He then sent him to Montreal."[58] Hilton Smith, Jackie Robinson's roommate when they were both with the Monarchs, supported this theory. After his first meeting with Rickey, Robinson told Smith, "Branch Rickey asked me how I would like to manage the Brooklyn black ballclub."[59]

Whatever the initial motives, Rickey's noble experiment caused a predictable outcry. White newspapers and major-league officials at first charged Rickey with robbing and exploiting the black leagues for publicity's sake. William Bramham, president of the minor-league association, accused Rickey of being "of the carpetbagger stripe," using blacks for his "own selfish interests that retard the race."[60] Some major-league owners questioned Rickey's right to destroy the black leagues, but undoubtedly their own interests outweighed any concern for the black teams. The New York Yankees management, for example, made almost $100,000 a year renting their four stadiums in New York, Newark, Kansas City, and Norfolk to black teams. And owners feared that the "preponderance" of black attendance "could conceivably threaten the value of the major league franchises" if baseball were integrated.[61] White players at first wavered in their acceptance, but the president of the National League, Ford Frick, issued a statement that illustrated management's total domination of labor in baseball "I do not care if half the league strikes. Those who do it will encounter quick retribution. All will be suspended. . . . This is the United States of America and one citizen has as much right to play as any other."[62]

For the owners of the black clubs, integration was bittersweet. The leagues had initially been formed as a temporary expedient, not as a substitute for the ultimate goal of integration into the major leagues. Recognition of equality was then a great victory. That the first black major leaguer should come from Wilkinson's team was a thread of continuity: he was the sole survivor of the first Negro National League, organized in 1920. But the owners of black clubs were also businessmen who saw that their very profitable organizations were being seriously threatened. Wilkinson expressed the ambivalence that club owners were feeling: "I think it would be a fine thing for the game, even though we would lose some of our stars."[63]

When integration finally came, the owners did not oppose the inevitable, but they did object to Rickey's methods. The debate over Robinson's contract broke out immediately. Wilkinson and Baird claimed that they did have a contract with Robinson—even though it was only verbal. Robinson maintained that he had no contract with the Monarchs. He said the secretary of the Monarchs had written to him before the

season started and had invited him to join the club; he had accepted the offer to play for the agreed amount. Rickey's position was simple. There was no contract, he said, because "there is no Negro league as such as far as I am concerned." The infusion of policy money had saved the Negro leagues during the depression, but it cast them now, as Rickey said, "in the zone of a racket."[64] Rickey contended that the Negro leagues were "simply a booking agents' paradise. They are not leagues and have no right to expect organized baseball to respect them."[65] At first, Baird wanted to lodge a protest with baseball's commissioner, Happy Chandler. Wilkinson and Baird eventually decided against doing this. They found themselves in a difficult position, because blocking Robinson's way would be labeled as racial treachery in the black community. One of the Newark team's owners, Effa Manley, who later experienced the same problem, explained that it was a "simple case of . . . being squeezed between intransigent racial considerations on one hand, and cold business reasoning on the other!"[66] Ultimately, Wilkinson issued a statement: "Although I feel that the Brooklyn club or the Montreal club owes us some kind of consideration for Robinson, we will not protest to Commissioner Chandler. I am very glad to see Jackie get this chance, and I'm sure he'll make good."[67] Hilton Smith, who was a close friend of Wilkinson's, recalled: "He used to talk to me quite a bit. The onliest thing that ever hurt him, he said, in baseball was for them to take Jackie Robinson from him without him getting compensated anything."[68]

The reaction among the black players was mixed. Many of them were surprised at the choice of Robinson to break the color line. Jesse Williams, whom Robinson replaced as the Monarchs' shortstop, expressed an eval-

Because he was passed over to break the color barrier, Bonnie Serrell played in Mexico for a number of years. Courtesy of John Holway.

uation that was commonly held: "He was a good ball player, but he wasn't the best ball player we had. But he was the best for that particular role that he played, being the first . . . to go up there and take the abuse he took. I wouldn't have took it. If they had picked me, you possibly wouldn't have heard of Mays and Campanella and all those other fellows cause I would possibly have gotten into a lot of trouble."[69] Pat Patterson agreed: "I could have named five or six baseball players that were better ball players at that time, but Jackie was a great athlete, he was able to pick things up fast, but the biggest thing was the getting along—that was the thing that he had to do."[70]

For the players who had been scouted and passed over, Robinson's signing occasioned some moments of bittersweet reflection and contemplation. How many of them echoed Satchel Paige's cry, "It still was me that ought to have been first"?[71] Bonnie Serrell, the second baseman for the Monarchs, who was Hilton Smith's choice to

break the color barrier, left the country. Smith sadly recalled: "Jackie couldn't touch that boy. He could do everything. It just killed him when they picked Jackie and not him. He left, went to Mexico and never came back."[72] Many players attributed Josh Gibson's early death to being "broken-hearted" that he was not chosen.[73] And many felt that a veteran should have been given the first shot. Jimmie Crutchfield put it simply, "How would you feel seeing a rookie selected?"[74]

Older players recognized that their age would keep them from having that "cup of coffee" in the majors. Hilton Smith quietly proclaimed: "Had I been three or four years younger, I probably would have been the first Negro signed in organized baseball. Satchel figured it was his age, just like me." Later, when Smith was approached about playing with the Dodgers, he turned down the offer. "I felt that it was too long a shot," he confided. "And I could feel myself that I was beginning to lose a little. And I had always prided myself [in knowing] when I see myself over the hill that I was going to retire, get out of baseball."[75] Pat Patterson summed up the best wishes offered by the older players: "To us it was an opportunity. We were so glad for them."[76] And for the younger players who still had time, it was a victory. "We all thought, 'Great! Great! The door is open!'" exclaimed Buck O'Neil. "It was what we had been praying for for a hundred years."[77]

Robinson angered the black baseball establishment with his vitriolic blast at the Negro leagues in a 1948 issue of *Ebony*. He complained of low salaries and poor travel conditions. Effa Manley rebuffed him by saying that he should attack, not the black leagues, but the racism that forced such segregation. His Monarchs roommate, Hil-

# A Hit!

The *Chicago Defender,* 19 July 1947.

ton Smith, said regretfully, "I felt bad about it because it was a stepping stone for him."[78]

For the black community, breaking the color barrier in baseball seemed to be a breakthrough for American-style democracy. The NAACP reported that most Americans saw the cracking of the color line in professional baseball as the "most visible sign of change" in race relations.[79] A sportswriter declared that "the elimination of the strictly colored game will help in the fight to make this country a stronger nation."[80] Robinson became someone to rally around, someone with "the hopes, aspirations and ambitions of thirteen million black Americans heaped on his broad, sturdy shoulders."[81] The majority of the

black community supported him loyally. Even those who previously had not cared about baseball loved Jackie Robinson and attended his games. "I know a gang of women," mused one observer, "who will pass up a fancy fashion show or a swank cocktail party to sweat it out in a baseball park" watching Jackie Robinson.[82]

Rickey quickly signed four other black players for the Dodgers organization, but the "noble experiment" remained his alone until finally, in 1947, Bill Veeck purchased Larry Doby for the Cleveland Indians. Even after Veeck had established the precedent of negotiating a player's sale with the team owner, Rickey tried to ignore the black leagues. Monarchs' coowner Baird remarked bitterly: "Rickey's acquisition of

Latin American fans dubbed Willard Brown "El Hombre Ese"—"That Man"—for his home-run-hitting prowess. By the time the St. Louis Browns signed him, Brown was well over thirty. Courtesy of John Holway.

Negro baseball players reminds me of a fellow who found a rope and when he got home there was a horse on the end of it. I have been informed that Mr. Rickey is a very religious man. If such is true, it appears that his religion runs toward the almighty dollar."[83] Effa and Abe Manley, owners of the Newark Eagles, battled Rickey over Monte Irvin's contract, thus settling the question of raiding without compensation and helping to establish a minimum payment of $5,000.[84]

In 1947 the Monarchs sent Willard Brown and Hank Thompson to the last place St. Louis Browns. Outfielder Brown was unhappy about going to St. Louis: "The first time they told me I was going to the Browns—I didn't want to go to the Browns in the first place! I said, 'No! I wasn't going.' But [the other players] just kept on, 'Why don't you go on, show them what you can do.' "[85] The *St. Louis Post-Dispatch* admitted that the other Browns were "none too happy over the addition of two Negro players."[86] Thompson and Brown found themselves excluded and taunted. Neither player performed well, and after about twenty games, they were returned to the Monarchs. Sportswriters argued that the "big jump from Negro baseball to the Major leagues" involved more than playing ability, and Brown and Thompson did not receive the needed support from the management. Sportswriters also urged black fans to support the major-league team long enough to give the black players time to adjust socially and psychologically and expressed the hope that the owners would retain black players until they became confident.[87]

When Satchel Paige signed with the Cleveland Indians in 1948, some fans and reporters ridiculed owner Bill Veeck for signing the "old man of baseball." But others knew that Satchel was ageless. Wendell Smith joked, "Satchel has difficulty proving that he was not pitching for the Indians when the Pilgrims landed."[88] And for many others, Paige still held his charm. Said one reporter, "The Satchmo has been a baseball legend for a long time, a Paul Bunyan in technicolor."[89] For all the grief that he caused managers by jumping contracts, Paige was still the hero of black baseball fans. The loss of Satchel Paige, even as surely as the signing of Jackie Robinson, signaled the end of black baseball.

# SIX

## "Black Baseball Ain't Dead—Yet!"

"All the people started to go Brooklynites. Even if we were playing here in Kansas City, everybody wanted to go over to St. Louis to see Jackie. So our league really began to go down, down, down."—Hilton Smith

**B**lack teams lost most of their appeal almost immediately after the major leagues became integrated. Nonetheless, they struggled on tenaciously for about fifteen years. At first, some sportswriters predicted a brighter future for the Negro leagues than before. They argued: "Negro fans would want to see the players whom the major league scouts were watching. So would the white fans."[1] But owners and most sportswriters knew that once a black player had appeared on a major-league team, the attraction of an all-black club was gone.

The NNL and the NAL started the 1947 season optimistically. But the eastern NNL teams lost thousands of dollars competing for crowds in "Jackie Robinson country." For example, the Newark Eagles attracted more than 120,000 fans in 1946. In 1947 the total was down to 57,000; and by 1948, only 35,000 attended their games.[2] When Effa Manley complained of poor attendance, the black press reprimanded her: "The day of loyalty to jim crow anything is fast passing away. Sister, haven't you hear the news? Democracy is a-coming, fast."[3] Teams in the NAL, by playing mostly in the Midwest and the South, managed to survive 1947, but patronage was about half of what it had been during the war years. Sportswriters noted that the desertion of black fans to the major leagues hit black baseball "like a Joe Louis right across to the jaw—and today Negro baseball finds itself flat on its back, attempting to rise after suffering a knockout blow."[4]

Owners reacted to the smaller crowds by promptly slashing the players' salaries. Athletes who had made as much as $1,000 a month during the war were shocked to learn that the Monarchs' payroll for the whole team in 1948 would be $6,000 a month.[5] This time, younger players did not react by jumping to the Mexican leagues. They took a chance on a more profitable future by staying in the United States in the hope of making the majors. But for older players who knew they had no chance at the big leagues, Latin America was still attractive. Jesse Williams jumped to Mexico in 1946 and then found himself suspended from the NAL. "They had been talking about suspension beforehand, but had never done anything about it, so I didn't think they'd do anything that time," he recalled. "So it just caught me. I stayed away four years because I couldn't play back here in the States. So I'd just go from one country to another." He played in Mexico for six months, then in Cuba, on to Puerto Rico, and then back to Mexico.[6]

By 1948, four blacks were playing on major-league teams: Robinson and Campanella with the Dodgers, Paige and Doby with the Cleveland Indians. Owners found that not even a reduction in salaries could compensate for the dwindling attendance. Several owners reported losses of over $20,000. At the end of the 1948 season, the Homestead Grays and the New York Black Yankees went out of business, and the Manleys sold the Newark Eagles to two Houston businessmen. Before the spring opener, black sports editors throughout the country lamented that after twenty-eight years, "Negro baseball . . . lost one of its finest and smartest men" when Wilkinson sold his interest in the Monarchs to coowner Tom Baird.[7] The Negro League establishment hailed the Monarchs as "the perennial

kingpin of mid-west teams—perhaps the best administrated of all Negro franchises."[8] But Wilkinson, who was seventy-four years old and nearly blind, clearly understood that the era of black baseball was over.

The Houston Eagles and the three remaining NNL clubs (the New York Cubans, the Baltimore Elite Giants, and the Philadelphia Stars) joined the NAL as part of a ten-club league. The end of the Negro National League did not daunt sportswriters' enthusiasm for black baseball. Wendell Smith insisted that the only thing that was wrong with black baseball was that "the men who made money out of the league in the past threw in the sponge the first time things got tough."[9]

But once things got tough, they got no better. As during the depression, the owners again reduced their schedules; teams were required to play only thirty games to be eligible for the Negro World Series. The Negro World Series had never been an important tournament, but with only one league, it had even less distinction. With teams split into eastern and western divisions, fans scorned the series as being "more like family members choosing sides and choking the bat to see who bats first."[10] Some teams continued to battle for the "World Championship" title even after fans abandoned the affair. But the games were little more than postseason barnstorming tours; the results themselves often went unrecorded.

The East-West Game initially gained in importance after integration. In earlier years the contest had been almost a holiday for players. Dr. J. B. Martin, president of the NAL, commented, "They came to Chicago to have a good time, to hold bull sessions, and celebrate!"[11] After integration they regarded it as a talent showcase for major-league scouts. But as more players signed with the majors, the annual classic became less and less glamorous. Crowds dropped from fifty-one thousand to ten thousand (see Appendix B). The owners turned to their tried-and-true attraction for increasing attendance: women. An "East-West Queen" was chosen in 1951, 1952, and 1955, but this event held little popular appeal. The annual East-West Game continued to be played as long as the league lasted. In 1963 the thirtieth annual East-West Game was held in Kansas City—the last such game was the first one to be played outside of Chicago.[12]

Integration was just one facet of postwar America, and the black leagues were not the only thing that suffered. After enduring the economic frustrations of the depression and the shortages of World War II, Americans entered an era of consumer extravagance. Of the grand array of new goods and services, television had the most profound effect on baseball. Fans outside the major-league cities were no longer isolated from the national pastime—television brought the game into their homes. In 1950 less than 10 percent of the American public owned a television set. By 1960, 94 percent of the families had at least one set. Minor leagues as well as the blacks suffered when attention on baseball shifted from the local talent to a fixation on the majors. Attendance at minor-league games dropped from 42.0 million to 15.5 million in the years right after the war. In addition, baseball began to encounter serious competition from other sports for the fan's entertainment dollar. Baseball had truly been the national pastime between the World Wars; but by 1950, professional football and basketball were wooing away the fans and some of the best athletes.[13]

Trying to survive, black teams reduced ticket prices, held raffles, and traveled to small towns where there were fewer opportunities for entertainment and recreation. A

Monarch Tony Stone prepares for a game in 1954. Stone batted a creditable .243 in the Negro leagues. Courtesy of Ted Rasberry.

couple of teams tried hiring women as an attraction. Promoter Syd Pollock of the Indianapolis Clowns signed the first woman to an NAL contract in 1953. Marcenia ("Tony") Stone had played with the New Orleans Creoles, the House of David, and the San Francisco Sea Lions before joining the Clowns at second base. Pollock sold the twenty-eight-year-old Stone to Baird's Monarchs the following year. Pollock then hired two more women, infielder Conni Morgan and pitcher Mamie ("Peanut") Johnson.[14]

A few NAL owners also tried to attract fans by integrating their own teams. As early as 1947, black sportswriters began a campaign to drive Jim Crow out of black baseball. Originally they made a democratic appeal: "We believe that it is inconsistent," wrote one reporter, "for Negroes to clamor for the right to participate in American sports without penalty for their color and yet maintain a color-locked policy as regards players of others races and colors.''[15] Their appeal soon took on economic overtones. Sports editors reasoned that attendance was declining because black fans no longer felt an obligation to support a team whose only asset was that it was all black. The American Giants signed the first white players to NAL contracts in 1949, hiring Louis Clarizio, Lou Chirban, and Ed Hammer. Monarchs outfielder Al Surratt remembered that the white players were accepted without problems by their black teammates but that they encountered racial difficulties in the South. ''They weren't accepted too well in the southern towns,'' he said. ''Mostly the older guys there, they didn't go for that. They'd ask him, 'Why with so many minor league clubs, why did you go with a black club?' ''[16] The police in Birmingham either halted games and forced white players into the stands with the fans, or they barred the white players from even entering the stadium.[17]

Ultimately, black teams found that they could survive only by becoming unofficial farm clubs for the major leagues. The American Giants had a ''working agreement'' with the St. Louis Browns, and the Monarchs had a similar setup with the New York Yankees, who owned Blues Stadium in Kansas City. Baird wrote to owner Lee MacPhail, ''I feel as though I am part of the Yankee organization and I want to give you first chance at any player that your organization might want.''[18] Baird sold Earl Taborn, Bob Thurman, Frank Barnes, and Elston Howard to the Yankees. The NAL also supplied players for Japan's two major leagues. Scout Abe Saperstein signed Negro leaguers Larry Raines, Jonas Gaines, James Newberry, and Johnny Britton to Japanese contracts.[19]

Developing and selling young players helped owners to break even but deprived the NAL of its independent existence. Teams still tried to win games, but owners no longer prized a championship title as much as they prized a promising rookie. Kansas City, for example, withdrew from the 1949 play-offs, conceding victory because the team had been crippled by selling so much talent to the major leagues. This farm-club status also meant that veteran players lost their traditional place of honor on the team. Previously, veterans had formed the core of the team. After integration, hard liners insisted that ''baseball is a young man's game.'' Men who were too old for a shot at the majors no longer had a place on the team.[20] Young players, even more than before, felt tremendous pressure to become stars immediately, as Baird explained: ''The mortality rate in the league is high, but that's a necessary evil with us. A boy can't be more than a year or two away from the big tent. Going with players who can't make it to the majors simply deprives other good youngsters of the chance.''[21]

Players who did not quickly ''make the big times'' also deprived owners of income. The *Chicago Defender* reported that only Kansas City and Birmingham showed a profit in 1949. Baird reportedly netted a profit in five figures in 1953, after selling Ernie Banks and Bill Dickey to the Cubs for $20,000—the most ever received for NAL recruits.[22] Most black teams, despite making sales to the majors, operated at a loss. Some owners lost as much as $15,000 in a season. Still the black press urged the league to continue. Several major-league farm clubs did not accept blacks. Black sportswriters worried that if the NAL training ground were to collapse, fans could ''kiss goodbye all hopes of ever seeing more than six or seven blacks in the major leagues.''[23] Reporters implored fans to ''unloosen your purse strings'' and to ''make the turnstiles click when they play in your vicinity.''[24]

Enthusiasts also encouraged more college, high-school, and local sandlot teams ''to help produce other Jackie Robinsons.''[25] One result of this drive was the establishment of the Delta Baseball School in Greenville, Mississippi. Homer (''Goose'') Curry, a former player and manager of the Memphis Red Sox, operated the school, which trained fifty-five youngsters annually. The Monarchs did their part by adopting a seventeen-and-under team in Kansas City's Jackie Robinson Baseball League. The Monarchs provided the Junior Monarchs with equipment and uniforms, and Sidney Duncan, son of Monarchs' catcher Frank Duncan, managed the team.[26]

Throughout these declining years, the Monarchs gained a reputation for being the ''foremost Negro preparatory school for the major leagues.''[27] By 1955 the Monarchs had sold twenty-five players to the predominantly white professional teams. To replenish his own roster, Baird relied on a traveling team to serve as a farm club for the Monarchs. When Wilkinson sold his half of the franchise, he reserved the right to maintain an independent team that would play west of Kansas City. His son Richard operated the Monarch Travelers, with Cool Papa Bell as manager, through 1949, when Baird took over the operation. Beginning in 1953 the Havana Cuban Giants served as the Monarchs' farm club. Managed by Oscar Rico, the Giants played in the United States during the summer. They developed future Monarchs Juan Armenteros, Francisco Herrera, and Dago Nuñez.[28] But as integration progressed, prospective players were signed by the majors right out of high school or were scouted in college, eliminating the need for the Negro-league training ground. The Monarchs offered fifteen-year-old Bob Gibson a pitching contract, but he turned

Manager Buck O'Neil tried to persuade Bob Gibson to join the Monarchs in 1952. Gibson declined, then signed with the Cardinals in 1959. Courtesy of Phil Dixon, Dixon Paper Company.

them down. He explained his decision thus: ''But this was 1952 and Negroes were beginning to appear in major-league uniforms more frequently, and thanks to Jackie Robinson and Branch Rickey and everybody who came after them, the Kansas City Monarchs were no longer the be-all and end-all for a Negro ball player.''[29] Monarchs' shortstop Ernie Banks, who signed with the Cubs in 1953, was the last of the great players produced in the Negro leagues.

Declining attendance forced many owners to abandon baseball. The NAL had ten teams in 1949; in 1951, six remained. By 1953 only the Monarchs, the Memphis Red Sox, the Birmingham Black Barons, and the Indianapolis Clowns persisted. The *Kansas*

When the Monarchs played the Indianapolis Clowns in Kansas City in 1953, 18,000 fans crowded the stadium. Courtesy of Phil Dixon, Dixon Paper Company.

*City Call*'s sportswriter encouraged the survivors: "Negro baseball ain't dead yet. Not by a long shot. It may not be as fat and sassy as it once was, or as robust at the gate, but it is still actively ambulatory."[30] With fewer league teams to play and with more competition in large cities, black teams hit the road again in barnstorming pairs. The Monarchs often teamed up against the Indianapolis Clowns, whose antics gave the game a circuslike atmosphere. Playing through small towns in the Midwest and in Canada, they sometimes drew two to seven thousand fans.[31]

Integration also affected the way in which fans perceived the teams. Players had once been an integral part of the community. Fay Young, a long-term friend of black baseball, recalled that "fans knew most of those players intimately . . . could tell all about their lives, where they came from, and what their batting and fielding averages were at

the time."[32] But players who were serving a two-year stint in the black leagues before going to the majors were merely passers-by. Attention was focused on their ultimate destination, the majors.

Though the Monarchs' relationship with the community was more tenuous, the Boosters continued their opening-day ritual. In the early 1950s their parade was a spectacle with more than a thousand participants. Every civic and fraternal organization in the black neighborhoods was represented—including the Wayne Minor American Legion's drum and bugle corps, St. Stephen's Baptist Church's band, the Koran Shrine Temple's patrol, bands and ROTC units from Lincoln and Sumner high schools, the Antlered Guard Patrol, the Past

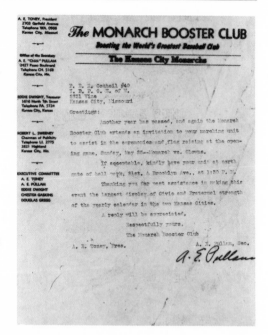

The letterhead of the Monarchs Booster Club. Courtesy of Black Archives of Mid-America.

The Booster Club at opening-game ceremonies, 1947. From the left: an unidentified person; A. E. ("Chick") Pullam, secretary; Douglass Gregg; Buck O'Neil, manager; Chester Gaskins; Eddie Dwight, publicity director; Arthur Toney, president. A fan said of opening day: "It was a big event—just like Easter and Christmas. You had to be there!" Courtesy of Georgia Dwight.

Band leader Lionel Hampton became an honorary Monarch and sometimes coached at first base. He posed (on the left) with manager Buck O'Neil and rookie Ernie Banks. Courtesy of Phil Dixon, Dixon Paper Company.

Daughters Ruler's Council, the Missouri National Guard, Mrs. Ophelia Jackson's majorettes, some Boy Scouts, and the Musicians Local Union's band. With the publicity help of Robert Sweeney (whom President Truman had honored with the title of Colonel) and former player Eddie Dwight, opening-day attendance ranged from fourteen to nineteen thousand. The Boosters made bandleader Lionel Hampton an official Monarch; he donned a uniform so that he could help to warm up pitchers and to coach at first base. The Boosters sponsored another "Baseball Bathing Beauty Contest" in 1948. From among the twenty-three contestants, Audrey Allen was chosen to represent Kansas City at the East-West Game. The Boosters kept high the enthusiasm for the team. One national sportswriter said admiringly, "Negro baseball may be dead, but you can't make the fans in this hospitable midwestern city believe it."[33]

As always, the Monarchs competed

The Negro American league owners in 1955, from the left: Dr. W. S. Martin, secretary; Ted Rasberry, vice-president; Dr. J. B. Martin, president; Dr. B. B. Martin, treasurer. Even as late as 1954, J. B. Martin was hoping that the curiosity of having blacks in the major leagues would wear off and that fans would return to the Negro leagues. Courtesy of Ted Rasberry.

against the Blues for fans. Even after the Blues had acquired two black players, the Monarchs continued to outdraw them. The farm-club system that developed talent for the majors created considerable unrest; fans in minor-league cities resented being rated as "second-class." Attendance was so poor that the Blues were disbanded in 1953. When the Boston Braves moved to Milwaukee (the first franchise to move in years), Kansas City fans became even more anxious for a major-league club. In the

summer of 1954 the *Kansas City Call*'s sportswriter shared rumors that a major-league team might move to the area. He urged readers to vote in favor of a bond issue to add a second level to Blues Stadium so that it would provide adequate seating for a major-league club. Little did these fans realize that what integration had not done to kill black baseball in Kansas City, a major-league team would do. The Philadelphia Athletics moved to Kansas City for the 1955 season. They became the Kansas City A's, who remained in last place in the league standings but led the circuit in attendance figures. Black Kansas Citians, too, adopted the "underdog A's." The *Call*'s reporter noted that with black players Vic Powers and Bob Trice, the A's took "a gripping interest on the Negro fan . . . who watched

them battle against great odds."[34] The Monarchs, besides losing their fans, also faced increased costs for renting the stadium, now city owned. The city charged 25 percent of the gate receipts and also required Baird to contract with the A's for ushers, ground crews, ticket agents, and janitors. Altogether, Baird paid out over $3,000 per game, which left him with less than half of the gross receipts to split with the visiting team. Baird's daughter correctly summed up the situation: "The Monarchs were priced out of Kansas City."[35] After the opening game in 1955, the Monarchs returned to Kansas City for only one other game that season.

At the end of that summer, only owners who had sold many players to the majors showed a profit. The league was so disorganized that some sportswriters were not certain that the season had ended and

Declining attendance forced the Monarchs to seek crowds in rural areas. One player recalled, "They were cutting salaries and bus-riding like mad." Courtesy of National Baseball Library, Cooperstown, N.Y.

had even less idea about who had won the pennant. That fall the Indianapolis Clowns severed their ties with the NAL. Tom Baird released manager Buck O'Neil to the Chicago Cubs as a scout, sold eight players to the majors (including George Altman and Lou Johnson), four to the minors, and the franchise and equipment to Ted Rasberry, a black businessman in Grand Rapids, Michigan. Baird went on to be a scout for the A's.[36]

Rasberry had played college baseball before organizing the semipro Grand Rapids Black Sox. He believed it was essential to keep the NAL alive in order for black youth to have a chance at the majors. He also knew that the Monarchs, the sole survivor

of the original NNL, were the mainstay of
the league. When Rasberry bought the
Monarchs in 1955, he already was operating
the NAL Detroit Stars, serving as vice-
president of the league, and scouting for the
Cleveland Indians.[37]

Rasberry succeeded in keeping the name
Monarchs alive, but the team no longer
belonged to Kansas City. Rasberry, like
Baird, could not afford the cost of using
Municipal Stadium, so he played only a
couple of games in Kansas City. Fans soon
lost interest in a Grand Rapids–based
traveling team and turned all of their
attention to the hometown Kansas City A's.
The *Kansas City Call* reported on the
Monarchs' activities for a short while, and
the Boosters supported the few games that
Rasberry did play in Municipal Stadium.
But in the black community, the Kansas City
Monarchs quickly became only a fond
memory.

Rasberry found that crowds could be
gathered only in small towns. He sold the
players' bus, and thereafter the team traveled around the country in station wagons.
Working with booking agent Harry Peebles,
Rasberry scheduled games in Kansas, Michigan, Minnesota, and Wisconsin. For barnstorming games, Rasberry sometimes
secured a guarantee of $250, sometimes a
promise of 60 percent of the $600–$700
gate. By playing seven or eight games a
week, he could afford to pay his stars $300
a month. Satchel Paige rejoined the Monarchs in 1955, but he admitted that "playing
for the Monarchs in 1955 wouldn't make
any man rich."[38] Working with Wilkinson
as his agent, Paige did free-lance pitching
for several midwestern teams and, as
always, attracted crowds.

The four teams in the black league still
depended on selling young talent in order to
balance their books at the end of the season.
Because of his scouting connections with the

Wilkinson continued to book Paige as a free-lance
pitcher after Paige's major-league career had ended.
Courtesy of Gladys Wilkinson Catron.

Cleveland Indians, Rasberry gave them first
choice of his players. If a player who had
been sold to the majors failed to maintain
major-league standards, most owners would
release the player back to Rasberry for more
training, with the possibility that he would
later be repurchased by the major-league
team. As NAL president, Rasberry estimated that each team needed $17,000 a year
to operate for fourteen weeks. He bargained
for a major-league subsidy, but nothing
concrete ever materialized from this effort.[39]

The NAL limped along with small
crowds and virtually no recognition from the
press until 1963. Then quietly and without
notice or regret, the owners yielded to
reality. Rasberry's Monarchs, often with
Satchel Paige, played a few games through
1964, but they were operating as a semipro
team. By 1965, only the Indianapolis
Clowns remained as a vestige of the era of
segregation.[40]

# SEVEN

## No Regrets

"The most important part of my life has been centered on baseball."—Quincy Trouppe

For thirty-five years the Monarchs were a major social institution for black Kansas Citians. People from every walk of life—ministers, merchants, gentlemen racketeers, musicians, janitors, and maids—all rallied around the team. Enthusiasm for the Monarchs inspired parades, dinners, beauty contests, and dances in the summer heat. When the season ended, fans would gather in barbershops and billiard halls to while away the winter afternoons, regaling each other with tales of past Monarchs glories.

As the most-traveled team in the leagues, the Monarchs had a magic that reached well beyond Kansas City. Sportswriters and fans recognized the Monarchs as one of the best teams in the country. Owners welcomed them as one of the best drawing cards. Sometimes with lights and Satchel Paige, but always with good baseball, the Monarchs entertained hundreds of thousands of rural Americans who had no other contact with professional sports.

Beyond its recreational value, baseball had deep implications, on a number of levels, for black Americans. As a business, the Negro leagues perhaps represented the highest achievement of black Americans during the era of segregation. The owners put together a complex network of fifteen or more franchises across the nation. Including support staff, the leagues employed members of as many as five hundred families. As America's largest black enterprise, the Negro leagues took in $2 million annually during the boom years of the World War II. As much as 75 percent of this went back

127

From the left: Newt Joseph, Frank Duncan, T. B. Watkins, Newt Allen, and Bullet Rogan, at a dinner honoring the Monarchs. Courtesy of Black Archives of Mid-America.

into the black community—either directly as salaries or trickling back by way of boardinghouses and restaurants.

The establishment of the Negro leagues also helped to establish baseball as a respectable livelihood. At the turn of the century, black and white parents alike viewed the game as a ragtag sport, hardly fitting for their children. By the Roaring Twenties, baseball had gained respectability. Major-league attendance more than doubled; Taft started the tradition of having the president throw out the first pitch of the season. Baseball became the National Pastime. For the lower-class German and Irish immigrants, organized baseball offered a glamorous opportunity for social mobility. The Negro leagues offered black youth a similar chance of "making it"—of escaping the drudgery of low-paying, menial jobs. Young Buck O'Neil, working on a celery

farm in Sarasota, Florida, exclaimed in exasperation, "Damn! Got to be something better than this!" His baseball talent earned him a scholarship, first to the high-school department and later to the college at Edward Waters in Jacksonville.[1] After a long career in the black leagues, O'Neil became a scout and the first black coach for the Chicago Cubs. John Donaldson went on from the Monarchs to become a scout for the rival Chicago White Sox. William ("Dizzy") Dismukes scouted for the White Sox and the Yankees. Othello ("Chico") Renfroe was the first black official scorer for the major leagues and later became the play-by-play announcer for the Atlanta Falcons. Chet Brewer taught baseball to Los Angeles youth for thirty years and earned a nomination for the coveted Martin Luther King, Jr., award.

Baseball served as a stepping stone in other directions too. Grady Orange and George Sweatt used their baseball earnings to pay for medical school. Pat Patterson became the superintendent of schools in Houston, Texas. Newt Allen became the

After more than twenty years in the Negro leagues, Buck O'Neil became a scout and coach for the Chicago Cubs. Courtesy of John Holway.

foreman at the county courthouse. Eddie Dwight worked as a chemist for the state of Kansas and reared a son who became the first black to be accepted into the astronaut program.

For many immigrants, participation in the national pastime was a way of identifying with the host society. The Negro leagues afforded black Americans the same opportunities to participate in the summer rituals of this archetypical American game. Opening-day ceremonies, the World Series, and the East-West games gave cause for celebration in a harshly repressed community. The society-page editor of the *Kansas City Call* explained the social significance: "Doesn't everybody in Kansas City go to the games? Isn't society and all social activities set aside for the games? This is due perhaps because

places of amusement in our city are limited and most of the social life is 'made.' Hence the great coming together to encourage a club that all Kansas City adores—The Monarchs."[2]

The Negro leagues were organized as a temporary expedient—not a substitute—for full integration. The *Pittsburgh Courier* heralded the NNL as a "direct slap at the inferiority complex."[3] With justifiable pride, black sportswriters pointed to the athletic and business achievements of the Negro leagues. But the assumptions of segregation were challenged most openly during the many interracial matches. Here, within the narrow confines of the sports setting, black athletes met the white man on his own terms and demonstrated their worth. The victories undermined the very ideology of segregation and chipped away at the status quo. "I'm sure we won more than we lost," mused Buck O'Neil. "But it was a different thing. It wasn't necessarily that we were better ball players. They were playing for that dollar they're going to make. But we had our pride. We going to play these major leaguers—we got to beat 'em!"[4]

Fans, too, saw athletic contests as microcosms of the race's struggle for equality. Author Maya Angelou explained how a defeat for boxing's heavyweight champion Joe Louis symbolized all the abuses and indignities that were suffered by blacks:

My race groaned. It was our people falling. It was another lynching, yet another Black man hanging on a tree. One more woman ambushed and raped. A Black boy whipped and maimed. It was the hounds on the trail of a man running through slimy swamps. It was a white woman slapping her maid for being forgetful.[5]

Conversely, athletic triumphs allowed

blacks to forget for a moment about the slights and the oppression. Athletic triumphs and athletes were sources of inspiration. After Jackie Robinson broke baseball's color barrier, the *Kansas City Call*'s sportswriter advised youth:

> When things look dark, void and altogether hopeless to the colored youth of America . . . , when they need an inspiring thought that should urge them onward to the road of achievement, despite forbidding obstacles, they will only need to read of and reflect upon the remarkable career of Jackie Robinson.[6]

Behind every victory many blacks saw a tiny step forward in their everyday relations with the white majority. The *Call*'s sportswriter contended that the best thing that baseball did for Kansas City was to allow the races to mingle and meet each other as fellow human beings:

> From a sociological point of view, the Monarchs have done more than any other single agent to break the damnable outrage of prejudice that exists in this city. White fans, the thinking class at least, can not have watched the orderly crowds at Association Park . . . and not concede that we are humans at least, and worthy of consideration as such.[7]

Sportswriters were adamant in calling for good behavior in the grandstands, believing, as one said, that "the same relations may be carried to the workshop, and the ball grounds may be the means of causing some one to be employed, where he would not otherwise have been considered."[8] Nightclub owner Milton Morris recalled his experiences as a fan at the Monarchs games when the issue of public accommodations came up for a vote in Kansas City. Morris was one of the few saloon keepers who

Jackie Robinson appeared in a comic-book series and tried to convince youths that hard work and sportsmanship would be recognized. The Kansas City Urban League sold copies of the hero's book. Courtesy of the Urban League of Greater Kansas City.

favored it, despite his being threatened by other owners. In an interview with Walter Cronkite on national television, Morris explained that he had seen the two races drink together successfully at the ball park and that it was foolish to say they couldn't.[9] The ball-park setting formed a basis for understanding and tolerance.

For civil-rights advocates, the noble experiment in baseball provided a model for later advances. For some black Kansas Citians, Robinson's connection with the Monarchs was an important factor in his being selected for this historic role. "The Monarchs baseball club was what you call ambassadors—not only for Kansas City, but for the Negro too," asserted Bob Sweeney. "It's an undeniable fact that the Monarchs were good for the race. When the Brooklyn Dodgers got ready for somebody to go into the big leagues, they came to the Kansas

City Monarchs and took Jackie Robinson."[10] Interracial contests had awakened white Americans to the undeniable fact of black talent. Integration forced them to confront their racial prejudices. As Roger Kahn eloquently explained in the preface to *The Boys of Summer:* "By applauding Robinson, a man did not feel that he was taking a stand on school integration, or on open housing. But for an instant he had accepted Robinson simply as a hometown ball player. To disregard color, even for an instant, is to step away from the old prejudices, the old hatred. That is not a path on which many double back."[11]

When looking back on their role in the integration struggle, the athletes were very proud to have played a part. Like many old-time Negro leaguers, Frank Duncan felt that "we were among the pioneers that paved the way for them."[12] Buck O'Neil elaborated:

Bullet Joe Rogan looks through a scrapbook of memories from his long career. Courtesy of Black Archives of Mid-America.

A lot of times they'll say to me, "Buck, you were before your time." But I don't think so. I think I was right on time. I was right in the midst of this thing . . . I had something to do with them getting there. I was playing before them, and the way we held ourselves when we played back there when—that is the reason that they're playing now. Everything happens in its season.[13]

The players now view their careers without bitterness, and they reject any sense of tragedy. Rather than dwell on the injustices and hardships that they endured, most Negro leaguers talk of the opportunities that baseball gave to them. Many echoed Connie Johnson's joy at being paid for doing what they loved to do: "I loved the game so much I would have played for nothing."[14] As professional baseball players they enjoyed glamour, recognition, and, in their wide travels, a bit of the "wild life."

Quincy Trouppe explained the game's significance for him: "Baseball opened doors for me which would have been barred. It revealed new vistas that were more educational than a doctor's degree . . . because of this great national game, I have lived a life comparable to the wealthiest man. There were tears too. But the happiness and sadness always blended into something that made my life more complete."[15] Hilton Smith said quietly, "Honestly true, if I had to live my life over, I'd live the same. No regrets."[16]

The last color barrier in baseball fell in 1970 when the commissioner appointed a special committee to select former Negro leaguers for the Baseball Hall of Fame in Cooperstown. To date, nine Negro leaguers and Rube Foster have been honored with a plaque in baseball's shrine to its greatest participants. Satchel Paige became the first black to be elected, in 1971. The plaque sums up the essence of Paige's career: "His pitching was a legend among major league hitters." Tales of the extraordinary talent had already passed into black folklore, where the legendary feats are fondly recounted. But Hall of Fame recognition meant that these men were no longer just black heroes. They are now recognized as American heroes.

# Appendix A
# Yearly Rosters for the
# Monarchs, 1920–55

After the passage of a generation, many players in the Negro leagues have become almost nameless. Yet, during their time, they were well-known members of the black community. They were so well known, in fact, that sportswriters often neglected to use their full names.

The following yearly rosters include full names when I could ascertain them. Alternate spellings are noted in parentheses. Players who used nicknames are cited in second and subsequent references by their popular nicknames. Because players frequently jumped their contract in midseason, rosters changed over the course of the summer. In the following lists, all players who were on the payroll for some part of the season are included. Also, players are identified by their position and hometown or home state as it was reported in the press. Players who were sold to major-league franchises have the name of such team or league in parentheses for the year in which they were sold.

## 1920

Arumi   rf, 2b
Baro, Bernardo   of
Blukoi, Frank   2b   Philippines
Carr, George ("Tank")   1b, rf   California
Crawford, Sam   p
Currie (Curry), Reuben ("Rube")   p   Kansas City, Mo.
Donaldson, John   p, cf   Glasgow, Mo.
Drake, Bill ("Plunk")   p, rf   Sedalia, Mo.
Fagin (Fagen), Bob   2b
Foreman, Zack   p, of   Parsons, Kans.

Harper  of
Harris, W.
Hawkins, Lemuel ("Hawk,"
    "Hawkshaw")  1b  Georgia
Jackson
Johnson, Oscar ("Heavy")  c  Atchison, Kans.
Johnson, Roy ("Bubbles")  2b  Detroit, Mich.
Lightner  p
McNair, Hurley ("Bugger")  p, lf
Mathol, Carroll ("Dink")  2b
Mendez, José ("Mendy")  p, 2b, mgr  Cuba
Moore, Walter ("Dobie")  ss
Muir, Walter
Portuando, Bartolo  3b, 2b  Cuba
Ray, Otto ("Jaybird")  rf, c
Rodrigues, J.  c  Cuba
Rogan, Wilbur ("Bullet Joe")  p, rf  Oklahoma
    City, Okla.
Washington, "Blue"  1b

## 1921

Barr  3b, ss
Bell, Cliff ("Cherry")  p  Texas
Blatner  rf, 1b, 2b
Carr, George  1b, 2b, rf
Cordova  3b
Crawford, Sam  p
Currie, Rube  p
Donaldson, John  p, cf
Duncan, Frank  c  Kansas City, Mo.
Fagin, Bob  2b
Foreman, Sylvester ("Hooks")  c, lf
Foreman, Zack  p, of
Hamilton  p
Hawkins, Lemuel  1b
Johnson, Roy  2b
King  of
Lloyd  ss
McAllister  of
McNair, Hurley  p, lf
Mendez, José  p, rf, ss, mgr
Moore, Dobie  ss
Mothel, Carroll  2b
Parpetti, Augustin  1b
Portuando, Bartolo  2b, 3b
Potter  c
Raglan  p
Ray, Jaybird  c
Rile, Ed  p
Rogan, Bullet Joe  p, rf

Smith, Lefty  p, rf
Taylor, ("Big")  p
Warfield, Frank  3b

## 1922

Allen, Newton ("Colt")  2b  Austin, Texas
Alsop, Clifford  p  Salina, Kans.
Anderson, Theodore ("Bubbles")  2b
Bell, Cliff  p
Carr, George  rf
Carter, William  c  Muskogee, Okla.
Crawford, Sam  p, mgr
Currie, Rube  p
Donaldson, John  p, cf
Drake, Bill  p
Duncan, Frank  c
Fagin, Bob  2b
Foreman, Hooks  c
Gissentanter (Gessantainer), Bill ("Lefty")  p
Hawkins, Lemuel  1b
Johnson, Heavy  c
Johnson, Roy  2b
Joseph, Walter ("Newt")  inf.  Muskogee,
    Okla.
Linder  p
McNair, Hurley  p, lf
Marshall, Jack  p
Mendez, José  p, 2b
Miller  p
Moore, Dobie  ss
Mothel, Carroll  2b
Murphy
Portuando, Bartolo  3b
Pullen, C. Neil  c
Ray, Jaybird  c
Redd, Gene  3b  Kansas City, Mo.
Rogan, Bullet Joe  p
Russell, Branch  3b, of
Shepperd  p  Oklahoma City, Okla.
Sweatt, George ("The Teacher")  1b,
    2b  Humboldt, Kans.
Taylor, Big  p
Williams, Henry  c  Oklahoma
Yokum  p  Ash Grove, Mo.

## 1923

Allen, Newt  2b
Anderson, Bubbles  2b

Bell, Cliff   p
Coley   p
Crawford, Sam   mgr
Currie, Rube   p
Donaldson, John   cf
Drake, Bill   p
Duncan, Frank   c
Foreman, Hooks   c
Gissentanter, Bill   p
Hawkins, Lemuel   1b
Johnson, Heavy   rf
Johnston, Wade   p, lf
Joseph, Newt   3b
McNair, Hurley   lf
Moore, Dobie   ss
Mothel, Carroll   c
Rogan, Bullet Joe   p
Sweatt, George   1b, 2b
Williams, Henry   c

## 1924

(NWS indicates those who were with the team for the first Negro World Series in 1924.)

Allen, Newt   2b   NWS
Bartlett, Homer ("Hop")   p
Bell, Cliff   p   NWS
Bell, William   p   Texas; NWS
Bobo, Willie   1b
Creacy, A. D. ("Dewey")   3b
Donaldson, John   cf
Drake, Bill   p   NWS
Duncan, Frank   c   NWS
Hawkins, Lemuel   1b   NWS
Johnson, Heavy   lf   NWS
Johnston, Wade   p, lf
Joseph, Newt   3b   NWS
McCall, Bill   p   NWS
McNair, Hurley   rf   NWS
Manese, E.   2b
Marshall, Jack   p
Mendez, José   p   NWS
Moore, Dobie   ss   NWS
Morris, Harold ("Yellowhorse")   p   NWS
Mothel, Carroll   c, cf   NWS
Ray, Jaybird   c
Rogan, Bullet Joe   p   NWS
Sweatt, George   cf   NWS

## 1925

Allen, Newt   2b
Bartlett, Hop   p
Bell, Cliff   p
Bell, William   p
Brewer, Chet   p   Des Moines, Iowa
Dean, Nelson   p
DeWitt, Fred   1b
Drake, Bill   p
Duncan, Frank   c
Foreman, Hooks   c
Hawkins, Lemuel   1b
Johnson, Heavy   lf
Johnston, Wade   p, lf
Joseph, Newt   3b
LaFlora, Louis
McNair, Hurley   p, of
Mendez, José   p
Moore, Dobie   ss
Mothel, Carroll   c, cf
Mullin
Rogan, Bullet Joe   p
Simms, William ("Simmy")   of
Sweatt, George   cf
Williams, Henry   c
Young, Tom ("T.J.")   c   Wichita, Kans.

## 1926

Allen, Newt   2b, ss
Bell, Cliff   p
Bell, William   p
Brewer, Chet   p
Dean, Nelson   p
Duncan, Frank   c
Hawkins, Lemuel   1b
Johnston, Wade   p, lf
Joseph, Newt   3b
McNair, Hurley   rf
Mendez, José   p
Miller, Dimps   p
Moore, Dobie   ss
Moore, Squire ("Square")   p
Mothel, Carroll   lf
Orange, Grady   2b
Primm   p
Rogan, Bullet Joe   p, mgr
Saunders, Bob   p
Torrienti, Cristobel   cf
Vaughn   cf

Young, Tom   c


## 1927

Allen, Newt   ss
Bell, Cliff   p
Bell, William   p
Brewer, Chet   p
DeWitt, Fred   1b
Duncan, Frank   c
Everett   ss
Foreman, Hooks   c
Giles, George   1b   Manhattan, Kans.
Grant
Hawkins, Lemuel   1b
Hughes, A.   of
Johnston, Wade   of
Joseph, Newt   3b
McNair, Hurley   of
Mitchell, George   p
Mothel, Carroll   2b
Orange, Grady   utility
Rogan, Bullet Joe   p, mgr
Smaulding, Owen   p
Walker, A.   p
Young, Maurice ("Doolittle")   p
Young, Tom   c
Young, William (Tom's brother)   p   Wichita,
   Kans.


## 1928

Allen, Newt   ss
Bell, William   p
Brewer, Chet   p
Brown   p
Cooper, Alfred ("Army")   p
Cooper, Andy ("Lefty")   p
Duncan, Frank   c
Dwight, Eddie ("Pee Wee")   cf   Dalton, Ga.
Giles, George   1b
Harding, A. ("Hallie")   inf, of
Hopwood   lf
Joseph, Newt   3b
Kenyon, Harry   p
Livingston, L. D. ("Googoo")   lf
Mothel, Carroll   2b
Rogan, Bullet Joe   utility, mgr
Taylor, Leroy   rf
Tyler, William ("Steel Arm")   p

Wilson, E.   p
Young, Tom   c


## 1929

Allen, Newt   2b
Bell, William   p
Brewer, Chet   p
Cooper, Andy   p
Cooper, Army   p
Duncan, Frank   c
Dwight, Eddie   cf   Kansas City, Kans.
Giles, George   1b
Harding, Hallie   ss
Joseph, Newt   3b
Livingston, L. D.   lf
Mothel, Carroll   1b
Rogan, Bullet Joe   cf, p, mgr
Taylor, Leroy   rf
Wilson, E.   p
Young, Tom   c


## 1930

Allen, Newt   2b
Bell, William   p
Cooper, Andy   p
Duncan, Frank   c
Harding, Hallie   ss
Joseph, Newt   3b
Livingston, L. D.   1b
McHenry, Henry   p
Markham (Marcum), John   p   Shreveport, La.
Mothel, Carroll   1b
Rogan, Bullet Joe   cf, mgr
Taylor, Leroy   rf
Turner   1b
Young, Tom   c


## 1931

Allen, Newt   2b
Beverly, Charles   p
Brown   lf
Byas, Richard ("Subby")   c, of
Clark   p
Cooper, Andy   p
Donaldson, John   of
Duncan, Frank   c

Foster, Willie   p
Harding, Hallie   ss
Harris, Chick ("Moocha")   p, lf
Hicks, Wesley   of
Joseph, Newt   3b
Livingston, L. D.   1b
Mothel, Carroll   1b
Orange, Grady   ss
Rogan, Bullet Joe   p, mgr
Rogers   rf
Sheppard   of
Stearnes, Norman ("Turkey")   of   Detroit, Mich.
Thompson, Samuel ("Sad Sam")   p
Young, Tom   c

## 1932

Allen, Newt   2b, capt
Bell, Cliff   of
Bell, James ("Cool Papa")   of
Bell, William   p
Beverly, Charles   p
Brewer, Chet   p
Clay   p
Cooper, Andy   p
Dean, Nelson   p
Duncan, Frank   c
Giles, George   1b
Harris, Chick   of
Hunter, Bertrum   p
Joseph, Newt   3b
Mothel, Carroll   3b, 2b
Thompson, Sad Sam   p
Trent, Theodore   p
Trouppe, Quincy   of   Georgia
Wells, Willie   ss
Young, Tom   c

## 1933

Allen, Newt   ss
Beverly, Charles   p
Boyd   of
Brewer, Chet   p
Cooper, Andy   p
Duncan, Frank   c
Dwight, Eddie   cf
Foreman, Hooks   c
Giles, George   1b

Joseph, Newt   3b
Mothel, Carroll   2b
Rogan, Bullet Joe   lf, mgr
Young, Tom   c

## 1934

Allen, Newt   2b, ss
Bankhead, Samuel   2b, 3b
Bell, Cool Papa   of
Beverly, Charles   p
Brewer, Chet   p
Cooper, Andy   p
Crawford, Sam   mgr
Davis   of
Donaldson, John   p
Duncan, Frank   c
Dwight, Eddie   cf
Giles, George   1b
Harris, Chick   of
Hunter, Bertrum   p
Joseph, Newt   3b
McNair, Hurley   rf
Mothel, Carroll   2b, 3b
Rogan, Bullet Joe   of, mgr
Stearnes, Turkey   cf
Taylor, Leroy   of
Trouppe, Quincy   of
Wells, Willie   ss
Young, Tom   c

## 1935

Allen, Newt   2b, capt
Berry, John Paul   p   Emerson, Ark.
Beverly, Charles   p
Brewer, Chet   p
Brown, Willard ("Big Bomb")   ss, 3b   Shreveport, La.
Cooper, Andy   p
Crawford, Sam   mgr
Dwight, Eddie   cf
Joseph, Newt   3b
Kransen (Kranson, Cranston), Floyd   p   Oakland, Calif.
Madison, Robert   p, ss
Mayweather, Eldridge ("Ed")   1b
Milton, Henry   2b, lf   East Chicago, Ind.
Rogan, Bullet Joe   utility
Taylor, Leroy   rf

Trouppe, Quincy   cf
Young, Tom   c

## 1936

Allen, Newt   2b
Berry, John   p
Brooks, E.   p
Brown, Willard   ss
Cooper, Andy   p, mgr
Dwight, Eddie   cf
Else, Harry ("Speedy")   c, p
Harris, Chick   of
Harris, Curtis ("Popsickle," "Popeye")   1b, utility
Kransen, Floyd   p
Madison, Robert   p
Mayweather, Ed   1b, 3b
Milton, Henry   lf
Morris   p
Paige, Leroy ("Satchel")   p   Mobile, Ala.
Patterson, Pat   3b
Rogan, Bullet Joe   1b, p, mgr
Taylor, Leroy   rf
Trouppe, Quincy   lf
Webster   p
Wilson, Woodrow ("Bo," "Lefty")   p

## 1937

Allen, Newt   2b
Barnes, Ed   p
Brooks, Jesse   3b
Brown, Willard   ss
Cooper, Andy   p, mgr
Duncan, Frank   c
Dwight, Eddie   cf
Else, Harry   c
Johnson, Byron ("Jewbaby")   ss
Kransen, Floyd   p
McHenry, Henry   p
Markham, John   p
Mays (reporters referred to him as Ed, Tom, Dave)   rf
Mayweather, Ed   3b, 1b
Milton, Henry   lf
Rogan, Bullet Joe   p, utility
Simms, Willie   cf   Shreveport, La.
Smith, Hilton   p   Giddings, Texas
Wilson, Lefty   p

## 1938

Adams, ("Packinghouse")   3b
Allen, Newt   2b
Betts   lf
Bibbs, Rainey   3b
Bowe, Randolph ("Bob," "Lefty")   p
Bradley, Frank   p   Benton, La.
Brown, Willard   of
Cooper, Andy   p
Cox, Roosevelt   3b, c
Duncan, Frank   c
Gilliard   lf
Jackson, ("Big Train")   p
Johnson, Byron   ss
Kransen, Floyd   p
Markham, John   p
Marshall   3b
Marvin, Alfred   p
Mayweather, Ed   1b, lf
Milton, Henry   rf, lf
Moses   p   Farmerville, La.
O'Neil, John ("Buck")   1b, rf   Sarasota, Fla.
Rogan, Bullet Joe   p
Simms, Willie   cf
Smith, Hilton   p
Stearnes, Turkey   cf
Strong, Ted   ss   Chicago

## 1939

Allen, Newt   2b
Bibbs, Rainey   3b
Bowe, Randolph   p
Bradley, Frank   p
Brown, Willard   lf
Cooper, Andy   p, mgr
DeCuir, Lionel   c   New Orleans, La.
Greene, James ("Joe")   c   New Orleans, La.
Hardy, Paul   c
Hutchinson, Willie ("Ace")   p   Oklahoma City, Okla.
Jackson, Big Train   p
Kransen, Floyd   p
Marcel   p
Metz
Milton, Henry   rf
Moses   p
O'Neil, Buck   1b
Smith, Hilton   p
Stearnes, Turkey   cf

Strong, Ted   ss
Treadway   p
Walker, George ("Little")   p   Waco, Texas
Williams, Jesse   3b   Corsicana, Texas

## 1940

Allen, Newt   2b
Barnes, V.   of   Hub, Miss.
Bibbs, Rainey   2b
Bradley, Frank   p
Bryant, Allen ("Lefty")   p   Kansas City, Mo.
Cooper, Andy   mgr
Cyrus, Herbert   3b   Monroe, La.
DeCuir, Lionel   c
Douglas, Jesse   2b   Longview, Texas
Greene, Joe   c
Kransen, Floyd   p
McDaniels, Booker T.   lf   Arkansas
Matchett, Jack ("Zip")   p   Odessa, Texas
Milton, Henry   rf
O'Neil, Buck   1b
Smith, Hilton   p
Stearnes, Turkey   cf
Walker, George   p
Williams, Jesse   ss

## 1941

Allen, Newt   ss, 3b, mgr
Bibbs, Rainey   2b
Bradley, Frank   p
Brewer, Chet   p
Brown, Willard   lf
Duncan, Frank   c
Greene, Joe   c
Johnson, Clifford ("Cliff," "Con-
   nie")   p   Stone Mountain, Ga.
McDaniels, Booker   p
O'Neil, Buck   1b
Paige, Satchel   p
Patterson, Pat   2b, 3b   Chicago
Simms, Willie   p, cf
Smith, Ford   p
Smith, G.   p
Smith, Hilton   p
Snead, Sylvester   rf
Strong, Ted   3b, rf
Walker, George   p
Williams, Jesse   cf, ss

Young, Tom   c

## 1942

Allen, Newt   2b
Bradley, Frank   p
Brown, Willard   cf
Cyrus, Herb   3b
Dawson, John   c
Dismukes, William ("Dizzy")   mgr
Duncan, Frank   c
Greene, Joe   c
Hardy, Paul   c
Johnson, Connie   p
LaMarque, James ("Lefty")   p   Potosi, Mo.
McDaniels, Booker   p
Matchett, Jack   p
O'Neil, Buck   1b
Paige, Satchel   p
Phillips, Norris   p   Houston, Texas
Serrell, William ("Bonnie,"
   "Bunny")   2b   Dallas, Texas
Simms, Willie   lf
Smith, Hilton   p
Strong, Ted   rf
Walker, George   p
Williams, Jesse   ss

## 1943

Alexander, Ted   p
Allen, Newt   utility
Barnhill, David ("Impo")   p
Brown, Willard   of
Bryant, Allen   p
Cyrus, Herb   3b
Duncan, Frank   mgr
Greene, Joe   c
Haynes (Hayes), Sam   c
Hoskins, William   lf
McDaniels, Booker   p
Matchett, Jack   p
O'Neil, Buck   1b
Paige, Satchel   p
Parker   p
Robinson, Frasier   1b   Odessa, Texas
Serrell, Bonnie   2b
Simms, Willie   1b
Smith, Hilton   p
Souell, Herbert ("Baldy")   3b

Thompson, Henry Curtis ("Hank")   rf   Okla-
   homa City, Okla.
Tyler   ss
Walker, George   p
Williams, Jesse   ss


## 1944

Alexander, Ted   p
Allen, Newt   1b, lf
Bumpus, Earl   rf   Kentucky
Duncan, Frank   c, mgr
Edwards   p
Harper, David   lf
Haynes, Sam   c
Johnson, Robert
LaMarque, Jim   p
Locke, Eddie   p   Kansas City, Mo.
McDaniels, Booker   p
McDaniels, Fred   of   Longview, Texas
Matchett, Jack   p
Moody, Lee   1b, lf
Paige, Satchel   p
Perkins   1b
Rivers   cf
Rochelle   p
Serrell, Bonnie   1b, 2b
Smith, Hilton   p
Smith, Mance   cf
Souell, Herb   3b
Taylor, Raymond   c
Thomas, Walter   rf
Vandever
Waldon   lf
Ward   c
Williams, Jesse   ss
Wingo, Doc   c
Wylie, Ensloe   p
Young, Edward ("Ned," "Pep")   c


## 1945

Berry, John   1b
Carlisle, Matthew   2b
Davis, Lee   p
Duncan, Frank   c, mgr
Gray   c
Harper, David   cf
Haynes, Sam   c
LaMarque, Jim   p
Locke, Eddie   p

McCullin, Clarence   of
McDaniels, Booker   p
Mack, John H.   p   Statham, Ga.
Matchett, Jack   p, lf
Moody, Lee   1b, cf
Moreland, Nate   p
Paige, Satchel   p
Radcliffe, Alex   c
Ray, John   cf
Renfroe, Othello ("Chico")   lf, 2b   Jackson-
   ville, Fla.
Robinson, John ("Jackie")   ss   Cairo, Ga.
   (Brooklyn Dodgers)
Scott, John   rf, cf
Serrell, Bonnie   1b
Smith, Hilton   p
Smith, Theolic ("Fireball")   p
Souell, Herb   3b
Thomas, Walter   lf
Walker, George   p
Washington, Lafayette   p
Williams, Eddie   lf
Williams, Jesse   2b, ss, 3b
Wylie, Ensloe   p
Young, Leandy   of   Shreveport, La.


## 1946

Alexander, Ted   p
Brown, Willard   3b, cf
Bryant, Allen   p
Duncan, Frank   mgr
Greene, Joe   c
Hamilton, J.   ss, cf
Hubbard, Larry   utility
Johnson, Connie   p
LaMarque, Jim   p
McCullin, Clarence   of
McKamey   ss
Moody, Lee   2b
Napoleon, Lawrence ("Lefty")   p
O'Neil, Buck   1b
Paige, Satchel   p
Renfroe, Chico   ss
Scott, John   lf
Smith, Fred   c
Smith, Hilton   p
Souell, Herb   3b
Strong, Ted   rf
Taborn, Earl ("Mickey")   c
Thompson, Hank   2b
Turner   c

Watson   p
Williams, Jesse   ss
Wylie, Ensloe   p

## 1947

Alexander, Ted   p
Berry, R.   p
Brown, Willard   of   (St. Louis Browns)
Collins, Eugene   p   Kansas City, Kans.
Cooper, Tom   of
Duffy, Bill   c
Duncan, Frank   mgr
Greene, Joe   c
Johnson, Connie   p
LaMarque, Jim   p
Moody, Lee   ss
Napoleon, Larry   p
O'Neil, Buck   1b
Paige, Satchel   p   (Cleveland Indians)
Renfroe, Chico   2b
Richardson, Gene   p   San Diego, Calif.
Roberts, Curtis   ss
Sanderson   utility
Scott, John   lf
Scroggins, John   p, of
Smith, Ford   p
Smith, Hilton   p
Souell, Herb   3b
Strong, Ted   of
Taborn, Earl   c
Thompson, Hank  2b, ss   (St. Louis Browns)
Wylie, Ensloe   p

## 1948

Baker, Eugene   ss   Davenport, Iowa
Brown, Willard   cf
Collins, Gene   p
Cooper, Tom   1b
Hall, Charley
Howard, Elston   c, 1b   St. Louis, Mo.
Howard, Herb
Johnson, Connie   p
Johnson, L.   p
LaMarque, Jim   p
O'Neil, Buck   mgr
Richardson, Gene   p
Roberts, Curtis   lf, 2b
Scott, John   rf
Smith, Ford   p   (New York Giants)

Smith, Hilton   p
Souell, Herb   3b
Taborn, Earl   c
Thompson, Hank   2b   (New York Giants)
Wright, Bill

## 1949

Baker, Gene   ss   (Chicago Cubs)
Barbee, Bud   of
Barnes, Frank   p   Greenville, Miss.
Bell, William R. ("Lefty")   p
Brown, Willard   of
Cartmill, Alfred   2b
Collins, Gene   p
Cooper, Tom   utility
Duncan, Melvin   p   Centralia, Ill.
Gaston, Isaac
Goshay, Samuel   of   Dayton, Ohio
Hayes, Jimmy   c
Henderson, Neal
Howard, Elston   1b, of
Hunt, Leonard   of   Kentucky
Johnson, Connie   p
Johnson, Ernest ("School Boy")   p   Jackson,
   Miss.
LaMarque, Jim   p
Landers, Robert Henry   p
Locke, Eddie   p
McDaniels, Booker   p   (Los Angeles Angels)
O'Neil, Buck   1b, mgr
Richardson, Gene   p
Roberts, Curtis   2b
Serrell, Bonnie   2b
Smith, Theolic   p
Souell, Herb   3b
Surratt, Alfred ("Slick")   of   Arkansas
Taborn, Earl   c   (New York Yankees)
Thompson, Harold   p
Thurman, Robert   p, of   Wichita, Kans. (New
   York Yankees)

## 1950

Alexander, Joe   c
Banks, Ernest ("Ernie")   ss   Dallas, Texas
Barnes, Frank   p   (New York Yankees)
Bell, Bili   p
Breda, William   lf
Chretian, Ernest   rf
Collins, Gene   cf

Cooper, Tom   c, rf
Duncan, Melvin   p, c
Everett, Curtis   lf
Fowikes, Samuel   p
Howard, Elston   lf   (New York Yankees)
Hughes, Lee   p
Jamerson, Londell ("Tincy")   p
Johnson, Connie   p
Johnson, School Boy   rf
LaMarque, Jim   p
O'Neil, Buck   1b, mgr
Peebles, Nathaniel ("Nate," "Nat")   1b, c
Pierre, Joseph   inf
Richardson, Gene   p
Roberts, Curtis   2b, ss
Serrell, Bonnie   ss, 2b
Souell, Herb   3b
Surratt, Al   of
Walker, George   p
Williams, Felix ("Jeff")   ss
Williams, LeRoy


## 1951

Banks, Ernie   ss
Battles, Charles
Bayliss, Henry ("Hank")   2b   Kansas City,
   Mo.
Bell, Bill   p
Betts, Russell   p
Breda, William   lf
Brown, Willard   of, 3b
Cartmill, Alfred   2b
Collins, Gene   p   (Chicago White Sox)
Cooper, Tom   p, 1b, c
Dooley   p
Duncan, Melvin   p
Everett, Curtis   lf
Givens, Virgil
Guyton, Miller ("San-Man")   3b
Head, John   of
Horn, Doc   rf
Hunt, Leonard   of
Jackson, Isiah ("Ike")   rf, c, 1b
Jamerson, Tincy   p
Johnson, Connie   p
LaMarque, Jim   p
Landers, Robert   p
Locke, Eddie   p
McGray, David
O'Neil, Buck   1b, mgr

Phiffe   ss
Pierre, Joseph   inf
Richardson, Gene   p
Roberts, Curtis   2b
Rowen   rf
Serrell, Bonnie   2b
Souell, Herb   3b
Surratt, Al   of
Taborn, Earl   c
Walker, George   p
W'gate   3b
Williams, Jesse   2b   (Vancouver: Western Inter-
   national League)
Williams, LeRoy


## 1952

Banks, Ernie   2b
Bayliss, Hank   2b
Bennett, Willie   ss
Booker, Richard   of
Brown, Willard   of, 3b   (Dallas Eagles)
Cooper, Tom   1b
Douse, Joe   p
Ensley, Frank   cf
Green   lf
Henderson, Duke   rf
Herrera, Francisco ("Pancho")   of   Santiago,
   Cuba
Humphreys, Carey   rf
Jackson, Ike   c
Jackson, John   p
Johnson, Connie   p   (Baltimore Orioles)
Johnson, James D.   p
Johnson, Ralph   ss
Landers, Bob   p
McCree, Earl   p
McDaniels, Booker   p
Mason, Henry ("Hank")   p   Marshall, Mo.
Murray   c
O'Neil, Buck   1b, mgr
Phillips, Richard   p
Richardson, Gene   p
Thompson, Hank   3b
Walker, George   p   (Seattle: Pacific Coast
   League)
White   p


## 1953

Armenteros, Juan   c

Banks, Ernie   ss   (Chicago Cubs)
Bayliss, Hank   3b
Bell, Bill   p
Brewer, Sherwood   2b
Cooper, Tom   c, asst. mgr
Dickey, Bill   p   (Chicago Cubs)
Douse, Joe   p
Henderson, Duke   of   (Carlsbad, N.M.)
Herrera, Francisco   1b
Holder, William   ss
Hunt, Leonard   of
Jackson, Ike   c
Jackson, John   p   (Cincinnati Reds)
Johnson, Ernest ("School Boy")   of   (Baltimore Orioles)
McCauley, Ben   of
Nuñez, Berto Daniel ("Dead Eye")   p
O'Neil, Buck   mgr
Phillips, Dick   p
Renfroe, Chico   utility
Richardson, Gene   p   (Carlsbad, N.M.)
Steele, Willie   3b, of
Williams, Jeff   lf   (Cincinnati Reds)

## 1954

Armenteros, Juan   c
Bayliss, Hank   3b
Bell, Bill   p
Brewer, Sherwood   2b
Conners, Doc   ss
Flores, Conrad   p
Gilmore, James   p
Harris, Leon   p
Herrera, Francisco   of   (Philadelphia Phillies)
Horn, Doc   of
Jones, Marvin   p
Kennedy, Ned   p
Ketchum
Maroto, Enrique   of
Mason, Hank   p   (Philadelphia Phillies)
Mitchell, Bob   p
Mobley, Dick   ss, 2b
Mobley, Ira
Nuñez, Berto   p
O'Neil, Buck   mgr

Phillips, Dick   p
Sands, Sam ("Piggy")   c, ss
Stone, Tony   2b
Thompson, Dick
Walls, James   of
Webster, Ernest   p

## 1955

Altmann, George   of   Goldsboro, N.C. (Chicago Cubs)
Armenteros, Juan   c
Bayliss, Hank   3b
Bennett, Arthur   of
Bennett, Willie   of
Cartmill, Alfred   2b
Clark, Estaban   1b
Duncan, Melvin   p
Forge, Willie   1b
Gautier, John   p
Gilmore, Jim   p
Hartman, J. C.   of
Hill, Bill   p
Incera, Victor   of
Johnson, Lou ("Sweet Lou")   of   Lexington, Ky. (Chicago Cubs)
Jones, Hank   of
Jones, Marvin   p
Maroto, Enrique   p
Mitchell, Bob   p
O'Neil, Buck   mgr
Paige, Satchel   p
Patterson, Joe   of
Phillips, Dick   p
Stephens, B. G.   p
Tiddle, Milton   c
Vaughn, Don   p
Whitney, Dave   ss
Williams, Larry   cf

Before Baird sold the franchise in 1955, he sold eight Monarchs to the majors and four to the minors. The details of the transaction were not reported.

# Appendix B
# The East-West Game

For thirty years the East-West Game was the highlight of the Negro leagues' summer season. For the twenty-three years that coverage is complete (1933–55), the West, in their "natty-colored cream" uniforms, defeated the blue-gray-clad East squad fourteen times. The following is a compilation of scores, attendance figures, and a list of Monarchs who participated for the West in these all-star games.

| Year | Score East | West | Attendance | Monarchs Who Participated |
|------|------|------|-----------|---------------------------|
| 1933 | 7 | 11 | 20,000 | None |
| 1934 | 1 | 0 | 20,000 | Monarchs were excluded, but fans nevertheless selected Chet Brewer |
| 1935 | 8 | 11 | 25,000 | Monarchs excluded |
| 1936 | 10 | 2 | 30,000 | Allen, Brown, Cooper, Dwight, Else, Harris, Kransen, Milton, Patterson, Rogan |
| 1937 | 7 | 2 | 20,000 | Allen, Brown, Mayweather, Milton, Smith |
| 1938 | 4 | 5 | 30,000 | Allen, Cooper (mgr.), Duncan, Johnson, Milton, Smith |
| 1939 | 2 | 4 | 33,489 | Cooper (asst. mgr.), Milton, Smith, Strong |
| 1940 | 11 | 0 | 25,000 | Cooper (asst. mgr.), Greene, Milton, Smith |
| 1941 | 8 | 3 | 50,256 | Allen, Paige, Smith, Strong |
| 1942 | 5 | 2 | 48,000 | Brown, Greene, O'Neil, Paige, Smith, Strong |
| 1943 | 1 | 2 | 51,723 | Brown, Duncan (mgr.), O'Neil, Paige, Williams |
| 1944 | 4 | 7 | 46,247 | Duncan (coach), Serrell |
| 1945 | 6 | 9 | 37,714 | Duncan (coach), McDaniels, Robinson, Williams |
| 1946 | 1 | 4 | 45,474 | None |
| 1947 | 2 | 5 | 48,112 | Souell |
| 1948 | 0 | 3 | 42,099 | Brown, LaMarque, Souell |
| 1949 | 4 | 0 | 31,097 | Brown, LaMarque, O'Neil, Richardson |
| 1950 | 3 | 5 | 24,614 | Cooper, Johnson, Souell |
| 1951 | 3 | 1 | 21,312 | Brewer, Cooper, O'Neil (mgr.), Williams |
| 1952 | 3 | 7 | 18,279 | Baylis, Henderson, I. Jackson, J. Jackson, O'Neil (mgr.), Phillips |
| 1953 | 1 | 5 | 7,000–10,000 | Armenteros, Banks, Baylis, Brewer, Cooper, Herrera, Jackson, Johnson, O'Neil (mgr.) |
| 1954 | 4 | 8 | 10,000 | Armenteros, Herrera, Mason, Nuñez, O'Neil (mgr.) |
| 1955 | 0 | 2 | 11,000 | Armenteros, Baylis, Hartman, Johnson, Maroto, O'Neil (mgr.), Paige, Whitney |

145

# Notes

Acronyms and short forms used in the notes:

ABCOHC   A. B. Chandler Oral History Collection, University of Kentucky Libraries, Department of Special Collections and Archives, Lexington, Kentucky

BAMA   Black Archives of Mid-America, Kansas City, Missouri

*Call*   *Kansas City Call*

*Courier*   *Pittsburgh Courier*

*Defender*   *Chicago Defender*

*Freeman*   *Indianapolis Freeman*

KCJOHP   Kansas City Jazz Oral History Project, in Joint Collection, Western Historical Manuscripts Collection and the State Historical Society of Missouri: Manuscripts, at University of Missouri, Kansas City

KCMOHC   Kansas City Monarchs Oral History Collection, in Joint Collection, Western Historical Manuscripts Collection and the State Historical Society of Missouri: Manuscripts, at University of Missouri, Kansas City

NBHFM   National Baseball Hall of Fame and Museum, Cooperstown, New York

NBHH   Negro Baseball Hall of History, Ashland, Kentucky

NLF   Negro Leagues File, at National Baseball Hall of Fame and Museum, Cooperstown, New York

SLOHP   St. Louis Oral History Project, Archive and Manuscript Division, University of Missouri, St. Louis

WHMC   Joint Collection, Western Historical Manuscripts Collection and the State Historical Society of Missouri: Manuscripts, at University of Missouri, Kansas City

## Chapter 1

1. *Defender,* 5 May 1923.

2. Jesse Fisher interview, KCMOHC.

3. John A. Lucas and Ronald A. Smith, *Saga of American Sport* (Philadelphia: Lea & Febiger,

1978), p. 269; Dale A. Somers, *The Rise of Sports in New Orleans, 1850–1900* (Baton Rouge: Louisiana State University Press, 1972), pp. 115, 119. The Negro Leagues File, NBHFM, contains clippings on games prior to the Civil War.

4. *Brooklyn* (N.Y.) *Daily Union,* 30 Sept. 1867, clipping in Robert Peterson File: Research Material for *Only the Ball Was White,* NBHFM; Harry C. Silcox, "Efforts to Desegregate Baseball in Philadelphia: The Pythian Baseball Club, 1866–1872," typescript, 1973, in NLF, p. 2.

5. William Carl Bolivar, "Pencil Pusher Points," *Philadelphia Tribune,* 24 Aug. 1912, cited in Silcox, "Efforts to Desegregate Baseball," pp. 2–3.

6. William Still to Pythian Baseball Club, 30 Jan. 1869, cited in Silcox, "Efforts to Desegregate Baseball," pp. 5–6; italics in original.

7. *Brooklyn* (N.Y.) *Daily Union,* 4 Oct. 1867, clipping in Peterson File.

8. Report from the Nominating Committee of the National Association of Base Ball Players, 11–12 Dec. 1867, cited in Harold Seymour, *Baseball,* vol. 1: *The Early Years* (New York: Oxford University Press, 1960), p. 42.

9. Raymond J. Burr, cited in Silcox, "Efforts to Desegregate Baseball," p. 4; Seymour, *Early Years,* p. 42.

10. Robert Peterson, *Only the Ball Was White* (Englewood Cliffs, N.J.: Prentice-Hall, 1970), p. 18.

11. Walker was also the first black on a college baseball team (see Ocania Chalk, *Black College Sport* [New York: Dodd, Mead & Co., 1976], pp. 2, 5). Walker was released at the end of the 1884 season, reportedly because of ill health. Walker was well enough, however, to play in the minor leagues for seven more years (see Ocania Chalk, *Pioneers of Black Sport* [New York: Dodd, Mead & Co., 1975], pp. 6–8).

12. Peterson, *Only the Ball Was White,* p. 18; Art Rust, Jr., *"Get That Nigger off the Field!"* (New York: Delacorte Press, 1976), p. 12; Lee Allen, *100 Years of Baseball* (New York: Bartholomew House, 1950), p. 282; *Sporting Life,* 24 Sept. and 1 Oct. 1884, clippings in NLF.

13. Anson claimed responsibility in his autobiography, *A Ball Player's Career: Being the Personal Experiences and Reminiscences of Adrian C. Anson* (Chicago: Era Publishing Co., 1900), pp. 148–50. Other sources that indict him

include the *Defender,* 4 Feb. 1933; Moses Walker's brother, Weldy, cited in Chalk, *Pioneers of Black Sport,* p. 16. Sol White, who played for the Cuban Giants, accused Anson in his *History of Colored Baseball:* "This same Anson, with all the venom of a hate which would be worthy of a [Senator Ben] Tillman or a [Senator James] Vardaman of the present day, made strenuous and fruitful opposition to any proposition looking to the admittance of a colored man in the National League" (cited in Peterson, *Only the Ball Was White,* p. 29).

14. *Sporting Life,* n.d., clipping attached to letter from Lee Allen to Bob Peterson, Thanksgiving Day 1959, in Peterson File.

15. David Q. Voigt examined *Sporting News* for its treatment of black athletes; his conclusions are presented in *America through Baseball* (Chicago: Nelson-Hall, 1976), pp. 112, 127.

16. *Richmond* (Va.) *Times,* cited in C. Vann Woodward, *The Strange Career of Jim Crow,* 3d rev. ed. (New York: Oxford University Press, 1974), p. 96; see also Kenneth C. Kusmer, *A Ghetto Takes Shape: Black Cleveland, 1870–1930* (Urbana: University of Illinois Press, 1976), 54–59.

17. *Freeman,* 11 Aug. 1888, clipping in NLF.

18. Despite a few disclaimers, the Cuban Giants have received credit for organizing the first professional black team in 1885. Both the *Cincinnati Enquirer,* 29 July 1882, and *Sporting Life,* 1884, referred to earlier professional teams (cited in Lee Allen to Bob Peterson, 7 Sept. 1967, in Peterson File).

19. *Newark* (N.J.) *Call,* 28 Sept. 1887, clipping in NLF.

20. Bill Pilot, "The Southern League of Colored Base Ballists," *Baseball Research Journal: Third Annual Report* (n.p., 1974), pp. 91–95.

21. *Sporting Life* referred to this league as the first. The league was also called the National Colored League and the Colored National League. There is some discrepancy about which teams were members, but all six were from New England. Edwin Bancroft Henderson, *The Negro in Sports,* rev. ed. (Washington, D.C.: Associated Publishers, 1949), p. 163, contended that the league was organized on paper only and never reached the field. *Sporting Life,* however, reported teams playing under the auspices of the league through May. See *Sporting Life,* 26 Jan.,

13 Apr., 18 May, and 1 June 1887, clippings in NLF; see also Peterson, *Only the Ball Was White*, pp. 26–27, and Chalk, *Pioneers of Black Sport*, pp. 35–38.

22. *Sporting Life*, 11 Oct. 1890, clipping in NLF.

23. "Historically Speaking," *Black Sports*, May/June 1972, p. 74, clipping in NLF.

24. *Chicago Broad Ax*, 21 Jan. 1911, cited in Allan H. Spear, *Black Chicago: The Making of a Negro Ghetto, 1890–1920* (Chicago: University of Chicago Press, 1967), p. 117.

25. Felix Payne and Tobe Smith attended the meeting, probably representing the Kansas City, Kansas, Giants (see *Defender*, 31 Dec. 1910, clipping in Peterson File; Peterson, *Only the Ball Was White*, p. 63).

26. John Holway, *Voices from the Great Black Baseball Leagues* (New York: Dodd, Mead & Co., 1975), p. 4.

27. A. W. Hardy interview, A. W. Hardy to Bob Peterson, 20 June (n.y.), and Dave Malarcher to Bob Peterson, 16 Dec. 1968—all in Peterson File; Peterson, *Only the Ball Was White*, pp. 63–64; William Brashler, *Josh Gibson: A Life in the Negro Leagues* (New York: Harper & Row, 1978), p. 4.

28. *Negro Baseball Yearbook: 1946*, p. 3, in NLF. The Indianapolis ABCs had a different origin. In the late 1880s the American Brewing Company in Indianapolis organized a black baseball club to advertise their beer. With their antics, jokes, and free beer, the ABCs drew large crowds. After the beer became well known, the brewers sold the team to a black saloon keeper, who retained the ABC trademark (see *Call*, 4 Jan. 1924).

29. Peterson, *Only the Ball Was White*, p. 63.

30. *Freeman*, 27 Jan. 1917.

31. *Sporting Life*, 2 Apr. 1892, clipping in NLF; Robert Smith, *Baseball*, rev. ed. (New York: Simon & Schuster, 1970), p. 318; Chalk, *Pioneers of Black Sport*, p. 43; *Freeman*, 17 Feb. 1917. Sol White, who played for the Cuban Giants, recalled these years as a "money period" for his team. From all accounts, the Cuban Giants earned about as much as a porter or waiter in a first-class hotel (see Peterson, *Only the Ball Was White*, p. 39; Rust, *"Get That Nigger,"* p. 22).

32. Sol White, *History of Colored Baseball* (1906), cited in Jackie Robinson, *Baseball Has Done It,* ed. Charles Dexter (Philadelphia: J. B. Lippincott Co., 1964), p. 17.

33. *Sporting Life*, 9 Aug. 1890, and *Boston Globe*, 1 Apr. 1897, cited in Voigt, *America through Baseball*, p. 112.

34. *St. Louis Post-Dispatch*, 1912, clipping in Peterson File.

35. *Sporting Life*, 3 July 1915, clipping in NLF.

36. *Defender*, 23 Feb. 1917, clipping in Peterson File.

37. *New York Age*, 1911, clipping in Peterson File.

38. Ibid., 28 Sept. 1911, cited in Chalk, *Pioneers of Black Sport*, pp. 22–24. Mendez later pitched for the Kansas City Monarchs.

39. *Sporting News*, cited in Richard Crepeau, *Baseball: America's Diamond Mind* (Orlando: University Presses of Florida, 1980), p. 172.

**Chapter 2**

1. St. Clair Drake and Horace R. Cayton, *Black Metropolis: A Study of Negro Life in a Northern City*, rev. ed. (New York: Harper & Row, 1962), p. 80.

2. *Freeman*, 27 Jan. 1917.

3. Ibid.

4. Chalk, *Pioneers of Black Sport*, p. 58.

5. *Defender*, 26 Apr. 1919.

6. Ibid., 14 and 21 Feb. 1920; *Call*, 25 Jan. 1924; *Freeman*, 21 Feb. 1920. In addition, W. A. Kelly of Washington, D.C., Charles Marshall of the *Indianapolis Ledger*, Nelson Crews of the *Call*, Robert Gilkerson of the Union Giants, A. Molina of the Cuban Stars, and Dr. Howard Smith and Q. J. Gilmore of Kansas City were listed as being in attendance according to some reports. Unfortunately, no issues of the *Kansas City Call* for 1919–21 are known to exist.

7. *Freeman*, 17 Jan. 1920.

8. Ibid.

9. *Defender*, 10 Jan. and 21 Feb. 1920. The league was incorporated in 1925 (see *Call*, 2 Jan. 1925).

10. *Defender*, 11 Dec. 1920. No copies of this constitution are known to exist today. In 1921 the constitution was amended, requiring a $1,000 deposit as a guarantee of good faith.

11. The NNL, like previous leagues, was unstable because of changing franchises. During the twelve-year life of the NNL (1920–31), teams

from the following cities were members at one time or another: Kansas City (Mo.), Chicago, Detroit, St. Louis, Indianapolis, Birmingham, Memphis, Cleveland, Havana (Cuba), Pittsburgh, Toledo, Dayton, and Milwaukee. Only the Chicago American Giants were members throughout the period. St. Louis was always represented as a city, but the Stars replaced the Giants after 1921.

12. *Defender,* 4 Oct. 1919.

13. *Call,* 27 July 1928; Bill Drake interview, SLOHP; unidentified clipping, 1927, in Bullet Joe Rogan Scrapbook, BAMA; Gladys Wilkinson Catron interview, KCMOHC; *Des Moines* (Iowa) *Sunday Register,* 20 May 1973, clipping in private collection of Richard Wilkinson, Mary-ville, Missouri. His initial ''J'' did not stand for anything. Players and sportswriters sometimes mistakenly called him ''Wilkerson.''

14. *Call,* 28 May 1948; see also ibid., 1 Feb. 1924 and 27 July 1928; William H. Young and Nathan B. Young, Jr., *Your Kansas City and Mine* (Kansas City: n.p., 1950), p. 69; Richard Wilkinson interview, KCMOHC.

15. *Sporting Life,* 3 July 1915, clipping in NLF.

16. *Defender,* 3 and 17 Sept. 1917; John Holway, ''Kansas City's Mighty Monarchs,'' *Missouri Life* 3 (March–June, 1975): 84; Peter-son, *Only the Ball Was White,* p. 72.

17. Wilkinson, cited in Young and Young, *Your Kansas City and Mine,* pp. 69–70; see also unidentified clipping, 1927, in Rogan Scrapbook. The Indianapolis ABCs disbanded because of the war draft (see Dave Malarcher to Bob Peterson, 20 Mar. 1969, in Peterson File). The entire pitching staff and two other members of the Chicago American Giants were drafted in 1917, but the team continued to play throughout the war (see *Defender,* 3 Sept. 1917; see also Mary Frances Berry and John W. Blassingame, *Long Memory: The Black Experience in America* [New York: Oxford University Press, 1982], p. 315).

18. *Sporting Life,* 3 July 1915, clipping in NLF; *Defender,* 23 June 1917; Catron interview; telephone conversation with Lee Wilkinson, 11 Feb. 1981.

19. *Call,* 15 Dec. 1922.

20. Telephone conversation with Bob Bailey, 12 Jan. 1981; telephone conversation with Richard Pullam, 12 Jan. 1981; telephone conver-sation with J. W. Jenkins IV, 2 July 1981; *Call,* 15 Dec. 1922 and 14 Aug. 1953; Hardy

interview, and A. W. Hardy to Bob Peterson, 20 June (n.y.), in Peterson File.

21. *Freeman,* 24 Feb. 1917; *Defender,* 22 July 1950. See Peterson, *Only the Ball Was White,* p. 65, for a discussion of the Giants' move from Topeka to Kansas City, Kansas.

22. Alberta Penn (Mrs. Q. J. Gilmore) interview, KCMOHC. Penn married Gilmore in 1921. See also telephone conversation with Lee Wilkinson, 11 Feb. 1981; Robert Sweeney interview, KCMOHC.

23. *Freeman,* 28 Feb. 1920.

24. *Defender,* 5 Feb. 1927; *Call,* 15 Dec. 1922. Wilkinson served from 1920 until 1922, at which time Joe Rush of Birmingham was elected. Q. J. Gilmore of Kansas City served as secretary from 1925 until 1929. The president acted as secretary that year; when Gilmore returned to Kansas City, he was reelected secretary. The secretary was the only league official to receive a salary (see *Call,* 15 Jan. 1925, 4 and 11 Jan. 1929).

25. Quincy Trouppe, *Twenty Years Too Soon* (Los Angeles: S & S Enterprises, 1977), p. 68; see also Drake interview; Newt Allen interview, KCMOHC.

26. *Call,* 27 July 1928.

27. *Defender,* 22 Aug. 1931.

28. *Call,* 15 Jan. 1926 and 13 May 1927; Malarcher to Peterson, n.d., in Peterson File; John O'Neil interview, KCMOHC. Effa Manley and Hilton Smith both reported having heard rumors that Wilkinson mortgaged his house to meet payroll (Hilton Smith interview, Donn Rogosin Collection, Austin, Texas).

29. Allen interview, KCMOHC.

30. Ibid.

31. Allen Bryant interview, KCMOHC; see also Maurice Young interview, KCMOHC; Willard Brown interview, ABCOHC.

32. Roy Johnson interview, KCMOHC.

33 *Call,* 7 Sept. 1928.

34. Sweeney interview.

35. Milton Morris interview, KCMOHC.

36. *Defender,* 27 Dec. 1919.

37. Ibid., 3 Jan. 1920.

38. Ibid., 10 and 17 Jan. 1920.

39. Ibid., 21 July, 15 Sept., and 1 Dec. 1917, and 21 Feb. 1920; Richard Wilkinson interview, KCMOHC; *Kansas City Star,* 11 Oct. 1920; Newt Allen interview, SLOHP.

40. This is the original roster approved by the NNL owners and sportswriters at the first NNL

meeting. See *Defender,* 21 Feb. and 22 May 1920; see Appendix A for the 1920 roster as it developed through the season.

41. *Defender,* 2 July 1921.

42. Ibid., 14 May 1921.

43. *Call,* 27 July 1928; see also *Call,* 28 May 1948 and 16 June 1950; *Defender,* 9 July 1949. When Wilkinson incorporated the team in 1920, he owned all but two shares of the stock. His wife owned one; the other was held by attorney Wilfred R. Waltner, who had drawn up the incorporation papers (see Articles of Association, Kansas City Monarchs Baseball and Amusement Company, 6 Feb. 1923, Secretary of State, Jefferson City, Missouri).

44. Penn interview.

45. *Call,* 21 Jan. 1922; *Courier,* 1 Nov. 1924.

46. Telephone conversation with Lee Wilkinson, 11 Feb. 1981; Richard Wilkinson interview; telephone conversation with Lawrence Benton, sports editor for the *Call,* 24 Nov. 1980.

47. Gilmore went to Texas in 1929 to help form the Texas-Oklahoma-Louisiana League. Lee Wilkinson, Richard Wilkinson, and former player William ("Dizzy") Dismukes then alternately served as traveling secretary (see Penn interview; Richard Wilkinson interview; Lee Wilkinson to author, 17 Feb. 1981).

48. Penn interview.

49. *Call,* 4 Feb. 1922, 14 Mar. 1924, and 27 July 1945; Penn interview.

50. Jesse Williams interview, KCMOHC; see also *Call,* 13 July 1922 and 14 Sept. 1928; Richard Wilkinson interview; Al Surratt interview, KCMOHC.

51. *Call,* 2 Apr. 1926. Wilkinson reportedly paid for Jewbaby's course in chiropractic (see *Call,* 11 Mar. 1949).

52. Ibid., 19 July 1940.

53. Ibid., 2 Apr. and 17 Sept. 1926, 9 Dec. 1927, 30 Oct. 1936, 26 Sept. 1941, and 29 May 1953.

54. Ibid., 7 Sept. 1928; Normal ("Tweed") Webb interview, SLOHP. A 1934 photograph of the team bears the inscription "Mascot Carey" (see unidentified newspaper clipping, 1934, in NLF).

55. *Call,* 3 June 1922.

56. *Courier,* 13 Dec. 1924; *Call,* 1 Apr. 1922, 4 and 11 Jan. 1929; *Defender,* 14 Jan. 1928 and 1 Feb. 1930.

57. Hilton Smith interview, KCMOHC.

58. *Call,* 15 Apr. 1922 and 16 Mar. 1928.

59. Allen interview, SLOHP.

60. Frank Duncan interview, John Holway Collection, Manassas, Va.

61. Chet Brewer interview, Donn Rogosin Collection, Austin, Texas.

62. *Call,* 1 Feb., 14 Mar., and 26 July 1924; Fisher interview; Richard Wilkinson interview; Smith interview, Texas; Pat Patterson interview, Donn Rogosin Collection, Austin, Texas.

63. Smith interview, Texas.

64. *Call,* 15 Apr. 1927; Richard Wilkinson interview; Georgia Dwight interview, KCMOHC; Allen interview, KCMOHC.

65. *Call,* 25 Mar. and 1 July 1922, 21 Mar. 1924; *Defender,* 21 Apr. 1923.

66. *Call,* 6 July 1923.

67. *Courier,* 27 Dec. 1924. After 1924 there are a few references to an All Nations team; in 1928 it was based in Kansas City. Wilkinson, however, had no financial interest in this team. Probably another organization adopted the name because of its established appeal with the crowds.

68. Unidentified newspaper clipping, ca. 1930–36, in Georgia Dwight Papers, Kansas City, Kans.

69. Ibid.; *Call,* 13 May 1927 and 4 Dec. 1936; Young interview; Dwight interviews.

70. O'Neil interview, KCMOHC; Brown interview.

71. Joe Greene, cited in Holway, *Voices from Black Baseball,* p. 304.

72. *Call,* 1 Apr. 1922.

73. Drake interview. Quincy Trouppe, who played with several teams, also discussed this tension between rookies and veterans (*Twenty Years Too Soon,* p. 96).

74. *Call,* 30 Aug. 1929.

75. Bryant interview; *Call,* 1 Apr. 1922 and 27 July 1928.

76. *Call,* 16 Mar. 1923; *Defender,* 29 Mar. 1930; Dwight interview.

77. Allen interview, SLOHP; Drake interview, SLOHP; Richard Wilkinson interview; Roy Johnson interview; *Call,* 27 Apr. 1923, 18 Feb. 1927, 27 Apr. 1928, 23 Apr. 1943. In the early 1950s the uniforms had a letter of the alphabet on the back instead of a number for player identification (see *Call,* 4 May 1951). Mrs. Eddie Dwight donated a gray and maroon uniform to the Smithsonian Institution in March 1981.

78. *Call,* 17 Apr. 1925.

79. Roy Campanella, *It's Good to Be Alive* (Boston: Little, Brown & Co., 1959), p. 76.

80. *Call*, 1 Feb. 1924 and 10 Feb. 1928; *Defender*, 27 Apr. 1929 and 29 Mar. 1930; *Courier*, 21 Feb. 1927.

81. *Call*, 3 Aug. 1923.

82. *Defender*, 19 Aug. 1922; see also *Call*, 21 Jan. 1927 and 3 Nov. 1922; Allen interview, KCMOHC. Wilkinson often hired Chick Wheeler and Tim Flood (a former National League umpire) to officiate at Monarchs games.

83. Young interview.

84. *Defender*, 19 Aug. 1922; see also ibid., 9 Oct. 1920 and 31 Dec. 1921.

85. Ibid., 21 Apr. 1923; *Courier*, 25 Aug. 1923; *Call*, 27 Apr. 1923.

86. This Milwaukee sportswriter was cited in the *Defender*, 5 May 1923.

87. *Call*, 20 Apr. 1923. For other reports of trouble see ibid., 28 Aug. 1925, 7 May 1926, 21 June 1929, and 12 July 1935; *Courier*, 25 Aug. 1923, 15 Dec. 1923, and 1 June 1935.

88. *Call*, 21 Jan. 1927; *Defender*, 11 Oct. 1941.

89. Drake and Cayton, *Black Metropolis*, p. 439.

90. Asa E. Martin, *Our Negro Population: A Sociological Study of the Negroes in Kansas City, Missouri* (Kansas City: Franklin Hudson Publishing Co., 1913), p. 42; see also *Call*, 29 Aug. 1924 and 16 Mar. 1923; Drake and Cayton, *Black Metropolis*, p. 440; Berry and Blassingame, *Long Memory*, p. 202; Thelma M. Dumas, ed., *Symbols of God's Grace: Seventy Years History of St. Stephen Baptist Church* (Kansas City: McWhirter Co., 1973), pp. 18, 21.

91. *Call*, 6 Feb., 28 Aug., 4 and 25 Sept. 1925.

92. Ibid., 15 Apr. 1927, 11 Jan. 1929, 15 Apr. 1927, and 24 May 1940.

93. *Defender*, 11 Sept. 1926 and 5 Jan. 1930.

94. Ibid., 6 Mar. 1920; *Courier*, 9 June 1931 and 9 June 1934.

95. *Courier*, 15 Dec. 1923; *Call*, 22 Dec. 1922 and 19 Jan. 1923; *Defender*, 4 Mar. 1922.

96. *Courier*, 7 July 1923.

97. *Defender*, 2 Feb. 1935.

98. Ibid., 5 Feb. 1927.

99. *Call*, 8 Mar. 1929; *Defender*, 6 Apr. 1929 and 6 Sept. 1924.

100. Patterson interview.

101. Williams interview; see also *Call*, 21 Jan. and 18 Feb. 1927.

102. *Defender*, 5 Feb. 1927.

103. Ibid.

104. Ibid., 13 Dec. 1919, 19 Jan. 1924, and 24 Dec. 1921; *Call*, 29 Oct. 1926, 23 Dec. 1927, and 27 Jan. 1928; Urban League, *The Negro Worker of Kansas City: A Study of Trade Unions and Organized Labor Relations* (Kansas City: Urban League, 1940), p. 22.

105. Francis Wallace, "College Men in the Big Leagues," *Scribner's Magazine* 82 (Oct. 1927): 492; U.S. Congress, House, Committee on the Judiciary, *Study of Monopoly Power: Organized Baseball, Hearings before the Subcommittee on Study of Monopoly Power of the Committee on the Judiciary,* 82d Cong., 1st sess., 1951, pp. 1361, 1367, 1384–85.

106. *Call*, 25 Jan. 1924 and 15 Jan. 1926; *Defender*, 6 Sept. 1924 and 16 Jan. 1926; *Courier*, 11 Aug. 1923. Reportedly, only Bolden avoided debts during this "war" (see *Call*, 2 Jan. 1925).

107. *Call*, 2 Jan. 1925.

108. Ibid., 19 Aug. and 9 Sept. 1922, 17 Aug. 1923, 19 Aug. 1925, 4 Feb. and 16 Dec. 1927; *Defender*, 30 Jan. 1926.

109. *Cleveland Advocate*, 13 Nov. 1915, cited in Kusmer, *Black Cleveland*, p. 106; see also *Defender*, 14 July 1923; David A. Gerber, *Black Ohio and the Color Line, 1860–1915* (Urbana: University of Illinois Press, 1976), pp. 417–21; Kusmer, *Black Cleveland*, pp. 106–13, 252; Spear, *Black Chicago*, p. 167; Drake and Cayton, *Black Metropolis*, pp. 64–75.

110. *Defender*, 10 Dec. 1921.

111. *Courier*, 21 Mar. 1931.

112. Brewer interview.

113. *Courier*, 27 Mar. 1926; see also *Defender*, 8 July 1911.

114. *Courier*, 25 Aug. 1923.

115. Ibid., 21 Mar. 1931.

116. Renfroe, cited in Holway, *Voices from Black Baseball*, p. 345. Others who discussed this dress code are Bryant interview; Cliff Johnson interview, KCMOHC; Guy Davis interview, KCMOHC.

117. Bryant interview.

118. *Call*, 25 Jan. 1924.

119. Ibid., 18 Feb. 1927.

120. Ibid., 7 Jan. 1922.

121. *Defender*, 1 Mar. 1930.

122. *Call*, 25 July 1930.

123. O'Neil interview, KCMOHC.

124. Allen interview, KCMOHC.

125. Young interview.

126. Holway, *Voices from Black Baseball*, p. 346.

127. *Defender,* 27 July 1929.

128. *Call,* 17 June 1922; see also *Defender,* 5 May 1923.

129. *Defender,* 1 Mar. 1930.

130. *Call,* 11 July 1924; *Defender,* 7 July 1928; *Courier,* 8 June 1929.

131. *Defender,* 1 Feb. 1930.

132. *Courier,* 12 Feb. 1927.

133. Harold Seymour, *Baseball,* vol. 2: *The Golden Age* (New York: Oxford University Press, 1971), pp. 17, 125–26.

134. Unidentified newspaper clipping, ca. 1930–36, in Dwight Papers.

135. *Defender,* 8 Jan. 1927.

136. *Courier,* 21 Mar. 1931; see also *Call,* 29 Oct. 1926.

## Chapter 3

1. Booker T. Washington interview, KCJOHP.

2. Gordon Stevenson, "A Brief History of Jazz in Kansas City," typescript in Missouri Valley Room, Kansas City Public Library, K.C., Mo.

3. Morris interview.

4. *Call,* 3 July 1925.

5. Howard Litwak and Nathan Pearson, Final Narrative Report, "Kansas City: The Oral History of a Jazz Scene, 1924–42," KCJOHP; Urban League, *Negro Worker of Kansas City,* p. 22; Clifford Naysmith, "History of Negro Population of Kansas City, Missouri, 1870–1930," in A. Theodore Brown Collection, WHMC; Martin, *Our Negro Population,* p. 9.

6. Fisher interview.

7. Williams interview.

8. Smith interview, KCMOHC.

9. O'Neil interview, KCMOHC; see also Drake and Cayton, *Black Metropolis,* p. 533, for a discussion of this "good moral character" within the black community.

10. *Call,* 27 July 1928.

11. Ibid., 25 Jan. 1924.

12. O'Neil interview, KCMOHC.

13. Brewer interview, Texas.

14. Lawrence Denton interview, KCJOHP.

15. Davis interview.

16. Fisher interview; see also James Carey Tate, "Kansas City Night Life: K.C. in the 30s," *Second Line,* Nov./Dec. 1961, p. 11; Fred Allhoff, "Thunder over Kansas City," *Liberty,* 17 Sept. 1938, pp. 4–8; *Call,* 7 Jan., 22 Apr., and 20 May 1922.

17. Davis interview.

18. Young interview.

19. *Defender,* 5 May 1923.

20. Davis interview.

21. Allen interview, KCMOHC.

22. Ibid.; see also Dwight interview. Some of the jazz musicians also talked of this "understanding" (e.g., see Booker T. Washington interview; Eddie Barefield interview, KCJOHP).

23. Fisher interview.

24. Penn interview.

25. Dwight interview; and Trouppe, *Twenty Years Too Soon,* p. 141, discussed the strain that travel put on marriages. See also Herman Walder interview, KCJOHP.

26. Bryant interview.

27. *Call,* 6 July 1923.

28. Count Basie interview, KCJOHP.

29. O'Neil interview, KCMOHC.

30. Fisher interview; see also Davis interview.

31. Advertisement for the Fashion Clothing Co. appeared in *Call,* 27 Apr. 1923.

32. *Call,* 6 Oct. 1922.

33. *Freeman,* 31 Mar. 1917.

34. Ibid., 28 Feb. 1920; see also *Call,* 1 Apr. 1922, 28 Sept. 1923, and 29 Feb. 1924.

35. *Call,* 28 Sept. 1923.

36. Ibid., 29 June 1923.

37. Sweeney interview.

38. O'Neil interview, KCMOHC; see also *Call,* 17 May 1940, 11 May 1928, and 30 May 1930; Penn interview; Fisher interview.

39. *Call,* 7 Aug. 1925, 27 May 1927, 5 Aug. 1938, and 9 Sept. 1927.

40. *Defender,* 5 May 1923. Many of the official cars were taxis that Wilkinson hired (see *Call,* 6 May 1922 and 1 May 1925).

41. *Call,* 15 May 1925 and 25 Feb. 1927. The *Call* announced "moving pictures" on 27 Apr. 1923, 1 May 1924, and 31 May 1929. The *Defender,* 8 Sept. 1929, also reported that films were taken of the Monarchs in Houston. MGM reportedly shot the 1929 films. I have not been able to locate the films.

42. Smith interview, KCMOHC.

43. *Call,* 16 Mar. 1923, 10 Oct. 1924, and 6 May 1927.

44. Buck O'Neil to Nancy Dickinson, 12 Jan.

1982, Negro Leagues File, NBHH. Newt Joseph's gold baseball charm is in the museum in Ashland, Ky.

45. *Call,* 2 Oct. 1925, 17 and 31 May 1929.

46. Ibid., 3 Oct. 1924 and 31 May 1929; Bill Drake, cited in Holway, *Voices from Black Baseball,* p. 32.

47. O'Neil interview, KCMOHC; see also *The Spirit of Freedom: A Profile of the History of Blacks in Kansas City, Missouri* (Kansas City: Office of Housing and Community Development, 1978), p. 13; *Call,* 3 Sept. 1926 and 30 May 1930; Berry and Blassingame, *Long Memory,* pp. 92–107; Penn interview; John R. Betts, "Organized Sport in Industrial America" (Ph.D. diss., Columbia University, 1951), pp. 645–47. When Wilkinson married Bessie Schisler, her family objected, not to his playing baseball, but to his playing Sunday baseball. Both families were Methodist, and Wilkinson withdrew from the church over this issue (see Catron interview).

48. Bryant interview.

49. *Call,* 30 Apr. 1926; see also Penn interview.

50. *Sporting News,* cited in Seymour, *Baseball: Early Years,* p. 328.

51. *Call,* 14 Feb. 1930; see also *Defender,* 2 June 1923.

52. *Call,* 3 June 1922; see also *Call,* 17 June 1922; *Defender,* 2 June 1923; Roy Johnson interview.

53. *Call,* 1 Apr. 1927.

54. Robert H. Boyle, *Sport: Mirror of American Life* (Boston: Little, Brown & Co., 1963), pp. 132–33, discussed the dream books. See also Drake and Cayton, *Black Metropolis,* pp. 468–70; Litwak and Pearson, Final Narrative Report.

55. *Call,* 3 June 1922.

56. Ibid., 19 Aug. and 3 Nov. 1922; Allen is cited in Holway, *Voices from Black Baseball,* p. 92. This park was known by various names during the years. It was Muehlebach Stadium from 1923 until 1938. It became Ruppert Field in 1938, when Jacob Ruppert purchased it for his New York Yankees organization. By 1946, fans were calling it Blues Stadium. In 1954 Arnold Johnson purchased the stadium from the Yankees and assigned the lease to the city; it then became known as Municipal Stadium.

57. Kansas City Monarchs Articles of Association, 6 Feb. 1923; Catron interview.

58. *Call,* 3 Nov. 1922; see also *Courier,* 20 Sept. 1947; Richard Wilkinson interview; Effa Manley, cited in Holway, *Voices from Black Baseball,* p. 321; *Call,* 4 Feb. 1949; *Defender,* 27 Aug. 1938; C. I. Taylor to Karl Finke, 28 Nov. and 5 Dec. 1920, in Peterson File.

59. Edgar Ray Chasteen, "Public Accommodations: Social Movements in Conflict" (Ph.D. diss., University of Missouri, 1966), p. 67; League of Women Voters, *The Negro in Kansas City* (Kansas City: n.p., 1944), pp. 12–14.

60. *Call,* 1 Feb. 1924 and 17 June 1938; Davis interview; Penn interview.

61. *Call,* 9 Oct. 1931; see also Gunnar Myrdal, *An American Dilemma: The Negro Problem and Modern Democracy* (New York: Harper & Brothers, 1944), pp. 908–11; Maxwell R. Brooks, *The Negro Press Re-examined* (Boston: Christopher Publishing House, 1959), pp. 11–12; Lee Finkle, *Forum for Protest: The Black Press during World War II* (London: Associated University Presses, 1975), pp. 45–46; Lawrence D. Hogan, *A Black News Service: The Associated Negro Press and Claude Barnett, 1919–1945* (Cranbury, N.J.: Associated University Presses, 1984), pp. 141–45.

62. *Defender,* 11 Sept. 1926.

63. Ibid., 8 July 1933; see also *Call,* 16 Mar. and 20 Apr. 1923, for promises of better coverage.

64. *Call,* 6 July 1923 and 11 Jan. 1929; *Courier,* 30 Jan. 1926.

65. Brewer interview. In 1944 the Negro leagues hired the Monroe Elias Baseball Bureau as official statisticians. This New York-based agency sent releases to thirty black and fifty white newspapers each week (see *Call,* 17 and 31 Mar. 1944).

66. John Holway, *Bullet Joe and the Monarchs,* foreword by Bob Feller (Washington, D.C.: Capital Press, 1984), n.p.

67. Drake, cited in Holway, *Voices from Black Baseball,* p. 90.

68. Holway, *Bullet Joe,* n.p.

69. Ibid.

70. Leonard, cited in Holway, *Voices from Black Baseball,* p. 279.

71. Allen, cited in Holway, *Voices from Black Baseball,* p. 93.

72. *Call,* 9 Sept. 1922.

73. Ibid., 12 Sept. 1924.

74. Ibid., 24 Oct. 1924.

75. *Courier*, 1 Nov. 1924. The attendance figures for the World Series were 14,027 for two games in Philadelphia; 6,087 for two games in Baltimore; 15,315 for three games in Kansas City; 10,428 for three games in Chicago (see *Call*, 19 Sept. 1924).

76. *Courier*, 7 Jan. 1926.

77. *Defender*, 23 Oct. 1926; see also *Call*, 25 Sept. and 23 Oct. 1925; *Defender*, 24 Oct. 1925.

78. *Defender*, 23 Oct. 1926.

79. *Call*, 29 Oct. 1926 and 14 Oct. 1927.

80. *Defender*, 23 Oct. 1926; *Call*, 29 Oct. 1926 and 24 Feb. 1928.

81. *Call*, 13 May 1922.

82. Dwight interview.

83. *Call*, 3 Mar. 1923.

84. Ibid., 10 June 1922, 29 Aug. 1924, 30 Mar. 1928, and 30 Aug. 1929; *Defender*, 28 Sept. 1929; Drake interview.

85. *Pittsburgh* (Kans.) *Times*, ca. 1964, clipping in Rogan Scrapbook.

86. Bill Yancey interview in Peterson File.

87. *Call*, 3 June 1922; *Courier*, 20 Dec. 1924; telephone conversation with Harry Peebles, 29 Dec. 1980.

88. O'Neil interview, Texas.

89. Allen interview, KCMOHC. Jazz musicians maintained that they found little prejudice among white musicians: e.g., William Saunders said, ''An entertainer was an entertainer and his feelings were just like yours'' (William Saunders interview, KCJOHP).

90. Patterson interview.

91. Roy Johnson interview.

92. Allen interview, KCMOHC.

93. O'Neil interview, KCMOHC.

94. Bryant interview.

95. *Call*, 3 Mar. 1923, 11 Apr. and 29 Aug. 1924, 12 Mar. and 23 July 1926; unidentified clipping, 1927, in Rogan Scrapbook.

96. *Call*, 23 July 1926.

97. Chet Brewer, cited in unidentified newspaper clipping in Dwight Papers.

98. *Call*, 13 Oct. 1922.

99. *Kansas City Star*, 19 Oct. 1922.

100. *Call*, 20 Oct. 1922; for other reports on the series see *Call*, 19 Aug. and 15 Dec. 1922 and 1 Feb. 1924; *Defender*, 28 Oct. 1922; *Kansas City Star*, 9 Oct. 1921.

101. James ''Cool Papa'' Bell interview, SLOHP; see also Allen, cited in Holway, *Voices from Black Baseball*, pp. 6–7; Fisher interview.

102. Brewer interview.

103. Patterson interview; see also Drake and Cayton, *Black Metropolis*, pp. 391–95.

104. *Call*, 14 Sept. 1923.

105. Drake, cited in Holway, *Voices from Black Baseball*, p. 35.

106. *Call*, 29 Aug. 1924. Sweatt was with Kansas City in 1924 and 1925 and with the Chicago American Giants in 1926 and 1927.

107. *Call*, 9 Feb. 1923.

108. Drake interview; see also Dave Malarcher to Bob Peterson, 16 Jan. 1969 and 20 Nov. 1968, in Peterson File.

109. For information on the California winter league see *Kansas City Star*, 13 Oct. 1920; *Call*, 24 Nov. 1922, 15 Oct. 1926, 4 Mar. and 1 July 1927; *Courier*, 15 Oct. 1927; *Defender*, 5 Mar. 1927; Brewer interview.

110. *Call*, 1 Mar. and 1 Apr. 1932.

111. Ibid., 4 Jan. 1929. The *Courier*, 13 Dec. 1924, discussed the financial lure. See also Peterson, *Only the Ball Was White*, pp. 60–61.

112. *Call*, 14 Oct. 1923.

113. Ibid., 25 Jan. and 1 and 8 Feb. 1929; *Defender*, 1 Jan. 1929.

## Chapter 4

1. *Call*, 17 May 1929.

2. Ibid., 1 Apr. 1932.

3. Ibid., 17 Apr. 1931; see also ibid., 3 Apr. 1931, and *Defender*, 3 Aug. 1929, for reports of Wilkinson's losing money.

4. *Call*, 1 Apr. 1932; see ibid., 17 Apr. 1931, and *Defender*, 3 Aug. 1929, for articles on the collapse of other teams.

5. Cum Posey, cited in *Courier*, 21 Mar. 1931.

6. The game between Salem and Lynne, Massachusetts, was originally scheduled as an exhibition game, but Secretary John Farrell of the National Association granted the teams permission to play it as a regular game (see Ernest J. Lanigan to George Baird, 9 Nov. 1951, Night Games File, NBHFM; see also ''Stadium Lighting,'' *G. E. Monogram*, Sept./Oct. 1977, p. 10, in Night Games File; Richard Wilkinson interview).

7. Telephone conversation with Ernest Selby, Benton Harbor, Mich., 5 May 1981. Other sources that describe the lighting system are *Call*, 10 Jan., 25 Apr., and 13 June 1930 and 26 Mar. 1941; *Defender*, 29 Mar. and 24 May 1930;

Holway, "Kansas City's Mighty Monarchs," pp. 84–85; *Kansas City Star,* 16 July 1972; *Courier-Journal & Times,* 11 May 1975, clipping in House of David File, NBHFM; Brewer interview; Lee Wilkinson to author, 17 Feb. 1981.

8. Richard Wilkinson interview. The *Call,* 28 Mar. and 25 Apr. 1930, estimated the cost of the system.

9. Harriett Baird Wickstrom interview, KCMOHC; Young and Young, *Your Kansas City and Mine,* p. 70. It is impossible to document the financial arrangements between the two men. Several people incorrectly identified Baird as Wilkinson's son-in-law.

10. *Defender,* 14 June 1930. The *Call,* 14 Mar. 1930, reported that the night game in Lawrence occurred "some weeks ago" but gave no specific date (see *Call,* 24 Apr., 2 May, and 20 June 1930, for other early reports).

11. *Defender,* 24 May 1930.

12. Brewer interview.

13. *Call,* 13 June 1930.

14. Ernest Selby, cited in Jerry Kirshenbaum, "The Hairiest Team of All," *Sports Illustrated,* 13 Apr. 1970, p. 114. For other players' opinions of playing under lights see *Independence* (Kans.) *Daily Reporter,* 28 Apr. 1930, in Night Games File; Brewer interview; Brashler, *Josh Gibson,* pp. 21–22; unidentified newspaper clipping, 18 July 1930, in Negro Leagues File; *Call,* 24 Jan. 1930.

15. *Call,* 28 Mar. 1930.

16. Ibid., 24 Jan. 1930.

17. *Defender,* 4 Mar. 1933; Betts, "Organized Sport in Industrial America," p. 478; *Call,* 20 and 27 June and 15 Aug. 1930; Bill Heward and Dimitri V. Gat, *Some Are Called Clowns: A Season with the Last of the Great Barnstorming Baseball Teams* (New York: Thomas Y. Crowell Co., 1974), pp. 77–78.

18. Frank Navin of the Detroit Tigers, Ed Barrow of the New York Yankees, and Sam Bredon of the St. Louis Cardinals are cited in Frederick G. Lieb, *The Baseball Story* (New York: G. P. Putnam's Sons, 1950), p. 259.

19. *Call,* 3 Apr., 22 May, 19 June, and 31 July 1931; *Defender,* 2 Apr. and 4 June 1932; unidentified newspaper clipping, ca. 1930–36, in Dwight Papers.

20. *Defender,* 10 June 1922; Robert S. Fogarty, *The Righteous Remnant: The House of David* (Kent, Ohio: Kent State University Press,

1981), pp. 121–24; Francis X. Sculley, "Do You Remember the House of David?" *Leatherstocking Journal,* Summer 1980, pp. 13–15, clipping in House of David File; Kirshenbaum, "The Hairiest Team," pp. 104–6; Young interview.

21. *Courier,* 18 Apr. 1936; telephone conversation with Selby; Lee Wilkinson's day book, 1932–37, in private collection of Lee Wilkinson, Glendale, Calif.; *Ames* (Iowa) *Daily Tribune Times,* 22 May 1935; Dwight Wilkinson to author, 3 Mar. 1981.

22. *Call,* 3 July 1931 and 8 July 1932.

23. Ibid., 10 Apr. 1931.

24. *Defender,* 21 Jan. 1933.

25. *Call,* 26 Jan. 1934.

26. Peterson, *Only the Ball Was White,* p. 121; Brashler, *Josh Gibson,* p. 97; Trouppe, *Twenty Years Too Soon,* p. 67; 1936 ledger sheet, in Dwight Papers.

27. *Call,* 2 Oct. 1931; see also ibid., 9 Oct. 1931; *Defender,* 28 Sept. 1935. Baird attended his first league meeting in 1939. The press continued to recognize only Wilkinson as "owner," however.

28. Unidentified clipping, 1927, in Rogan Scrapbook.

29. David Kemp to author, 23 Oct. 1984.

30. *Courier,* 18 Apr. 1936; Fogarty, *Righteous Remnant,* p. 121; telephone conversation with Lee Wilkinson, 21 Feb. 1981.

31. *Call,* 9 Oct. 1931.

32. *Courier,* 21 Apr. 1934; see also *Colored Baseball and Sports Monthly* 1 (Sept. 1934), clipping in NLF; *Courier,* 22 July 1933.

33. *Courier,* 21 Apr. 1934; see also *Defender,* 21 Apr. 1934.

34. Unidentified newspaper clipping, ca. 1934, in Dwight Papers; see also *Courier,* 18 Aug. 1934; *Call,* 21 Sept. 1934; *Defender,* 21 Apr. and 18 Aug. 1934.

35. Donn Rogosin, *Invisible Men: Life in Baseball's Negro Leagues* (New York: Atheneum, 1983), p. 138.

36. *Call,* 29 Sept. 1934.

37. Unidentified newspaper clipping, ca. 1930–36, in Dwight Papers; see also *Call,* 7 Oct. 1932, 19 Oct. 1934, and 4 Sept. 1937; *Defender,* 3 Feb. and 13 Oct. 1934; Allen interview, KCMOHC.

38. Johnny Buss, cited in *Courier,* 19 Aug. 1933; see also *Defender,* 21 Apr. and 16 June 1934; Richard Wilkinson interview.

39. *Defender,* 25 Aug. 1934.

40. Unidentified newspaper clipping, ca. 1932, in private collection of Gladys Wilkinson Catron, St. Joseph, Mo.; *Call,* 18 Nov. 1932; *Defender,* 27 Aug. 1932.

41. *Call,* 28 Oct. and 11 Nov. 1932.

42. Rogosin, *Invisible Men,* p. 127.

43. Campanella, *It's Good to Be Alive,* pp. 65–66.

44. Smith, cited in Holway, *Voices from Black Baseball,* p. 289.

45. Morris interview.

46. For reports of doctoring the ball see *Courier,* 21 Mar. 1931; Leroy Paige, *Maybe I'll Pitch Forever,* ed. David Lipman (Garden City, N.Y.: Doubleday, 1962), p. 51; Holway, *Voices from Black Baseball,* pp. 35, 114; Brashler, *Josh Gibson,* pp. 28–29; *Kansas City Star,* 16 July 1972; Leroy Paige, *Pitchin' Man,* ed. Hal Lebovitz (n.p.: By the editor, 1948), p. 64.

47. Allen interview, KCMOHC.

48. Connie Johnson interview, Donn Rogosin Collection, Austin, Texas.

49. *Call,* 8 and 15 Apr. and 3 June 1932, 21 Sept. 1934, and 22 Sept. 1939; *Courier,* 18 Aug. 1934; Brashler, *Josh Gibson,* p. 74; Allen interview, SLOHP.

50. Sol White, cited in Peterson, *Only the Ball Was White,* p. 151; see also Rust, *"Get That Nigger,"* p. 26; George Eugene Hungerford, *Diamond Dust* (Peetz, Colo.: Advocate Publishing Co., 1941), p. 26; Hardy interview, in Peterson File.

51. Rogosin, *Invisible Men,* p. 145.

52. Dwight interview; see also Drake, cited in Holway, *Voices from Black Baseball,* pp. 26–27.

53. Rogosin, *Invisible Men,* p. 148; see also O'Neil interview, Texas.

54. Lorenzo Piper Davis and Theodore Rosengarten, "Reading the Hops: Recollections of Lorenzo Piper Davis and the Negro Baseball League," *Southern Exposure* 5 (1977): 79.

55. Paige, *Pitchin' Man,* p. 74.

56. Ibid., p. 67; *Courier,* 22 Aug. 1936.

57. Connie Johnson interview, KCMOHC.

58. *Defender,* 28 Sept. 1935.

59. Sam Lacy, "Will Our Boys Make Big League Grade?" *Negro Baseball Yearbook: 1945,* p. 29, in Peterson File; Tristram Potter Coffin, *The Old Ball Game: Baseball in Folklore and Fiction* (New York: Herder & Herder, 1971), pp. 126–29, 133–35; Paige, *Maybe I'll Pitch For-*ever, pp. 34, 43, and *Pitchin' Man,* p. 82; Young interview.

60. *Defender,* 13 July 1929 and 6 Feb. 1932; *Courier,* 9 Feb. 1935; Effa Manley and Leon Herbert Hardwick, *Negro Baseball . . . before Integration* (Chicago: Adams Press, 1976), p. 41.

61. Rogosin, *Invisible Men,* pp. 14–17, 103–8.

62. Patterson interview.

63. Rogosin, *Invisible Men,* p. 105; see also Drake and Cayton, *Black Metropolis,* pp. 468–88, 524–25, 546.

64. *Defender,* 21 Jan. 1933. These cities were members sometime during the first four years: Pittsburgh, Cleveland, Indianapolis, Chicago, Nashville, Akron, Cincinnati, Columbus, Detroit, Baltimore, Washington, Philadelphia, Newark, Havana (Cuba), New York, Brooklyn, Memphis, Birmingham, and Harrisburg. In 1936 Abe and Effa Manley combined their Newark Dodgers and Brooklyn Eagles clubs. Other sources for the early years of the NNL include: *Defender,* 1 Feb. 1936, 14 Jan., 11 Feb., and 4 Mar. 1933, and 23 Mar. 1935; Manley and Hardwick, *Negro Baseball,* p. 49; Peterson, *Only the Ball Was White,* p. 94.

65. *Defender,* 1 July 1933.

66. Dave Malarcher to Bob Peterson, 16 Jan. 1969, in Peterson File; see also *Call,* 19 Dec. 1930; *Defender,* 5 Jan. 1930.

67. *Defender,* 22 Aug. 1931. Robert A. Cole reorganized the American Giants as a traveling club in 1932. See *Defender,* 25 May 1940, for a detailed account of the American Giants' problems after Foster's death.

68. *Defender,* 10 Feb. 1934. See *Defender,* 29 Aug. 1931 and 30 Jan. 1932, and *Courier,* 9 Feb. 1935, for more information on Wilkinson's proposed move to Chicago.

69. A. Theodore Brown, *The Politics of Reform: Kansas City's Municipal Government, 1925–1950* (Kansas City: Community Studies, 1958), p. 168.

70. *Kansas City Rising Son,* 25 Oct. 1906, cited in Lyle W. Dorsett, *The Pendergast Machine* (New York: Oxford University Press, 1968), p. 44.

71. Fisher interview.

72. Urban League, *Negro Worker of Kansas City,* pp. 22–23; see also "History of Negro Population," Brown Collection.

73. *Call,* 3 June 1932; see also "Money

Disbursements of Wage Earners: Clerical Workers in Five Cities in the West North Central Mountain Region, 1934–36,'' U.S. Department of Labor, Bureau of Labor Statistics, 1939, cited in Urban League, *Negro Worker of Kansas City,* pp. 60–62.

74. Barefield interview.

75. Dwight interview; 1936 ledger sheet in Dwight Papers.

76. *Call,* 17 Oct. 1930; see also ibid., 21 May 1926 and 27 Jan. 1928; *Defender,* 12 Feb. and 24 Dec. 1921; Morris interview; Barefield interview; Allen interview, KCMOHC.

77. *Defender,* 21 Oct. 1933 and 27 Jan. 1934; *Courier,* 21 Apr. 1934; Allen interview, KCMOHC; Carroll Mothel's passport in private collection of Phil Dixon, K.C., Kans.

78. *Defender,* 9 Mar. 1940.

79. Ibid., 27 Jan. 1934 and 13 Mar. 1937; *Courier,* 21 Apr. and 17 Nov. 1934 and 27 July 1935.

80. *Call,* 18 Aug. 1933. Cum Posey, owner of the Homestead Grays; Gus Greenlee, owner of the Pittsburgh Crawfords; Robert Cole, owner of the Chicago American Giants; Roy Sparrow, of the *Pittsburgh Sun-Telegraph;* and Bill Nunn, of the *Courier,* were the original planners of the East-West Game (see *Courier,* 15 Aug. 1942).

81. *Courier,* 10 Aug. 1935.

82. *Call,* 18 Aug. 1933.

83. In 1933 the leagues were not operating, and all major teams were eligible. In 1934 and 1935 only members of the new NNL were eligible. In 1936 not even all members of the NNL were considered in the voting, but the Monarchs were included. After the Negro American League organized in 1937, the NNL represented the East and the NAL the West. See *Defender,* 5 Aug. 1933 and 1 Aug. 1936; *Call,* 5 July 1935; *Courier,* 18 Aug. 1934 and 8 Aug. 1936; Peterson, *Only the Ball Was White,* pp. 291–92.

84. Peterson, *Only the Ball Was White,* pp. 291–92; *Call,* 8 Sept. 1933; *Defender,* 29 July 1939. Several white sportswriters attended the games, but the *Defender* (9 Sept. 1939 and 2 Aug. 1941) estimated that whites made up only 5 to 10 percent of the crowd.

85. *Defender,* 15 Aug. 1936; also *Call,* 26 July 1935.

86. *Call,* 16 Aug. 1935.

87. Ibid., 5 July 1935; *Courier,* 18 Aug. 1934

and 13 July 1935; *Defender,* 27 Aug. and 15 Oct. 1938 and 10 Aug. 1940.

88. Williams interview.

89. Nat Trammell, ''Baseball Classic—East vs. West,'' *Colored Baseball and Sports Monthly* 1 (Oct. 1934): 6, in NLF.

90. *Defender,* 25 May and 7 Sept. 1940.

91. Ibid., 10 Sept., 8 and 15 Oct. 1938. In 1942, 1946, 1947, and 1948, the teams chosen for the East-West Game played a second game on the East Coast. These games were billed as All Star Classics. They were not as successful or prestigious as the Chicago contests. North-South All Star games were played periodically, but again, they were not major sporting events.

92. The NAL was composed of teams from Kansas City, Mo., Chicago, Cleveland, Memphis, St. Louis, New Orleans, Birmingham, Toledo, Atlanta, Jacksonville, Indianapolis, Cincinnati, and Detroit.

93. *Courier,* 27 Apr. 1940.

94. *Defender,* 2 Mar., 10 and 24 Aug. 1940; *Courier,* 20 Apr. 1940; telephone conversation with Peebles.

95. *Defender,* 29 June and 14 Sept. 1940.

96. Manley and Hardwick, *Negro Baseball,* pp. 56–57; *Courier,* 15 June 1940; *Call,* 30 Apr. 1937; Brashler, *Josh Gibson,* pp. 104–7; *Defender,* 10 July 1937.

97. Williams interview. ''The Latin Connection'' chapter in Rogosin, *Invisible Men,* has a detailed discussion of the Latin American experience.

98. W. E. B. DuBois, ''The Black Vote in Philadelphia,'' *Charities* 15 (7 Oct. 1905): 31.

99. Williams interview; see also Berry and Blassingame, *Long Memory,* p. 373.

100. Willie Wells to Wendell Smith, cited in Brashler, *Josh Gibson,* p. 73.

101. *Defender,* 29 June 1940 and 10 July 1937; *Call,* 1 June 1940 and 28 Feb. 1941; Chalk, *Pioneers of Black Sport,* p. 66; Brashler, *Josh Gibson,* p. 108. Paige's only punishment was being banned from the East-West Game in 1940.

102. *Courier,* 15 June 1940. Newark was allowed to keep two Kansas City recruits: James Clarkson and Ernest Carter (see Manley and Hardwick, *Negro Baseball,* p. 57).

103. *Call,* 11 Mar. 1949.

104. Paige, *Maybe I'll Pitch Forever,* p. 130; see also ibid., pp. 131, 141, for his comments on

Wilkinson. This team was also billed as "Satchel Paige's Kansas City Colored All Stars" and the "Kansas City Travelers."

105. Paige, *Maybe I'll Pitch Forever*, p. 131.

106. Peterson, *Only the Ball Was White*, pp. 142–43.

107. *Defender*, 29 Apr. 1939; *Call*, 2 June, 27 Sept., and 6 Oct. 1939, and 17 May 1940.

108. *Courier*, 6 June 1942; see also Davis and Rosengarten, "Reading the Hops," p. 74.

109. Bryant interview; see also Brewer interview; Fisher interview.

110. O'Neil interview, KCMOHC.

111. Smith interview, Texas.

112. Ibid.

113. Ted Rasberry interveiw, KCMOHC.

114. Chester Washington of the *Courier* is cited in Brashler, *Josh Gibson*, p. 106.

115. Renfroe is cited in Holway, *Voices from Black Baseball*, p. 340. For other discussions of Paige see Smith, who is cited in Holway, *Voices from Black Baseball*, pp. 280–81; Smith interview, KCMOHC; Dwight interview; *Defender*, 20 Sept. 1941; Jimmie Crutchfield, cited in Rogosin, *Invisible Men*, p. 100.

116. *Call*, 24 Mar. 1939.

117. Ibid., 26 Mar. 1937.

118. Ibid., 14 May 1937.

119. Ibid., 16 Apr. 1937 and 12 May 1939.

120. Mary Jo "Josette" Weaver Owens interview, KCMOHC; see also *Call*, 2 and 30 June and 7 July 1939, 28 June, 19 July, 2 Aug., and 6 Sept. 1940; Penn interview; *Defender*, 8 July 1939. Josette Owens donated her loving cup to the Smithsonian Institution in 1981.

121. *Call*, 22 May 1942.

## Chapter 5

1. *Call*, 2 May 1941 and 23 June 1944; *Defender*, 19 July 1941 and 3 Mar. 1945; David S. Neft et al., *The Sports Encyclopedia: Baseball* (New York: Grosset & Dunlap, 1974), p. 278. *Sporting News*, 25 Feb. 1978, said that fifty-four professional black baseball players served in World War II. This estimate seems low considering that there were twelve teams and that fourteen men went from the Monarchs alone. The Monarchs who served were John O'Neil, Ted Strong, Ted Alexander, Willard Brown, Hilton Smith, Jesse Williams, Norris Phillips, Frank Bradley, Cliff Johnson, Joe Greene, Allen Bryant, Leroy James, Lee Moody, and Sam Haynes.

2. Trouppe, *Twenty Years Too Soon*, pp. 136–44; *Call*, 17 May 1946.

3. C. A. Franklin to Congressman [Jasper C.] Bell, 19 Apr. 1943, in Jasper Bell Papers: 2306, f161, WHMC.

4. C. A. Franklin to Joseph Eastman, 9 Apr. 1943, Bell Papers.

5. *Call*, 2, 9, and 16 Apr. 1943 and 18 Feb. 1944; *Courier*, 5 June 1943; Manley and Hardwick, *Negro Baseball*, p. 60.

6. *Call*, 17 Dec. 1943; *Defender*, 6 Jan. and 10 Mar. 1945; Frederick W. Cozens and Florence Scovil Stumpf, *Sports in American Life* (Chicago: University of Chicago Press, 1953), pp. 213–14.

7. *Call*, 2 May 1941. "Sawbuck" was slang for a ten-dollar bill. See also *Spirit of Freedom*, p. 20; Berry and Blassingame, *Long Memory*, pp. 198–99.

8. *Call*, 26 Mar. 1941.

9. O'Neil interview, KCMOHC; see also *Defender*, 10 July 1943; Brashler, *Josh Gibson*, p. 124; Peterson, *Only the Ball Was White*, pp. 97–98; *Call*, 8 Sept. 1944.

10. *Call*, 15 May 1942 and 12 Feb. 1943; *Courier*, 18 July 1942. Arthur Toney was president of the Boosters from 1942 until Baird sold the team in 1955. Sweeney was publicity director. Leading Boosters at this time included John Gregg, Roy Dorsey, attorney James Herbert, A. E. ("Chick") Pullam, and state representative J. McKinley Neal.

11. In the *Call*, 31 Aug. 1945, Leland ("Larry") MacPhail, owner of the Yankees and the Blues, confirmed that the Monarchs attracted more fans than the Blues.

12. Owens interview.

13. Allen interview, Texas.

14. Connie Johnson interview, KCMOHC.

15. Dave Hawkins is cited in Paige, *Pitchin' Man*, p. 71.

16. *Call*, 23 June 1944.

17. Bryant interview. The average weekly wage in 1945 was $44.39 (see Neil A. Wynn, *The Afro-American and the Second World War* [London: Paul Elek, 1976], p. 14).

18. *Courier*, 20 Sept. 1947 and 25 Oct. 1941.

19. Bryant interview.

20. *Courier*, 5 Sept. 1942.

21. Paige, *Maybe I'll Pitch Forever*, p. 159.

22. *Defender,* 5 Aug. 1944.

23. Ibid., 5 Aug. 1944; Paige, *Pitchin' Man,* p. 75; Paige, *Maybe I'll Pitch Forever,* pp. 163–66. The NNL and the NAL played a second All Star Game in Cleveland in 1942 to benefit the Army-Navy Relief Fund.

24. *Defender,* 2 June and 17 Aug. 1945; 1946, 1947, 1948 East-West Game Reports, in NLF.

25. *Defender,* 28 July 1944; *Call,* 27 July 1944. In 1950 the fans voted for eight players for each team; the managers chose the pitchers and the reserves. In 1955, sportswriters and fans nominated the players for the game (see *Call,* 28 July 1950 and 15 July 1955).

26. *Call,* 4 Sept. 1942 and 8 Sept. 1944; Smith interview, Texas; *Defender,* 16 Oct. 1943. The arbitration commission was composed of three sportswriters: Fay Young, *Defender;* Wendell Smith, *Courier;* and Sam Lacy, *Baltimore Afro-American.*

27. *Defender,* 14 Sept. 1946. Victors in the Negro World Series during the 1940s were the Kansas City Monarchs, 1942; the Homestead Grays, 1943, 1944, and 1948; the Cleveland Buckeyes, 1945; the Newark Eagles, 1946; and the New York Cubans, 1947.

28. Smith interview, Texas.

29. *Call,* 3 July 1946; see also O'Neil interview, KCMOHC; Rogosin, *Invisible Men,* p. 125.

30. Smith interview, Texas; Brewer interview.

31. *Defender,* 10 Mar. 1945. Robinson signed for $400 a month. For more information on Robinson's early career see *Courier,* 5 Oct. 1940; *Call,* 2 Mar. 1945; Jackie Robinson, *I Never Had It Made,* ed. Alfred Duckett (New York: G. P. Putnam's Sons, 1972), p. 35, and *Jackie Robinson: My Own Story,* ed. Wendell Smith, foreword by Branch Rickey (New York: Greenberg Publishers, 1948), p. 7.

32. Allen interview, KCMOHC.

33. Jules Tygiel, *Baseball's Great Experiment: Jackie Robinson and His Legacy* (New York: Oxford University Press, 1983), p. 33.

34. Paige, *Maybe I'll Pitch Forever,* p. 85. the economic potential of integration was also discussed in *Courier,* 8 Sept. 1934; Holway, *Voices from Black Baseball,* p. 11; *Defender,* 28 Oct. 1933 and 3 Aug. 1935; O'Neil interview, KCMOHC.

35. Smith interview, Texas.

36. Dave Malarcher is cited in Stephen

Banker, "Black Diamonds," *Black Collegian* 9 (Jan./Feb. 1979): 34.

37. *Defender,* 22 July 1939.

38. *Call,* 18 Sept. 1942.

39. Ibid., 5 Jan. 1940; Chasteen, "Public Accommodations," pp. 97–98.

40. Drake and Cayton, *Black Metropolis,* pp. 747–48; August Meier and Elliott Rudwick, *CORE: A Study in the Civil Rights Movement, 1942–1968* (New York: Oxford University Press, 1973), pp. 3–4; Wynn, *Afro-American and the Second World War,* p. 100.

41. *Courier,* 27 Feb. 1943.

42. *Defender,* 13 Jan. 1945.

43. Tygiel, *Baseball's Great Experiment,* p. 32.

44. *Defender,* 5 Feb. 1938.

45. *Call,* 19 Mar. 1943; see also *Defender,* 12 Aug. 1939 and 27 Feb. 1937; *Call,* 14 July 1939.

46. Buck Leonard, cited in Holway, *Voices from Black Baseball,* p. 269; see also Berry and Blassingame, *Long Memory,* p. 175.

47. *Courier,* 23 Aug. 1947.

48. Ibid.

49. Smith interview, Texas. For reports of these early tryouts see Peterson, *Only the Ball Was White,* pp. 179–80; Rust, *"Get That Nigger,"* pp. 17–19; A. S. ("Doc") Young, *Great Negro Baseball Stars and How They Made the Major Leagues* (New York: A. S. Barnes & Co., 1953), p. 11; Manley and Hardwick, *Negro Baseball,* p. 61; Rogosin, *Invisible Men,* pp. 191–96; Tygiel, *Baseball's Great Experiment,* pp. 43–46.

50. Landis, cited in *Defender,* 25 July 1942.

51. Bill Veeck, with Ed Linn, *Veeck as in Wreck: The Autobiography of Bill Veeck* (New York: G. P. Putnam's Sons, 1962), pp. 170–71.

52. Chandler, cited in Holway, *Voices from Black Baseball,* p. 14. Though he made this public statement, some believe that Chandler was personally less enthusiastic about integration (see especially Dan W. Dodson, "The Integration of Negroes in Baseball," *Journal of Educational Sociology* 28 (Oct. 1954): 76.

53. *Call,* 20 Apr. 1945; *Sporting News,* 22 June 1974, in NLF.

54. Bostic, cited in Tygiel, *Baseball's Great Experiment,* p. 46; see also *Call,* 13 Apr. 1945; Rust *"Get That Nigger,"* p. 20.

55. "Report of the Mayor's Committee on

Baseball to Mayor F. H. La Guardia,'' by John H. Johnson, chairman, New York, 31 Oct. 1945, pp. 6–8.

56. *Defender,* 26 May 1945. For other reports on the USL see *Call,* 12 Jan. 1945 and 3 May 1946; *Defender,* 6 Jan. 1945.

57. *Call,* 9 Mar. 1945.

58. Rogosin, *Invisible Men,* pp. 209–10.

59. Smith interview, Texas.

60. Unidentified newspaper clipping, 25 Oct. 1945, in NLF. See Dodson, ''Integration of Negroes in Baseball,'' for Rickey's efforts to minimize the antagonism.

61. In August 1946 a special committee of major-league owners presented a report to the baseball commissioner discussing the ''Race Question.'' This report endorsed segregated teams (see *Sporting News,* 25 Feb. 1978, in NLF).

62. Frick, cited in Smith, *Baseball,* pp. 327–28.

63. Wilkinson, cited in *Courier,* 8 Aug. 1942; see also *Call,* 14 Jan. 1944.

64. Rickey, cited in *Defender,* 27 Oct. 1945; see also Robinson, *My Own Story,* pp. 54–55.

65. *Courier,* 3 Nov. 1945.

66. Manley and Hardwick, *Negro Baseball,* pp. 72–73.

67. Wilkinson, cited in Peterson, *Only the Ball Was White,* p. 192.

68. Smith interview, Texas.

69. Williams interview.

70. Patterson interview.

71. Paige, *Maybe I'll Pitch Forever,* p. 173.

72. Smith interview, Texas.

73. Ibid.

74. Crutchfield, cited in Rogosin, *Invisible Men,* p. 204.

75. Smith interview, KCMOHC.

76. Patterson interview.

77. O'Neil interview, KCMOHC.

78. Smith interview, Texas; see also Jackie Robinson, ''What's Wrong with Negro Baseball?'' *Ebony Magazine,* 12 June 1948, pp. 13–17; Effa Manley, ''Negro Baseball Isn't Dead!'' *Our World,* Aug. 1948, pp. 27–28, in Effa Manley File, NBHFM.

79. Walter White, secretary of the NAACP, ''Time for a Progress Report,'' *Saturday Review of Literature,* 22 Sept. 1951, p. 38.

80. *Call,* 23 Sept. 1949.

81. *Courier,* 29 Dec. 1945.

82. Ibid., 7 June 1952.

83. T. Y. Baird to Fresco Thompson, scout for the Dodgers, cited in *Call,* 28 Jan. 1949.

84. Manley and Hardwick, *Negro Baseball,* pp. 90–92; *Call,* 21 Jan. 1949; *Courier,* 30 Aug. 1947.

85. Brown interview.

86. Tygiel, *Baseball's Great Experiment,* p. 221.

87. *Courier,* 30 Aug. and 6 Sept. 1947.

88. Ibid., 14 June 1952.

89. Tom Meany, cited in Paige, *Maybe I'll Pitch Forever,* pp. 198–99.

## Chapter 6

1. *Defender,* 6 Jan. 1945.

2. Manley and Hardwick, *Negro Baseball,* pp. 94–96.

3. *Call,* 24 June 1949.

4. *Courier,* 11 Sept. 1948.

5. Both the NNL and the NAL adopted this salary limit (see *Defender,* 10 Jan. 1948).

6. Williams interview; see also *Call,* 17 May 1946 and 18 June 1954.

7. *Call,* 14 Jan. 1949. The terms of the sale were not disclosed. For reports on the decline of Negro League teams see *Call,* 18 Feb. 1949; Manley and Hardwick, *Negro Baseball,* p. 96; *Courier,* 21 Feb. 1948 and 6 Sept. 1947.

8. *1946 Negro Baseball Yearbook,* p. 11, in NLF.

9. *Courier,* 6 June 1953.

10. *Call,* 23 Sept. 1949. The Western Division included the Chicago American Giants, the Kansas City Monarchs, the Memphis Red Sox, the Birmingham Black Barons, and the Houston Eagles. The Eastern Division had the Baltimore Elite Giants, the New York Cubans, the Philadelphia Stars, the Indianapolis Clowns, and the Louisville Buckeyes. The Negro World Series was played in 1949, 1951, and 1952.

11. *Courier,* 15 Aug. 1953.

12. Ibid.; the scorebook for the 30th Annual East-West Game, in Dwight Papers. Carolyn Combs was crowned in 1951. Maranie Mitchell of Chicago was selected ''Miss West'' and Bobbie Holman of Memphis as ''Miss East'' in 1952. Gale Patricia Hunt reigned in 1955 (see *Defender,* 11 Aug. 1951 and 23 Aug. 1952; *Call,* 5 Aug. 1955).

13. O'Neil interview, KCMOHC; *Call,* 20

May 1955, 27 Aug. and 10 Sept. 1948; Benjamin G. Rader, *American Sports: From the Age of Folk Games to the Age of Spectators* (Englewood Cliffs, N.J.: Prentice-Hall, 1983), pp. 242, 285. Negro-leagues ball games were not televised, but radio station KPRS in Kansas City began broadcasting the games in 1954 (see *Call,* 4 June 1954).

14. *Courier,* 9 July 1949 and 13 Mar. 1954; *Call,* 27 Feb. 1953.

15. *Call,* 11 Feb. 1949; see also ibid., 17 Oct. 1947 and 24 June 1949.

16. Surratt interview.

17. *Call,* 4 Mar. 1949; *Defender,* 8 July 1950 and 2 June 1951.

18. T. Y. Baird to Lee MacPhail, 17 Jan. 1949, in NLF; see also *Courier,* 8 Sept. 1951; *Defender,* 29 Apr. 1950.

19. *Chicago Herald-Tribune,* 4 Mar. 1953, in NLF.

20. *Courier,* 17 June 1950.

21. Ibid., 16 Apr. 1955.

22. Ernie Banks and Jim Enright, *"Mr. Cub"* (Chicago: Follett Publishing Co., 1971), p. 76; *Defender,* 7 Jan. 1950; *Courier,* 17 Apr. 1954.

23. *Courier,* 11 Sept. 1948; see also ibid., 2 June and 1 Sept. 1951, and *Call,* 9 May 1952, for other articles encouraging the teams to continue.

24. *Defender,* 30 Apr. 1949; *Courier,* 20 Mar. 1948.

25. *Call,* 20 June 1947.

26. *Courier,* 6 Jan. 1951; *Call,* 26 July 1946.

27. *Call,* 1 Aug. 1947. Players who were sold to major-league franchises are listed in Appendix A.

28. Ibid., 7 Apr. and 16 May 1950 and 29 May 1953; *Courier,* 30 May 1953; Richard Wilkinson interview; Bell interview; Davis and Rosengarten, "Reading the Hops," p. 78.

29. Bob Gibson, *From Ghetto to Glory: The Story of Bob Gibson,* ed. Phil Pepe (Englewood Cliffs, N.J.: Prentice-Hall, 1968), pp. 21–22.

30. *Call,* 27 Feb. 1953.

31. Ibid., 18 June 1954; *Courier,* 31 May and 6 June 1955.

32. *Defender,* 16 Apr. 1955.

33. Ibid., 28 May 1953. For other Kansas City activities see *Kansas City Star,* 25 May 1953 and 23 May 1954; *Call,* 12 May 1950, 12 May 1953, 23 July and 13 Aug. 1948, 24 June and 18 Nov. 1949; Dwight interview.

34. *Call,* 8 Apr. 1955; see also ibid., 20 May 1955, 16 July 1954, and 9 Sept. 1955; Ernest Mehl, *The Kansas City Athletics* (New York: Henry Holt & Co., 1956), pp. 33–42.

35. Wickstrom interview; see also *Call,* 26 Aug. 1955, and Heward and Gat, *Some Are Called Clowns,* pp. 211–12, for other reports of difficulties encountered in renting stadiums.

36. *Call,* 6 May, 23 Sept., and 30 Dec. 1955; *Courier,* 5 Mar. 1955; unidentified newspaper clipping, 14 July 1962, in T. Y. Baird File, NBHFM.

37. Rasberry interview; *Courier,* 19 June 1954; Ted Rasberry to "Gentlemen," 20 Sept. 1960, in NLF.

38. Paige, *Maybe I'll Pitch Forever,* p. 266. Financial information is located in NAL contracts, 1955–63, in private collection of Ted Rasberry, Grand Rapids, Mich.; telephone conversation with Peebles, 29 Dec. 1980.

39. Ted Rasberry to "Gentlemen," 26 Sept. 1960, in NLF; Rasberry interview; Ted Rasberry to Ford Frick, 3 July 1959, in Officials' Correspondence File, NBHFM; unidentified newspaper clipping, 31 July 1960, in NLF.

40. *Kansas City Star,* 25 Aug. 1964; *Sporting News,* 17 Apr. 1965, clipping in NLF. Ed Hamman organized the Clowns every year until 1973 (see Heward and Gat, *Some Are Called Clowns,* pp. 3, 79, 174).

## Chapter 7

1. O'Neil interview, Texas.

2. *Call,* 31 May 1929

3. *Courier,* 13 Dec. 1930.

4. O'Neil interview, Texas.

5. Maya Angelou, *I Know Why the Caged Bird Sings* (New York: Random House, Bantam Books, 1971), p. 113.

6. *Call,* 15 July 1949.

7. Ibid., 27 Oct. 1922.

8. Ibid., 3 Nov. 1922.

9. Morris interview.

10. Sweeney interview.

11. Roger Kahn, *The Boys of Summer* (New York: Harper & Row, 1971), p. xvi.

12. Duncan, cited in Holway, *Voices from Black Baseball,* p. 16.

13. O'Neil interview, KCMOHC.

14. Connie Johnson interview, KCMOHC.

15. Trouppe, *Twenty Years Too Soon,* p. 11.

16. Smith interview, KCMOHC.

# Sources Consulted

## Manuscript Sources

Ashland, Kentucky
  Negro Baseball Hall of History: Negro
  Leagues File

Austin, Texas
  Donn Rogosin Collection: recorded interviews
  with Newt Allen, Chet Brewer, Cliff Johnson,
  John O'Neil, Pat Patterson, and Hilton Smith

Cooperstown, New York
  National Baseball Hall of Fame and Museum:
  T. Y. Baird File; Rube Foster File; House of
  David File; Effa Manley File; Negro Leagues
  File, Night Games File; Officials' Correspond-
  ence File; Robert Peterson File; J. L. Wilkin-
  son File

Glendale, California.
  Lee Wilkinson Papers

Grand Rapids, Michigan
  Ted Rasberry Papers

Hyde Park, New York
  Franklin D. Roosevelt Library: President's
  Personal File 5939

Kansas City, Kansas
  Phil Dixon Collection
  Mrs. Eddie (Georgia) Dwight Papers

Kansas City, Missouri
  Author's Correspondence File
  Black Archives of Mid-America: Wilbur "Bul-
  let Joe" Rogan Scrapbook; Kansas City
  Monarchs File
  Kansas City Public Library, Missouri Valley
  Room: Kansas City Monarchs File; Jazz
  History File
  University of Missouri, Kansas City: Joint
  Collection, Western Historical Manuscripts
  Collection and the State Historical Society of
  Missouri: Manuscripts
    Kansas City Monarchs Oral History Collec-
    tion: recorded interviews of Newt Allen;
    Hank Baylis; Allen Bryant; Gladys Wilkin-

son Catron; Guy Davis; Mrs. Eddie (Geor-
gia) Dwight; Jesse Fisher; Cliff Johnson;
Roy Johnson; Milton Morris; John O'Neil;
Mary Jo ("Josette") Weaver Owens; Al-
berta Gilmore Penn; Ted Rasberry; Othello
Renfroe; Hilton Smith; Robert Sweeney;
Alfred Surratt; Harriett Baird Wickstrom;
Richard Wilkinson; Jesse Williams; Maurice
Young
Kansas City Jazz Oral History Project:
recorded interviews of Eddie Barefield;
Count Basie; Lawrence Denton, William
Saunders; Herman Walder; Booker T. Wash-
ington; and Final Narrative Report
Jasper C. Bell Papers
A. Theodore Brown Collection

Lexington, Kentucky
University of Kentucky Libraries, Department
of Special Collections and Archives
A. B. Chandler Oral History Collection:
recorded interviews of Willard Brown and Effa
Manley

Manassas, Virginia
John Holway Papers

Maryville, Missouri
Richard Wilkinson Papers

St. Joseph, Missouri
Gladys Wilkinson Catron Papers

St. Louis, Missouri
University of Missouri, St. Louis, Archive and
Manuscript Division
St. Louis Oral History Project: recorded
interviews of Newt Allen, James Bell, Bill
Drake, and Normal Webb

## Personal Reminiscences

Bailey, Bob. Kansas City, Mo. Telephone Con-
versation, 12 Jan. 1981.
Benton, Lawrence. Kansas City, Mo. Telephone
conversations, 24 Nov. 1980 and 26 Jan. 1981.
Dwight, Mrs. Eddie (Georgia). Kansas City,
Kans. Telephone conversation, 11 May 1981.
Jenkins, J. W., IV. Kansas City, Mo. Telephone
conversation, 7 Feb. 1981.
Mehl, Ernest, Sun City, Ariz. Telephone conver-
sation, 12 Jan. 1981.
Peebles, Harry. Wichita, Kans. Telephone con-
versation, 29 Dec. 1980.

Pullam, Richard. Kansas City, Mo. Telephone
conversation, 12 Jan. 1981.
Selby, Ernest. Benton Harbor, Mich. Telephone
conversation, 5 May 1981.
Wilkinson, Dwight. Boring, Oreg. Telephone
conversation, 11 May 1981.
Wilkinson, Lee. Glendale, Calif. Telephone
conversations, 1 and 11 Dec. 1980 and 11
Feb. 1981.

## Public Records

Missouri. Secretary of State. Articles of Associa-
tion, Kansas City Monarchs Baseball and
Amusement Company.
Missouri, Kansas City, Office of Housing and
Community Development. *The Spirit of Free-
dom: A Profile of the History of Blacks in
Kansas City, Missouri.* 1978.
New York City, New York. "Report of the
Mayor's Committee on Baseball to Mayor F.
H. La Guardia," by John H. Johnson,
chairman, 31 Oct. 1945.
U.S. Congress, House, Committee on the Judici-
ary. *Study of Monopoly Power: Organized
Baseball,* in *Hearings before the Subcommittee
on Study of Monopoly Power of the Committee
of the Judiciary,* 82d Cong., 1st sess., 1951.

## Newspapers

*Chicago Defender,* July 1909 to Dec. 1960.
Chicago: University of Chicago Library, De-
partment of Photographic Reproduction, n.d.
*Indianapolis Freeman,* Jan. 1917 to Dec. 1924.
Chicago: Recordak Newspaper Services, n.d.
*Kansas City Call,* Jan. 1922 to Dec. 1964.
Kansas City, Mo.: American Micro Co., 1966.
*Kansas City Star,* Jan. 1918 to Aug. 1926.
Chicago: Recordak Newspaper Services, n.d.
*Pittsburgh Courier,* Jan. 1923 to Dec. 1960.
Pittsburgh: Microfilm Corporation of Pennsyl-
vania, n.d.

## Books and Dissertations

Allen, Lee. *100 Years of Baseball.* New York:
Bartholomew House, 1950.

Angelou, Maya. *I Know Why the Caged Bird Sings.* New York: Random House, Bantam Books, 1971.

Anson, Adrian C. *A Ball Player's Career: Being the Personal Experiences and Reminiscences of Adrian C. Anson.* Chicago: Era Publishing Co., 1900.

Banks, Ernie, and Enright, Jim. *"Mr. Cub."* Chicago: Follett Publishing Co., 1971.

Berry, Mary Frances, and Blassingame, John W. *Long Memory: The Black Experience in America.* New York: Oxford University Press, 1982.

Betts, John R. "Organized Sport in Industrial America." Ph.D. dissertation, Columbia University, 1951.

Boyle, Robert H. *Sport: Mirror of American Life.* Boston: Little, Brown & Co., 1963.

Brashler, William. *Josh Gibson: A Life in the Negro Leagues.* New York: Harper & Row, 1978.

Brooks, Maxwell R. *The Negro Press Re-examined.* Boston: Christopher Publishing House, 1959.

Brown, A. Theodore. *The Politics of Reform: Kansas City's Municipal Government, 1925–1950.* Kansas City: Community Studies, 1958.

Campanella, Roy. *It's Good to Be Alive.* Boston: Little, Brown & Co., 1959.

Chalk, Ocania. *Black College Sport.* New York: Dodd, Mead & Co., 1976.

————. *Pioneers of Black Sport.* New York: Dodd, Mead & Co., 1975.

Chasteen, Edgar Ray. "Public Accommodations: Social Movements in Conflict." Ph.D. dissertation, University of Missouri, 1966.

Coffin, Tristram Potter. *The Old Ball Game: Baseball in Folklore and Fiction.* New York: Herder & Herder, 1971.

Cozens, Frederick W., and Stumpf, Florence Scovil. *Sports in American Life.* Chicago: University of Chicago Press, 1953; reprint ed., New York: Arno Press, 1976.

Crepeau, Richard. *Baseball: America's Diamond Mind.* Orlando: University Presses of Florida, 1980.

Detweiler, Frederick G. *The Negro Press in the United States.* Chicago: University of Chicago Press, 1922.

Dorsett, Lyle W. *The Pendergast Machine.* New York: Oxford University Press, 1968.

Drake, St. Clair, and Cayton, Horace R. *Black Metropolis: A Study of Negro Life in a Northern City.* Rev. ed. New York: Harper & Row, 1962.

Dumas, Thelma M., editor. *Symbols of God's Grace: Seventy Years History of St. Stephen Baptist Church.* Kansas City: McWhirter Co., 1973.

Finkle, Lee. *Forum for Protest: The Black Press during World War II.* London: Associated University Presses, 1975.

Fogarty, Robert S. *The Righteous Remnant: The House of David.* Kent, Ohio: Kent State University Press, 1981.

Franklin, John Hope. *From Slavery to Freedom: A History of Negro Americans.* 3d ed. New York: Alfred A. Knopf, 1967.

Gerber, David A. *Black Ohio and the Color Line, 1860–1915.* Urbana: University of Illinois Press, 1976.

Gibson, Bob. *From Ghetto to Glory: The Story of Bob Gibson.* Edited by Phil Pepe. Englewood Cliffs, N.J.: Prentice-Hall, 1968.

Gregory. Paul M. *The Baseball Player: An Economic Study.* Washington, D.C.: Public Affairs Press, 1956.

Henderson, Edwin Bancroft. *The Negro in Sports.* Rev. ed. Washington, D.C.: Associated Publishers, 1949.

Heward, Bill, and Gat, Dimitri V. *Some Are Called Clowns: A Season with the Last of the Great Barnstorming Baseball Teams.* New York: Thomas Y. Crowell Co., 1974.

Hogan, Lawrence D. *A Black National News Service: The Associated Negro Press and Claude Barnett, 1919–1945.* Cranbury, N.J.: Associated University Presses, 1984.

Holway, John. *Bullet Joe and the Monarchs.* Foreword by Bob Feller. Washington, D.C.: Capital Press, 1984.

————. *Voices from the Great Black Baseball Leagues.* New York: Dodd, Mead & Co., 1975.

Hungerford, George Eugene. *Diamond Dust.* Peetz, Colo.: Advocate Publishing Co., 1941.

Kahn, Roger. *The Boys of Summer.* New York: Harper & Row, 1971.

Kusmer, Kenneth C. *A Ghetto Takes Shape: Black Cleveland, 1870–1930.* Urbana: University of Illinois Press, 1976.

League of Women Voters. *The Negro in Kansas City.* Kansas City: n.p., 1944.

Lieb, Frederick G. *The Baseball Story.* New York: G. P. Putnam's Sons, 1950.

Litwak, Howard, and Pearson, Nathan. *Goin' to Kansas City.* Kansas City: Kansas City Museum, 1980.

Loy, John W., and Kenyon, Gerald S., eds. *Sport, Culture, and Society: A Reader on the Sociology of Sport.* London: Macmillan Co., 1969.

Lucas, John A., and Smith, Ronald A. *Saga of American Sport.* Philadelphia: Lea & Febiger, 1978.

Manley, Effa, and Hardwick, Leon Herbert. *Negro Baseball . . . before Integration.* Chicago: Adams Press, 1976.

Martin, Asa E. *Our Negro Population: A Sociological Study of the Negroes in Kansas City, Missouri.* Kansas City: Franklin Hudson Publishing Co., 1913.

Mehl, Ernest. *The Kansas City Athletics.* New York: Henry Holt & Co., 1956

Meier, August, and Rudwick, Elliott. *CORE: A Study in the Civil Rights Movement, 1942–1968.* New York: Oxford University Press, 1973.

Myrdal, Gunnar. *An American Dilemma: The Negro Problem and Modern Democracy.* New York: Harper & Brothers, 1944.

Neft, David S.; Johnson, R. T.; Cohen, R. M.; and Deutsch, J. A. *The Sports Encyclopedia: Baseball.* New York: Grosset & Dunlap, 1974.

Osofsky, Gilbert. *Harlem: The Making of a Ghetto: Negro New York, 1890–1930.* New York: Harper & Row, 1963.

Ostransky, Leroy. *Jazz City: The Impact of Our Cities on the Development of Jazz.* Englewood Cliffs, N.J.: Prentice-Hall, 1978.

Paige, Leroy. *Maybe I'll Pitch Forever.* Edited by David Lipman. Garden City, N.Y.: Doubleday, 1962.

———. *Pitchin' Man.* Edited by Hal Lebovitz. N.p.: By the editor, 1948.

Peterson, Robert. *Only the Ball Was White.* Englewood Cliffs, N.J.: Prentice-Hall, 1970.

Rader, Benjamin G. *American Sports: From the Age of Folk Games to the Age of Spectators.* Englewood Cliffs, N.J.: Prentice-Hall, 1983.

Robinson, Jackie. *Baseball Has Done It.* Edited by Charles Dexter. Philadelphia: J. B. Lippincott Co., 1964.

———. *I Never Had It Made.* Edited by Alfred Duckett. New York: G. P. Putnam's Sons, 1972.

———. *Jackie Robinson: My Own Story.* Edited by Wendell Smith. Foreword by Branch Rickey. New York: Greenburg Publishers, 1948.

Rogosin, Donn. *Invisible Men: Life in Baseball's Negro Leagues.* New York: Atheneum, 1983.

Rust, Art, Jr. *"Get That Nigger off the Field!"* New York: Delacorte Press, 1976.

Seymour, Harold. *Baseball.* Vol. 1: *The Early Years.* New York: Oxford University Press, 1960.

———. *Baseball.* Vol. 2: *The Golden Age.* New York: Oxford University Press, 1971.

Smith, Robert. *Baseball.* Rev. ed. New York: Simon & Schuster, 1970.

Somers, Dale A. *The Rise of Sports in New Orleans, 1850–1900.* Baton Rouge: Louisiana State University Press, 1972.

Spear, Allan H. *Black Chicago: The Making of a Negro Ghetto, 1890–1920.* Chicago: University of Chicago Press, 1967.

Thorn, John. *A Century of Baseball Lore.* New York: Hart Publishing Co., 1974.

Trouppe, Quincy. *Twenty Years Too Soon.* Los Angeles: S & S Enterprises, 1977.

Tygiel, Jules. *Baseball's Great Experiment: Jackie Robinson and His Legacy.* New York: Oxford University Press, 1983.

Urban League. *The Heartland: The State of Black Kansas City, 1984.* Kansas City: Urban League, 1984.

———. *The Negro Worker of Kansas City: A Study of Trade Unions and Organized Labor Relations.* Kansas City: Urban League, 1940.

Veeck, Bill, with Ed Linn. *Veeck as in Wreck: The Autobiography of Bill Veeck.* New York: G. P. Putnam's Sons, 1962.

Voigt. David Q. *America through Baseball.* Chicago: Nelson-Hall, 1976.

Woodward, C. Vann. *The Strange Career of Jim Crow.* 3d rev. ed. New York: Oxford University Press, 1974.

Wynn, Neil A. *The Afro-American and the Second World War.* London: Paul Elek, 1976.

Young, A. S. ("Doc"). *Great Negro Baseball Stars and How They Made the Major Leagues.* New York: A. S. Barnes & Co., 1953.

Young, William H., and Young, Nathan B., Jr. *Your Kansas City and Mine.* Kansas City: n.p., 1950.

## Articles

Allhoff, Fred. "Thunder over Kansas City." *Liberty,* 17 Sept. 1938, pp. 4–8.

Banker, Stephen. "Black Diamonds." *Black Collegian* 9 (Jan./Feb. 1979): 33–36.

Davis, Lorenzo Piper, and Rosengarten, Theodore. "Reading the Hops: Recollections of Lorenzo Piper Davis and the Negro Baseball League." *Southern Exposure* 5 (1977): 62–79.

Dodson, Dan W. "The Integration of Negroes in Baseball." *Journal of Educational Sociology* 28 (Oct. 1954): 73–82.

DuBois, W. E. B. "The Black Vote in Philadelphia." *Charities* 15 (7 Oct. 1905): 27–48.

Grothaus, Larry. "Kansas City Blacks, Harry Truman and the Pendergast Machine." *Missouri Historical Review* 69 (Oct. 1974): 65–82.

Holway, John. "Kansas City's Mighty Monarchs." *Missouri Life* 3 (Mar.–June 1975): 83–89.

Kirshenbaum, Jerry. "The Hairiest Team of All." *Sports Illustrated,* 13 Apr. 1970, pp. 104–6.

McCoy, Donald R., and Ruetten, Richard T. "The Civil Rights Movement, 1940–54." *Midwest Quarterly* 11 (Oct. 1969): 11–34.

Meier, August. "Negro Class Structure & Ideology in the Age of Booker T. Washington." *Phylon* 23 (Fall 1962): 258–66.

Pilot, Bill. "The Southern League of Colored Base Ballists." *Baseball Research Journal: Third Annual Report.* N.p.: 1974, pp. 91–95.

Robinson, Jackie. "What's Wrong with Negro Baseball?" *Ebony Magazine,* 12 June 1948, pp. 13–17.

"Satchelfoots." *Time,* 3 June 1940, p. 44.

Tate, James Carey. "Kansas City Night Life: K.C. in the 30s." *Second Line,* Nov./Dec. 1961, pp. 11–12, 32.

[Tobin, Richard L.] "Sports as an Integrator." *Saturday Review,* 21 Jan. 1967, p. 32.

Wallace, Francis. "College Men in the Big Leagues." *Scribner's Magazine,* Oct. 1927, pp. 489–93.

White, Walter. "Time for a Progress Report." *Saturday Review of Literature,* 22 Sept. 1951, pp. 9–10, 38.

# Index

169